美術品収集家のチョイス

Contemporary
Art Station
C A

現代美術局発行

The Art Collector's Choice bookは、日本をはじめ世界のアートコレクター、美術館関係者、ギャラリーのオーナー、アート愛好家の方々のための、世界中の投資価値の高いアート作品を集めたガイドブックです。

The Art Collector's Choice book is committed for Japanese and international art collectors, curators, gallery owners and art enthusiasts, containing a curated selection of the most investable artworks that will inspire art collectors around the globe.

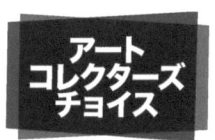

現代美術局発行

Published by Contemporary Art Station

表紙 | **Front Cover:** Francesco Ruspoli, "Harmony".
裏表紙 | **Back Cover:** Eriko Kaniwa, "Inner Tropics - Flamingo".
次頁 | **Next Page:** Kat Kleinman, "Collage".

現代美術局/ICMグループ株式会社によって2020年に英国で出版されました。すべての作品@2020年個人アーティスト。
作品の寸法と表題はアーティストによって提供。

ISBN 978-1-913179-47-2
英国出版、英国印刷
現代美術ステーションによって作成。
2020© ICMグループ限定
初版7500部

無断複製禁止
本書のいかなる部分も、事前の許可なくコピー、記録、その他の情報保存及び検索システムを含む電子又は機械的ないかなる形態でも複製または送信することはできません。
英国図書館の出版中のデーター
この本の目録レコードはイギリスの図書館から入手できます。

First published in the United Kingdom in March 2020 by the Contemporary Art Station / ICM Group Ltd.
All artworks @ 2020 the individual artists.
Measurements and titles of artworks are supplied by the artists.

ISBN 978-1-913179-47-2
Printed in the United Kingdom by UK Book Publishing.
Curated by Contemporary Art Station.
2020 © ICM Group Limited
First Edition 7500 copies

All Rights Reserved.
No part of this publication may be reproduced or transmitted in any form or by any means, electronic or mechanical, including photocopy, recording or any other information storage and retrieval system, without prior permission.
British Library Cataloguing-in-Publication Data.
A catalogue record for this book is available from the British Library.

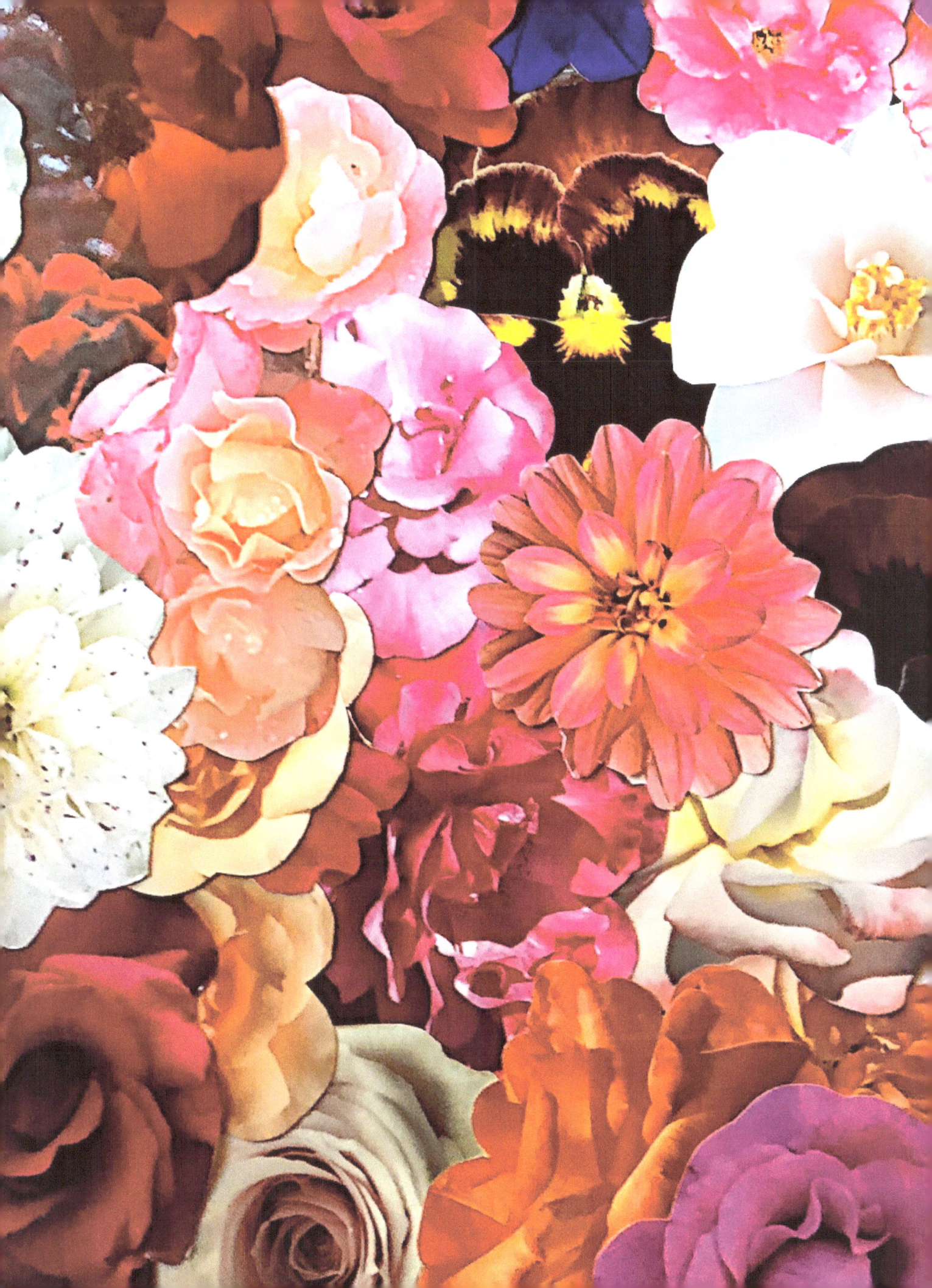

アート
コレクターズ
チョイス

注目のアーティスト ｜ Featured Artists

August Vilella	Jaana Heikkinen
Alexander Saner	Jasmine Seo
Amarnath Viswanath	Jessica Alazraki
Antwan Thompson	Josephine Pititto
Belle Roth	Jøran Juveli Marstrander
Betty Collier	Kaoru Kobayashi
Bj Formento	Karin Monschauer
Bo Kyung Song	Kat Kleinman
Bob Vanderbob	Laurent Pheulpin
Caspar Baum	Linda Lasson
Chace Gray	Ludmila Budanov
Chan Suk On	Makotu Nakagawa
Christo Anto Francis	Marina Koraki
Claudia Mayer-Mallenau	Maria Linares Freire
Daniel Johananoff	Max Werner
David Whitfield	Mayuko Ono Gray
Derwin Leiva	Michal Ashkenasi
Edmund Ian Grant	Mika Yajima
Eriko Kaniwa	Mira Satryan
Francesco Ruspoli	Nora Komoroczki
Gloria Keh	Paul Ygartua
Gro Folkan	Paula Menchen
Gustavs Filipsons	Peter Higgins
Haruka Harada	Pia Kintrup
Herbert Hermans	Ursa Schoepper
Helene Deserres	Vardan Ghumashyan
Howard Harris	Veronica Ibargüengoitia
Irena Orlov	Woonhyoung Choi
Irene Hoff	Yaroslava Liseeva

ICM Group Ltd. | ICMグループ限定

現代美術局発行

Published by Contemporary Art Station

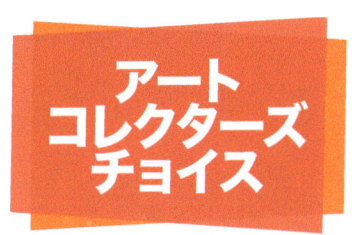

Irene Hoff
オランダ | Netherlands

独学でアートを学んだオランダ人アーティストIrene Hoff氏は、現在人間と環境における厳しい状況からみられるように、世界はバランスを失っていると考えている。彼女は、思いやり、直観、調和が生きるための重要な要素となる世界を望んでいる。その作品は、希望とインスピレーションに満ちており、それは鑑賞者に自分の感情と信念に気づき、自分らしくなれるきっかけを与えている。功績として、野生動物を描いた作品は自然保護士やレオナルド・ディカプリオによって署名されている。最近では、The Contemporary Art Curator Magazine 監修で2019年に出版された「100 Artists of the Future（アーティスト100人の未来）」に収録された。

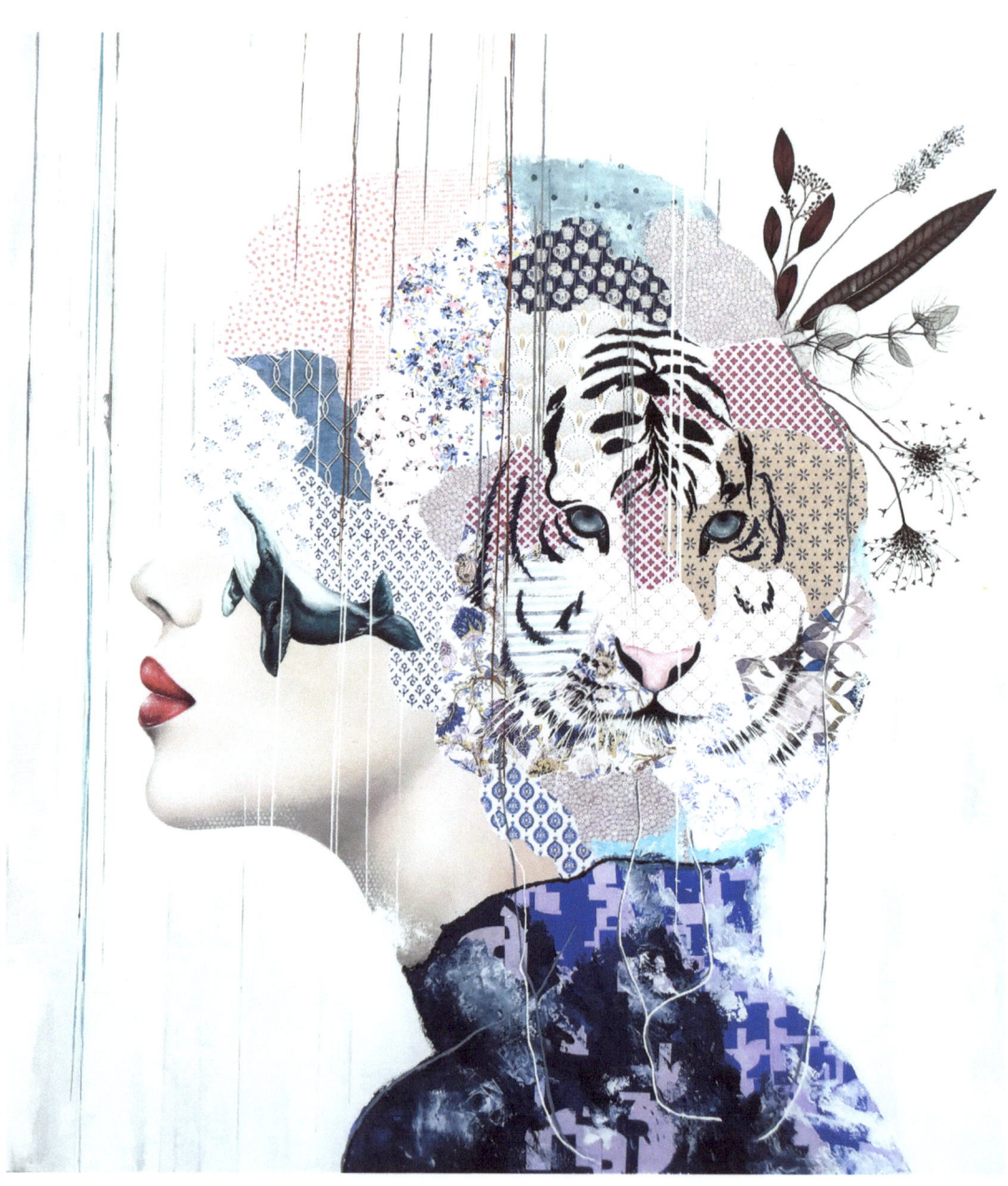

技術 | 絵画
価格帯 | USD 3000 - USD 6000
販売レポート | 要求に応じて [2018年] - 要求に応じて [2019年]
有効な年数 | 8年

Powerplay
Mixed media on canvas. 120x100 cm. 2019
USD 4300

irenehoff.com

For self-taught Dutch artist Irene Hoff, the world is out of balance which can be seen in the human & environmental challenges we are currently faced with. She craves a world where compassion, intuition and harmony are key elements for living. Irene's art is filled with hope and inspiration that encourages viewers to become aware of their feelings and beliefs, making space for their true self. Among her achievements, Irene is proud to have had one of her wildlife paintings signed by nature warrior and actor Leonardo DiCaprio. More recently, she was published in '100 Artists of the Future', A Collector's Edition curated by The Contemporary Art Curator Magazine (2019). Instagram: art_irenehoff

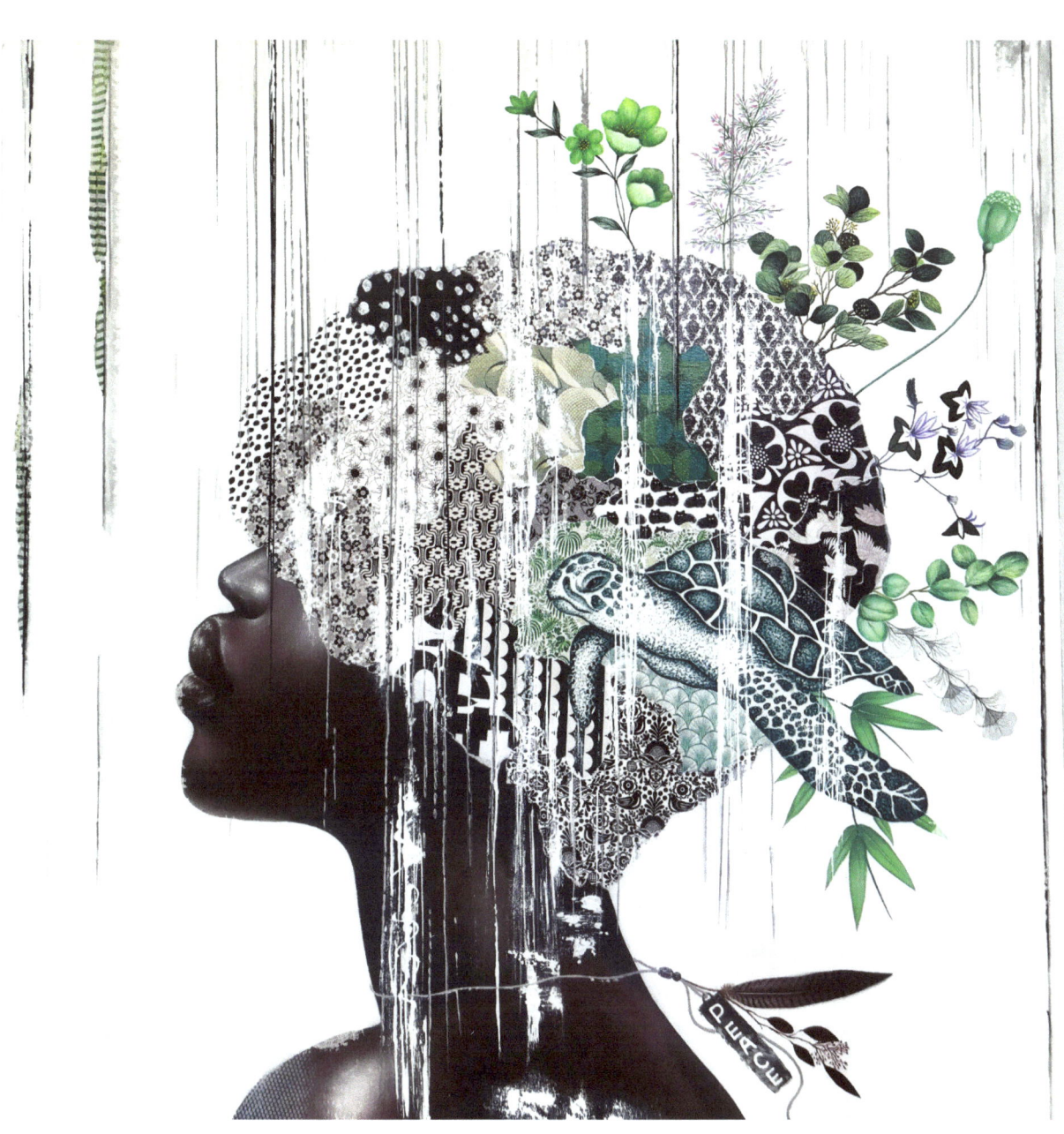

Technique | Painting
Price Range | USD 3000 - USD 6000
Sales Report | On request (2018) - On request (2019)
Active Years | 8 years

Slowing Down
Mixed media on canvas. 130x130 cm. 2019
USD 4800

Irene Hoff
オランダ | Netherlands

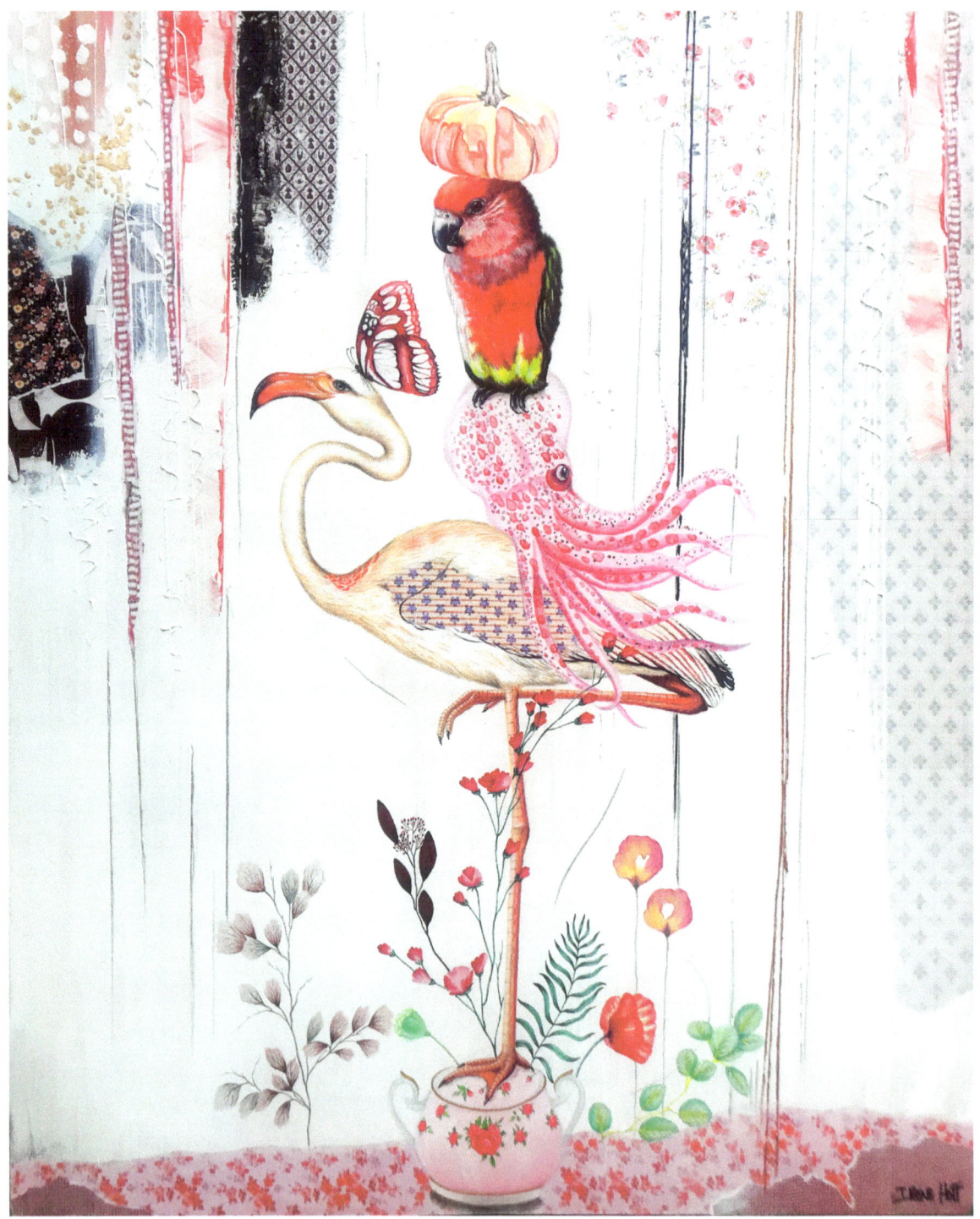

The Harmony of Things
Mixed media on canvas. 120x100 cm. 2019
USD 4300

irenehoff.com

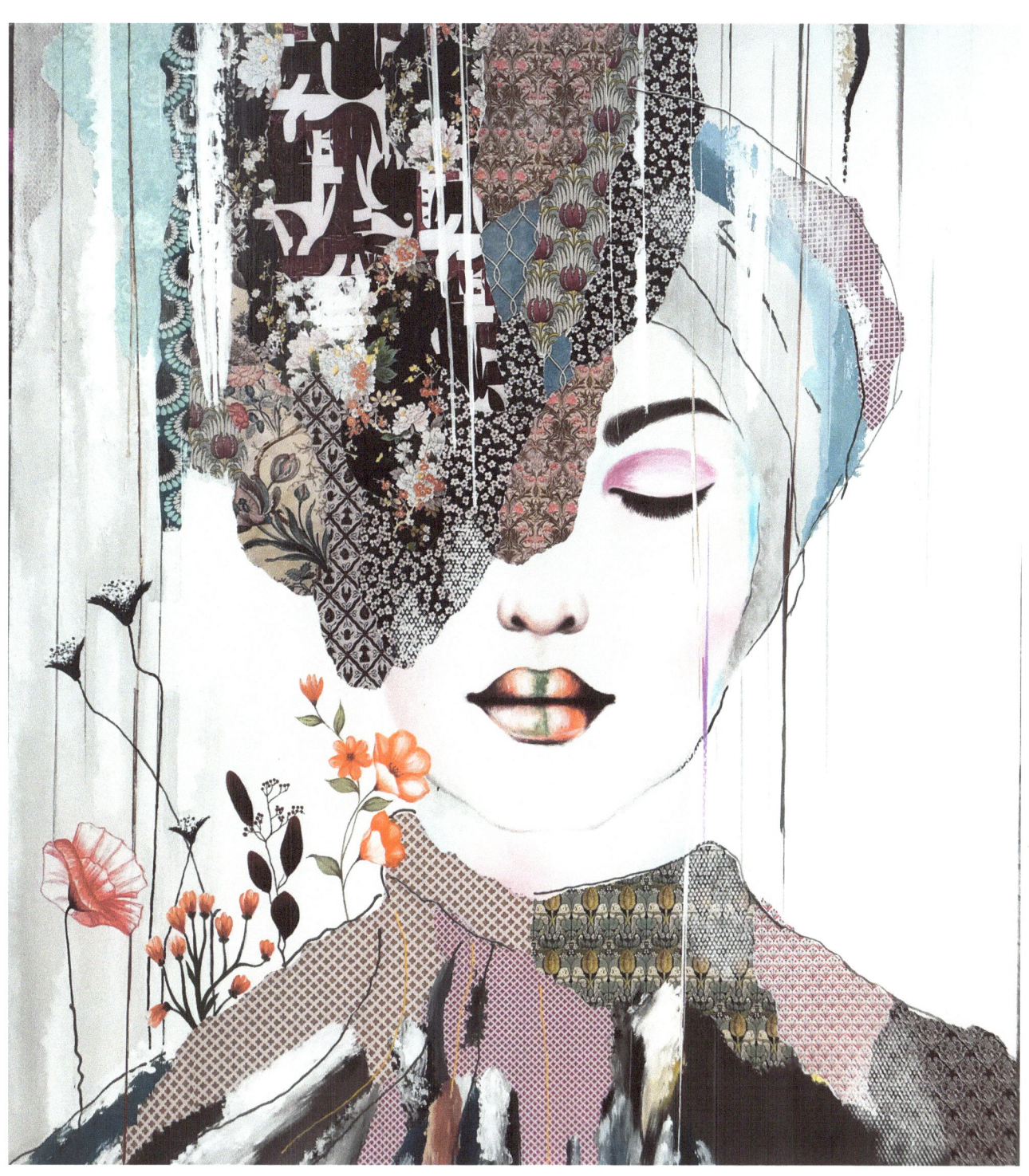

Showing Up
Mixed media on canvas. 130x120 cm. 2019
USD 4800

Kat Kleinman
ハンガリー | United States

Kat Kleinman氏はカリフォルニア北部出身で、2016年より花のコラージュアーティストとして活動。ポジティブな気持ちと、一時的であっても人の気持ちを和らげることに焦点をあてている。癒しのプロセスとして、何十本もの花を組み合わせ、まとまりのある新しい形を作っている。自身の写真を使用することにより作品に誠実さが増し、ネットのダウンロード素材などを使用した人間味のない方法とは一線を画している。全ての花は自身で切り、このプロセスを瞑想的だと考えている。彼女は色が持つ感情への前向きな作用とそれによって人々の関係性を向上させる可能性に強い関心を寄せている。彼女の作品は書籍やアメリカでの主要な展覧会などで紹介され、世界的に認知されている。

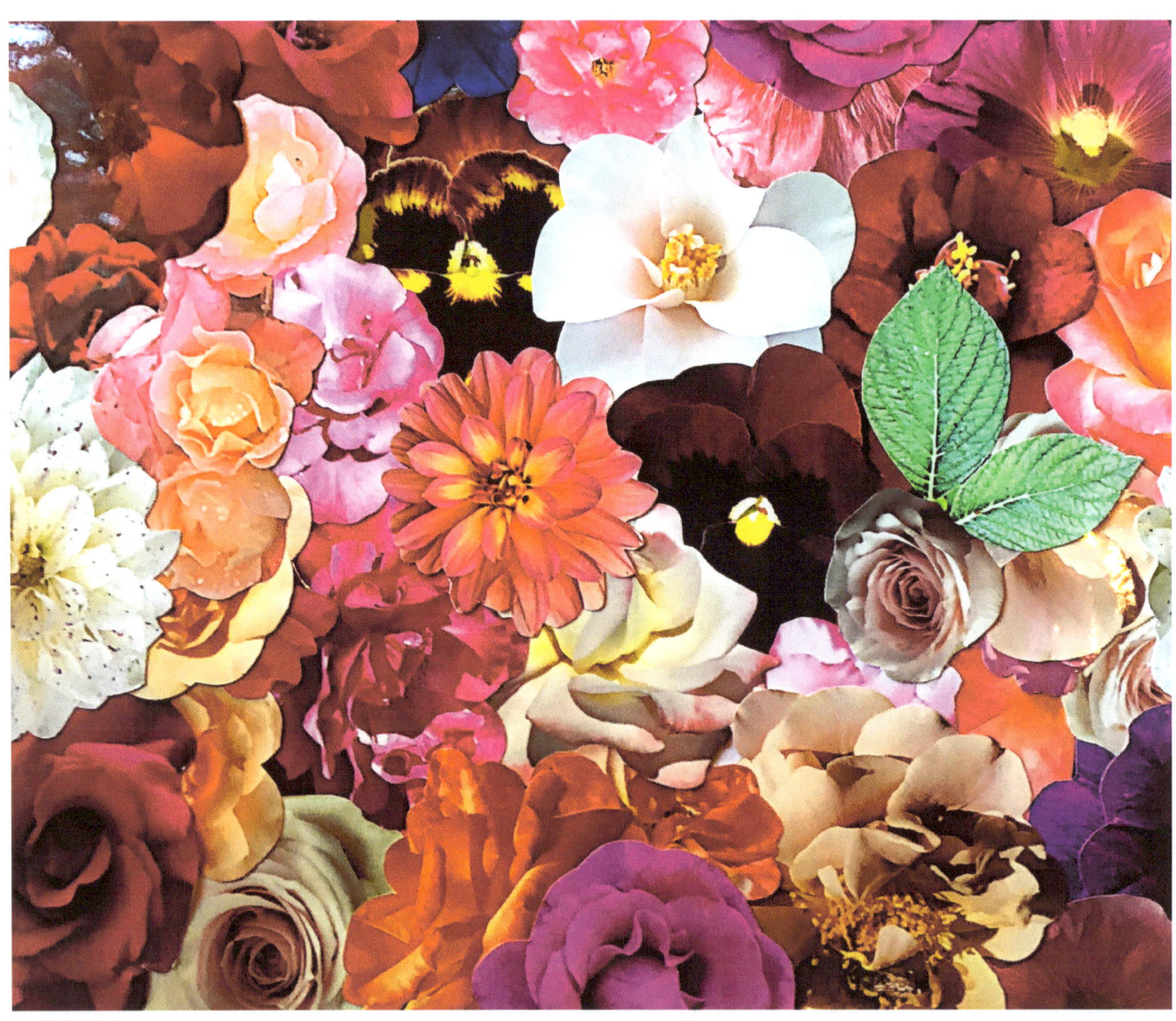

技術 | 写真 - 混合メディア
価格帯 | 200 US$ - 1200 US$
販売レポート | n/a US$ [2018年] - n/a US$ [2019年]
有効な年数 | 3年

Collage
(24x36 in.) 2019
USD 750

katkleinman.com

Kat Kleinman is a floral collage artist from Northern California. She began her career as an artist in 2016, with a focus on positivity and making people feel better, if only for a moment. Kat combines dozens of flowers to create a new and cohesive form, reflective of the healing process. Using her own photography separates the integrity of Kat's work from those who use more impersonal internet downloads as a source. Each flower is hand cut, a process she calls meditative. Kat is enthusiastic about the potential for color to positively influence emotions, ultimately leading to better relationships between people. Her work has been featured in books, in major exhibitions in the United States, and has been recognized internationally.

Collage
(24x36 in.) 2019
USD 750

Technique | Photography - Mixed Media
Price Range | 200 US$ - 1200 US$
Sales Report | n/a US$ (2018) - n/a US$ (2019)
Active Years | 3 years

Kat Kleinman
ハンガリー | United States

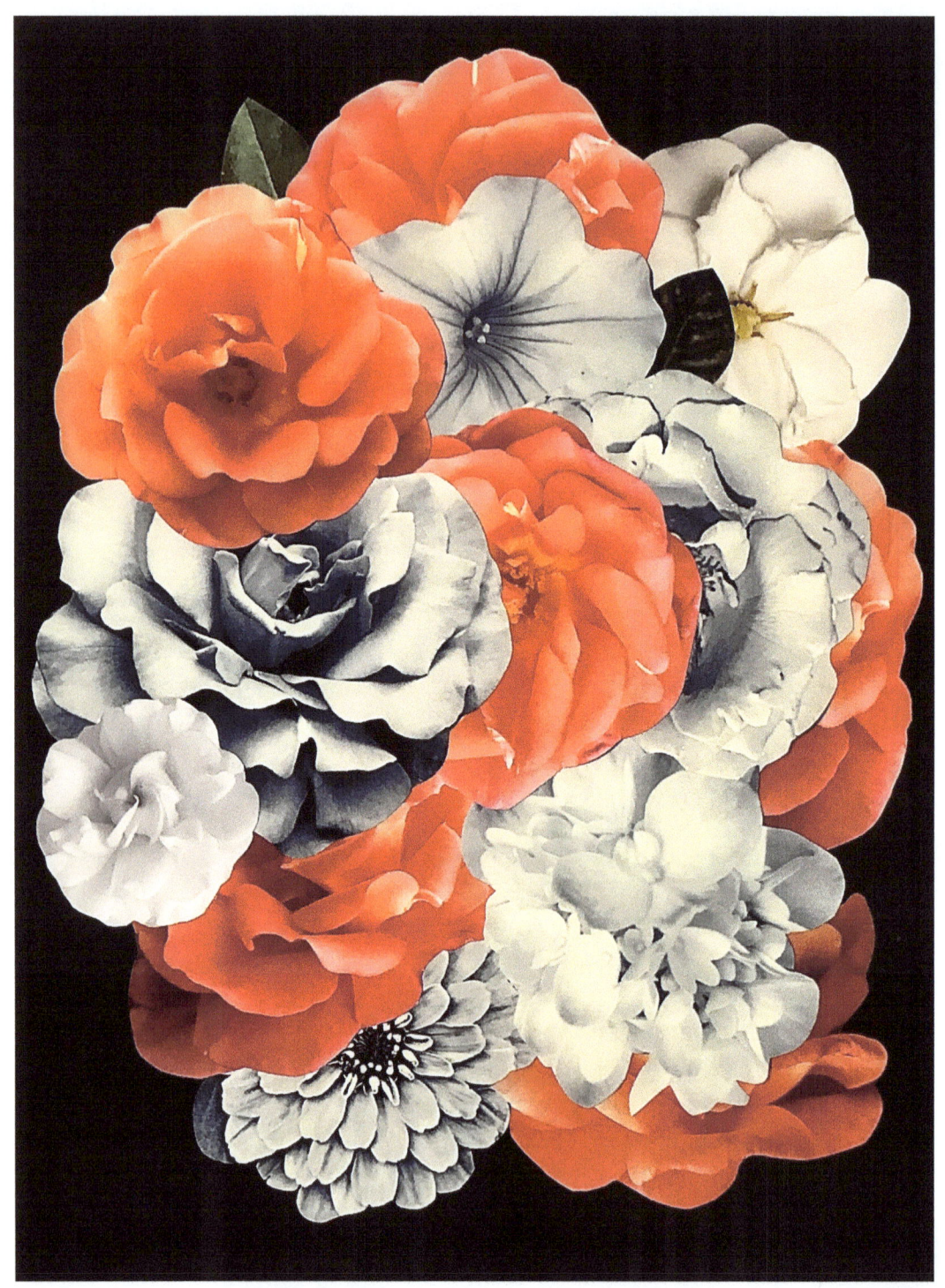

Collage
(20x16 in.) 2019
USD 300

katkleinman.com

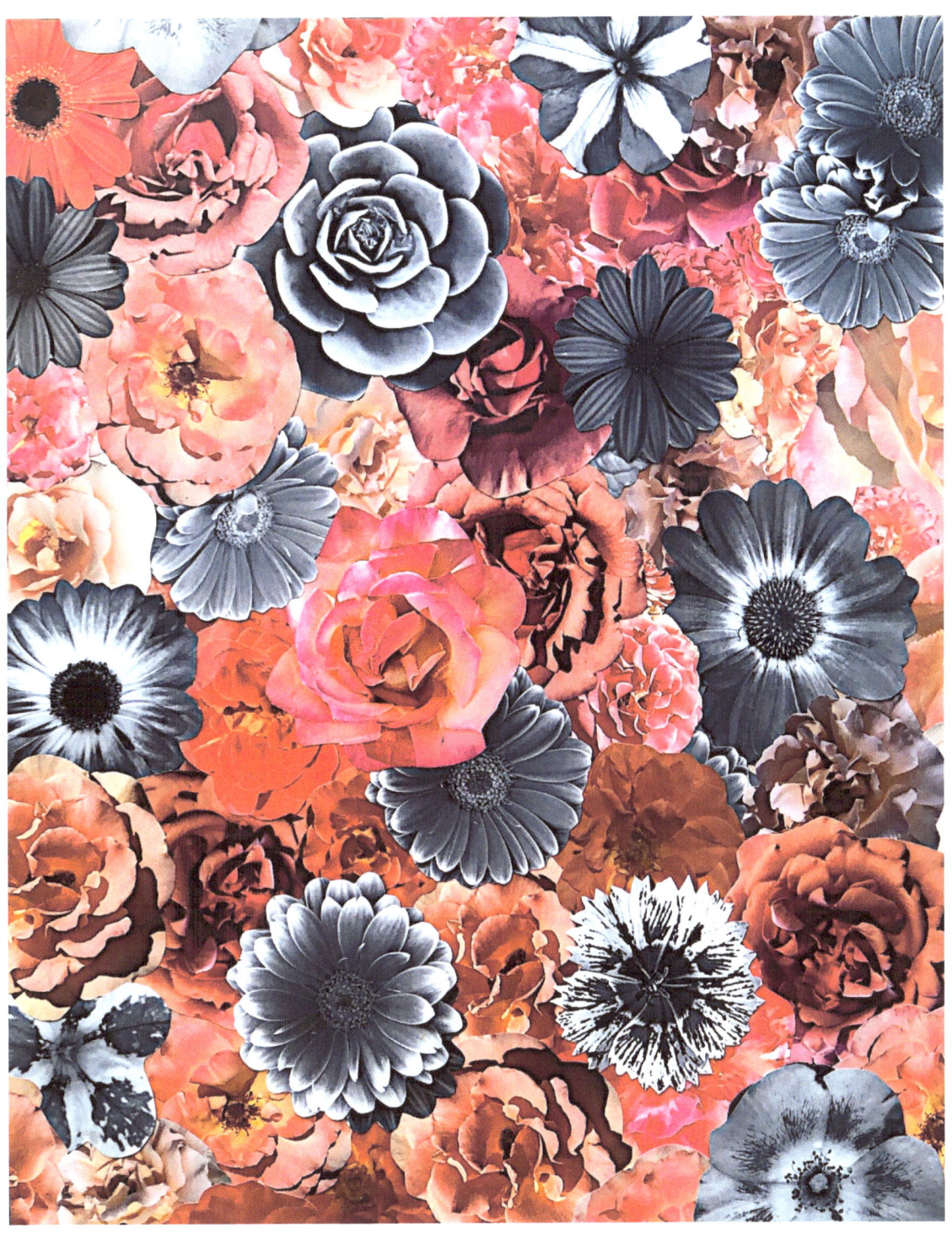

Collage
(20x16 in.) 2019
USD 300

Eriko Kaniwa
日本 | Japan

東京在住のカニワエリコ氏は世界的な賞の受賞歴がある写真デジタル・アーティストで、そのユニークな独自の哲学に基づき、よりデジタルな技法を用いた写真作品を制作している。また、彼女はSensegraphiaアートの創設者でもある。Sensegraphiaとは、写真の視覚的美しさを使って、人間は自然の一部であり、自然の力学に関わっているということを認識することができる自然感を発達させ表現することにより、写真の概念を再定義することである。

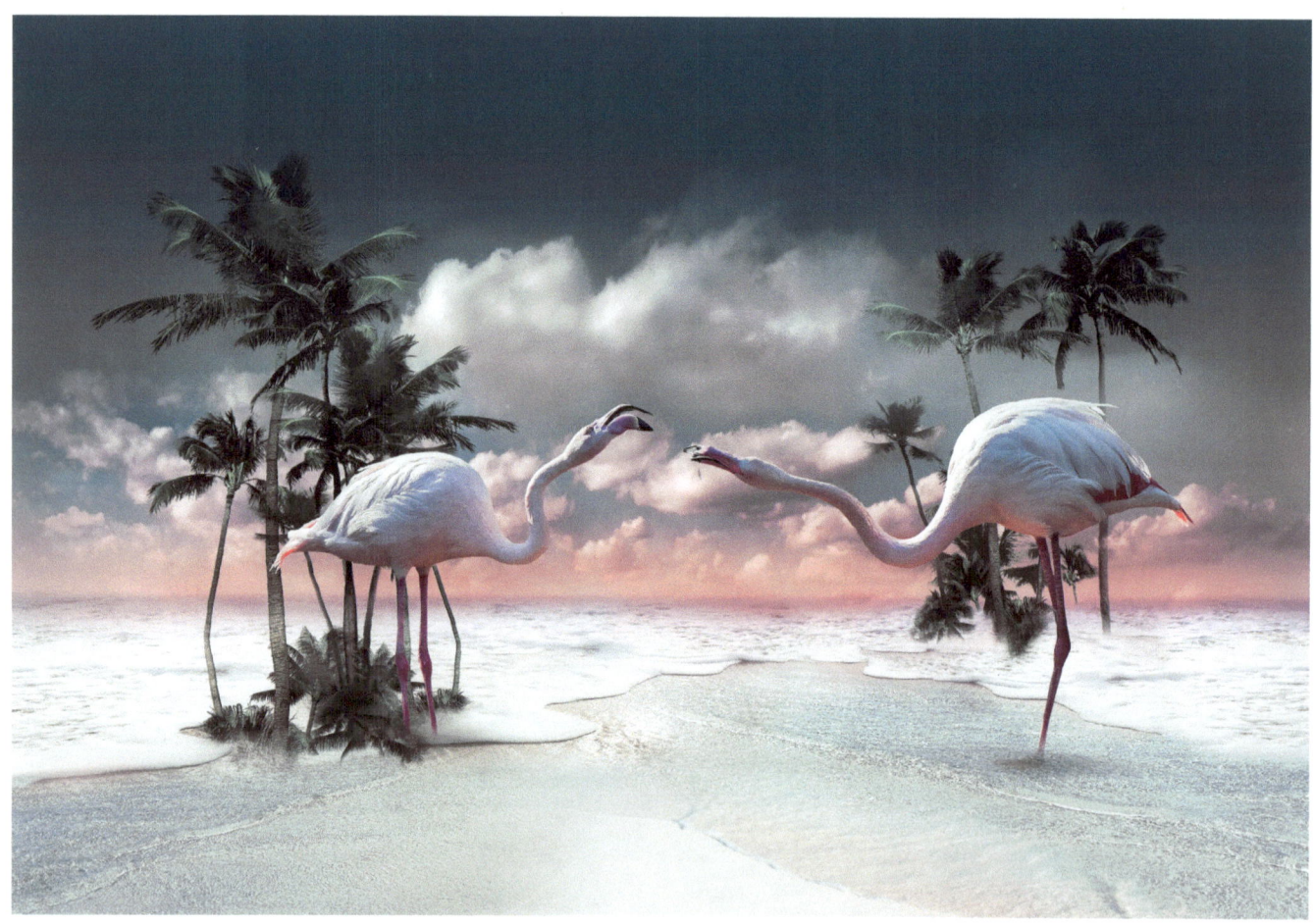

技術	写真 - デジタルアート
価格帯	650 US$ - 4000 US$
販売レポート	n/a US$ [2018年] - n/a US$ [2019年]
有効な年数	5年

Inner tropics - Flamingo (2020). Limited edition 5+2APs.
W120 cm x H80 cm. Print on CANSON Platine Fibre Rag.
Price Upon Request.

sensegraphia.jp

Eriko Kaniwa is an international award-winning photographic digital artist based in Tokyo, creates digitally enhanced photographic artwork based on her unique philosophy, and the creator of Sensegraphia fine art. Sensegraphia is a conceptual redefinition of photography, in which the visual aesthetics of the photograph are used to develop and express the sense of nature that enables us to recognize that humans are a part of nature and that we are involved in nature's dynamics. Sensegraphia puts forward a philosophy and creative activities that reestablish the essential unity between people and nature through fine art. Also she and her artworks has been featured in the magazines such as British GQ, London Life, Wired and more.

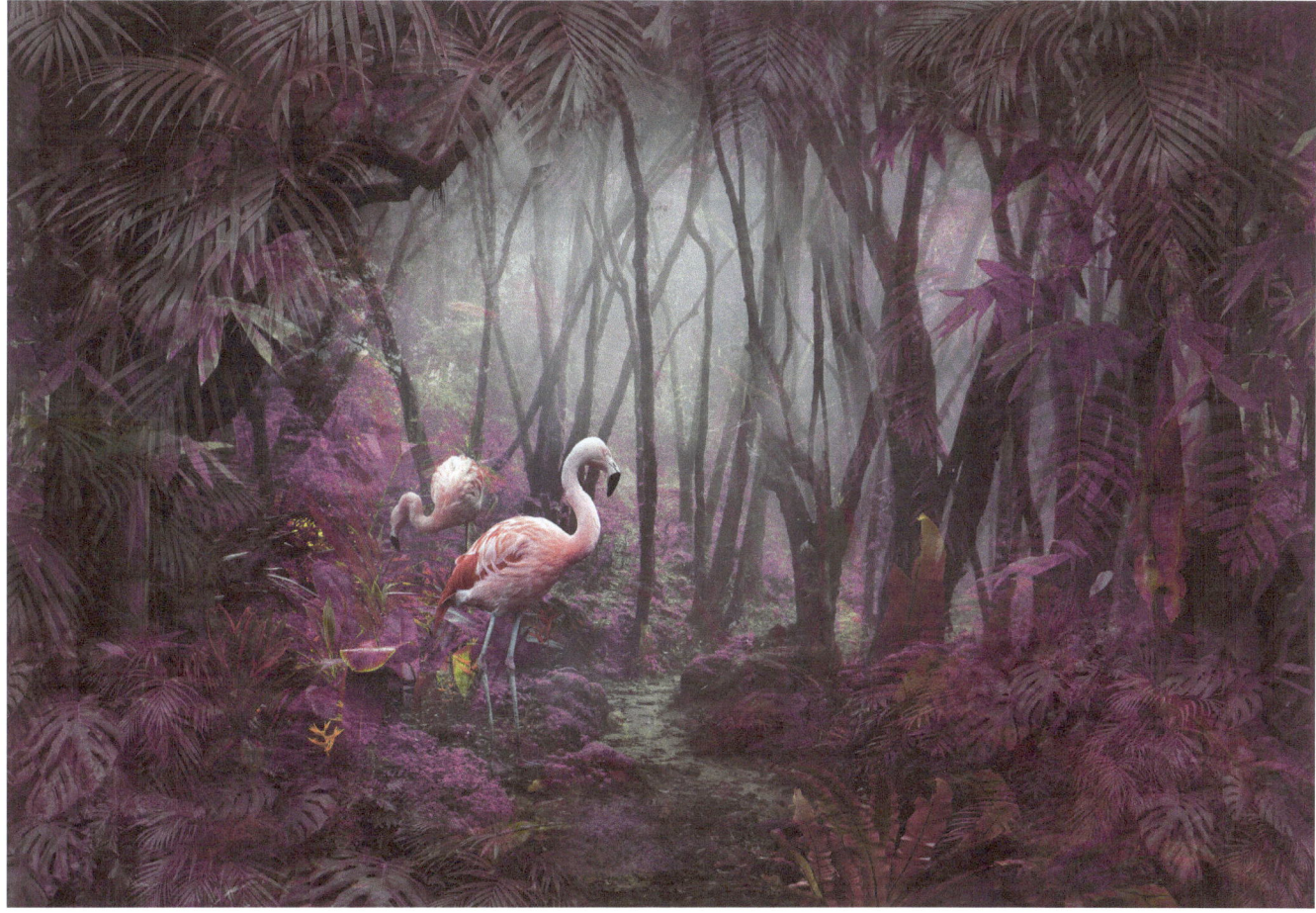

Technique | Photography - Digital Art
Price Range | 650 US$ - 4000 US$
Sales Report | n/a US$ (2018) - n/a US$ (2019)
Active Years | 5 years

Another Tropics (2019) - Limited Edition 5+2APs.
W130 cm x H86.5 cm. Print on CANSON Platine Fibre Rag
Price Upon Request

Eriko Kaniwa
日本 | Japan

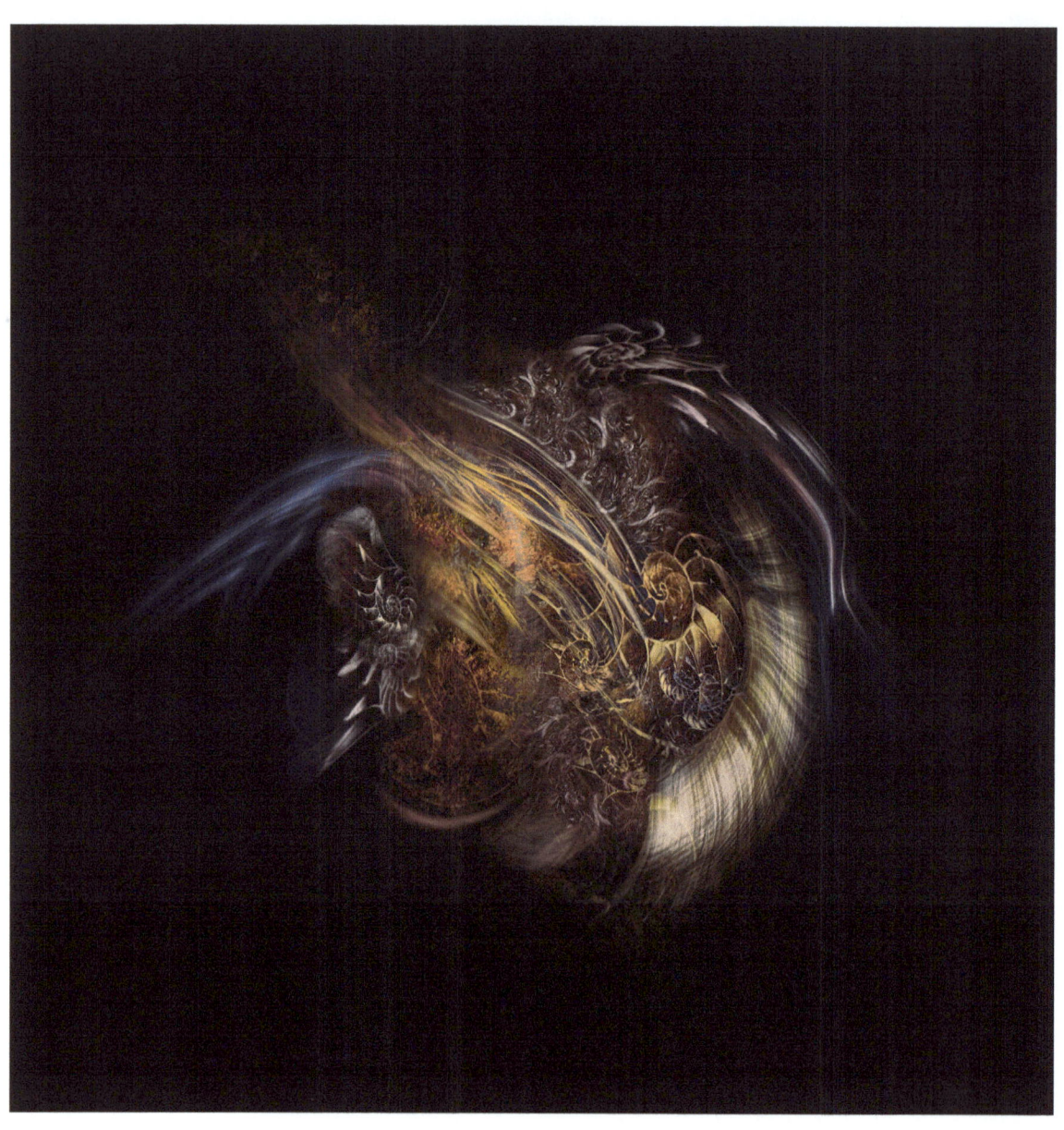

Nautilus Universe - Wind Flare (2020) Limited Edition. 5+2APs.

W100cm x H100 cm. Print on CANSON Platine Fibre Rag

Price Upon Request

sensegraphia.jp

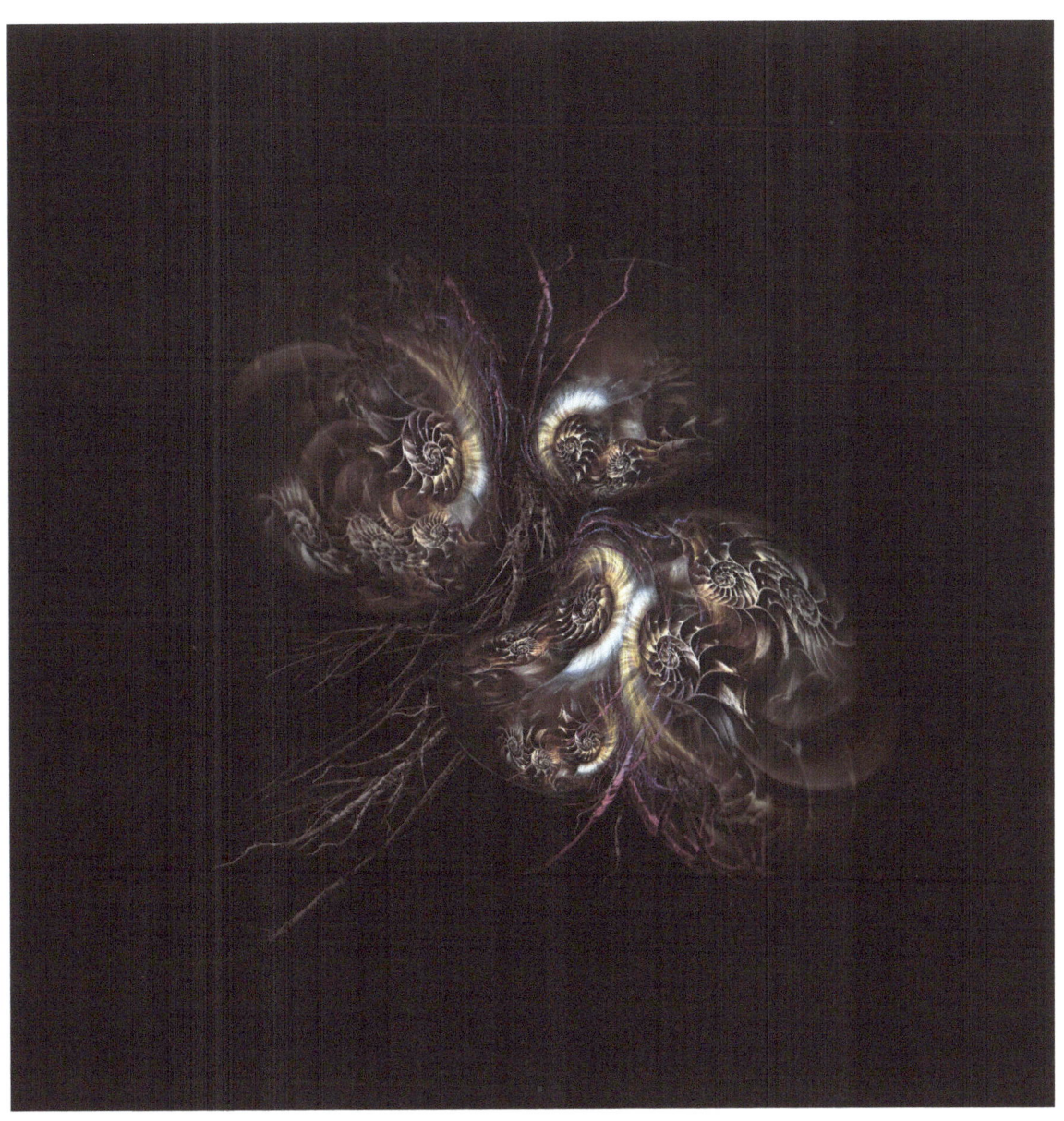

Nautilus Universe meets branching #2 (2020) Limited Edition
5+2APs. W100cm x H100 cm. Print on CANSON Platine Fibre Rag
Price Upon Request

Danny Johananoff
ハンガリー | United States

私は心の底から楽しんでいるこれらの春の甘い朝のように、素晴らしい静寂が私の魂全体を所有しています。　私は一人で、私のような魂の至福のため
写真家のDanny Johananoff氏は、アートはどこにでも存在し、彼が見たアートをレンズを通じてとらえるのが自身の役割だと考えている。彼は、鑑賞
者が作品を写真家としての彼の眼を通してイメージをとらえることを可能にしている。彼にとっての写真作品は、カメラを使った絵画なのである。作品の
多くはぼやけた幻想的なもので、それらは自然が持つ様式と純粋な美しさを表現している。また、撮影はあえて撮影対象に何の期待も概念も持たずに
始める。そうすることで、感性を刺激するどんな情景も受け入れられるからである。そして、その感情と観点を鑑賞者へ伝えたいと考えている。

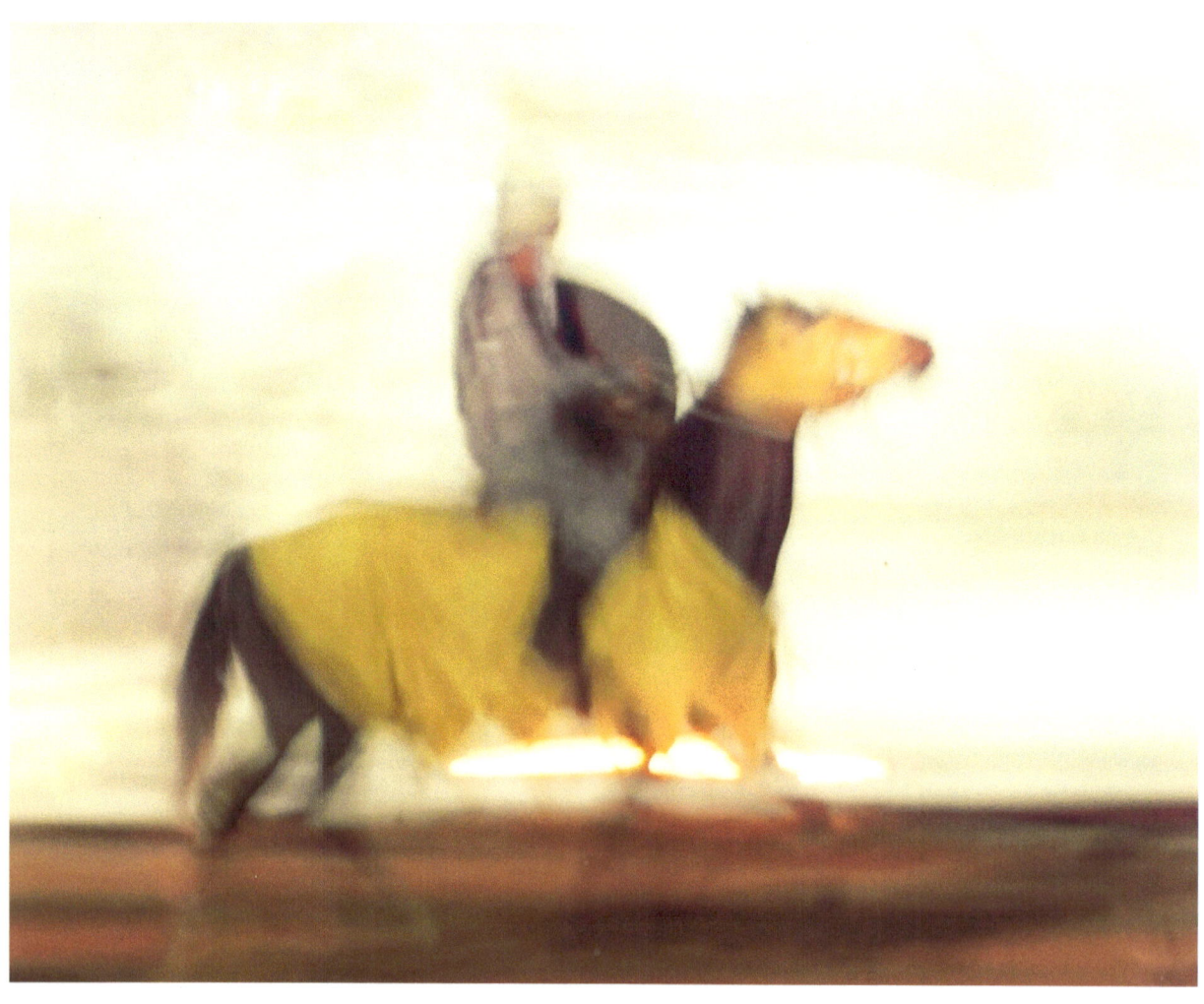

技術 | 写真
価格帯 | USD 1900 - USD 5200
販売レポート | USD n/a [2018年] - USD n/a [2019年]
有効な年数 | 2年

Persian Miniature

15.5"x20.5"

USD 1900

art-mine.com/artistpage/danny_johananoff.aspx

As a photographer, Danny Johananoff believes art is always there, and that it is his job to capture it in the lens through which he sees it. Danny allows the viewer to observe the image through his eyes as a photographer. Johananoff refers to his work as painting with his camera. His images are often blurred and dreamy, depicting the culture and the pure beauty found in nature. Johananoff begins each photo expedition with no expectations or notions on what he may see and shoot. Thus, he opens himself up to receive any scenery that emits an emotion to him. It is this feeling and point of view he wishes to transmit onto the viewer.

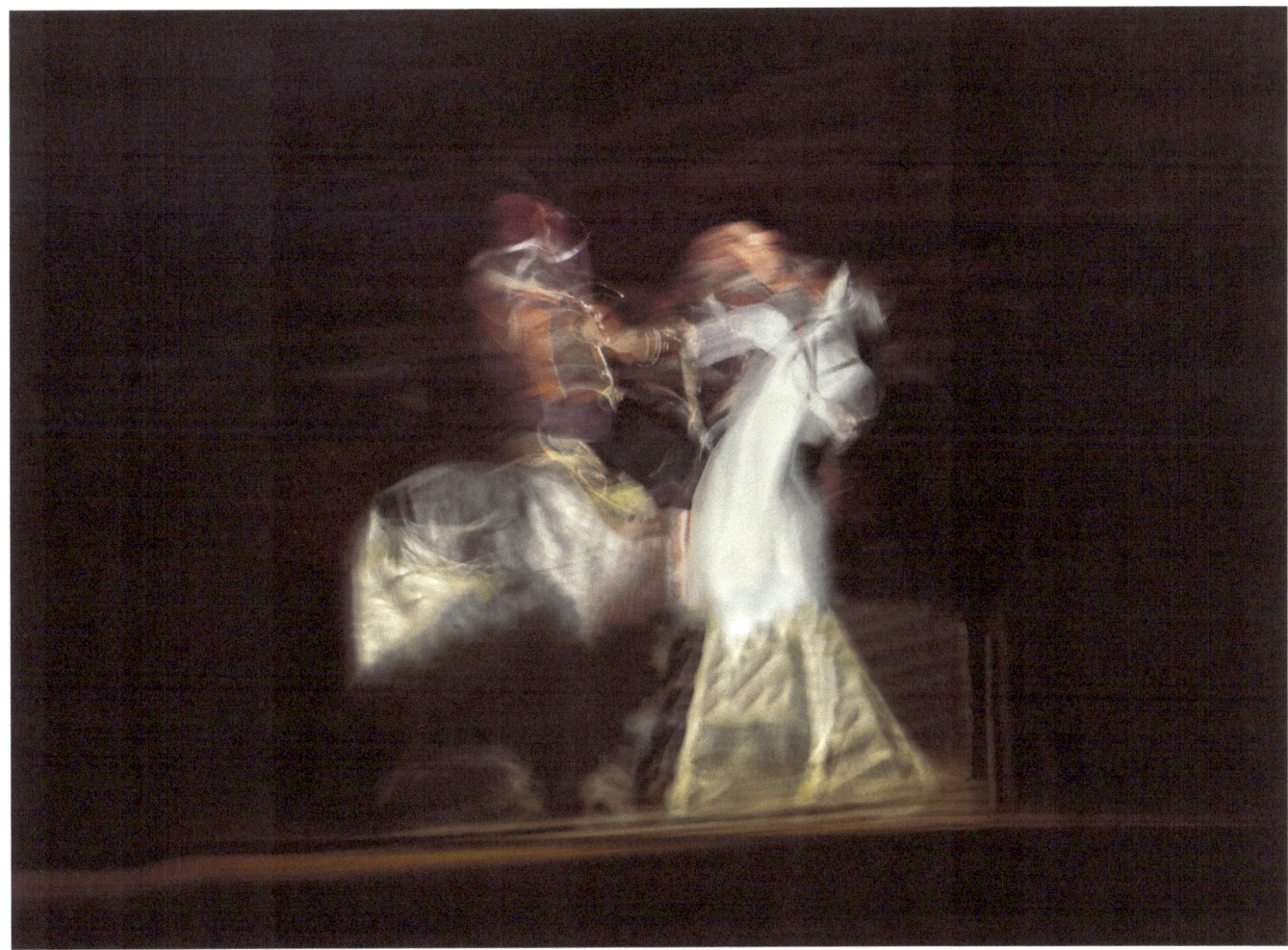

Technique | Photography
Price Range | USD 1900 - USD 5200
Sales Report | USD n/a (2018) - USD n/a (2019)
Active Years | 2 years

Friendly Collision
30"x42"
USD 3200

Danny Johananoff
ハンガリー | United States

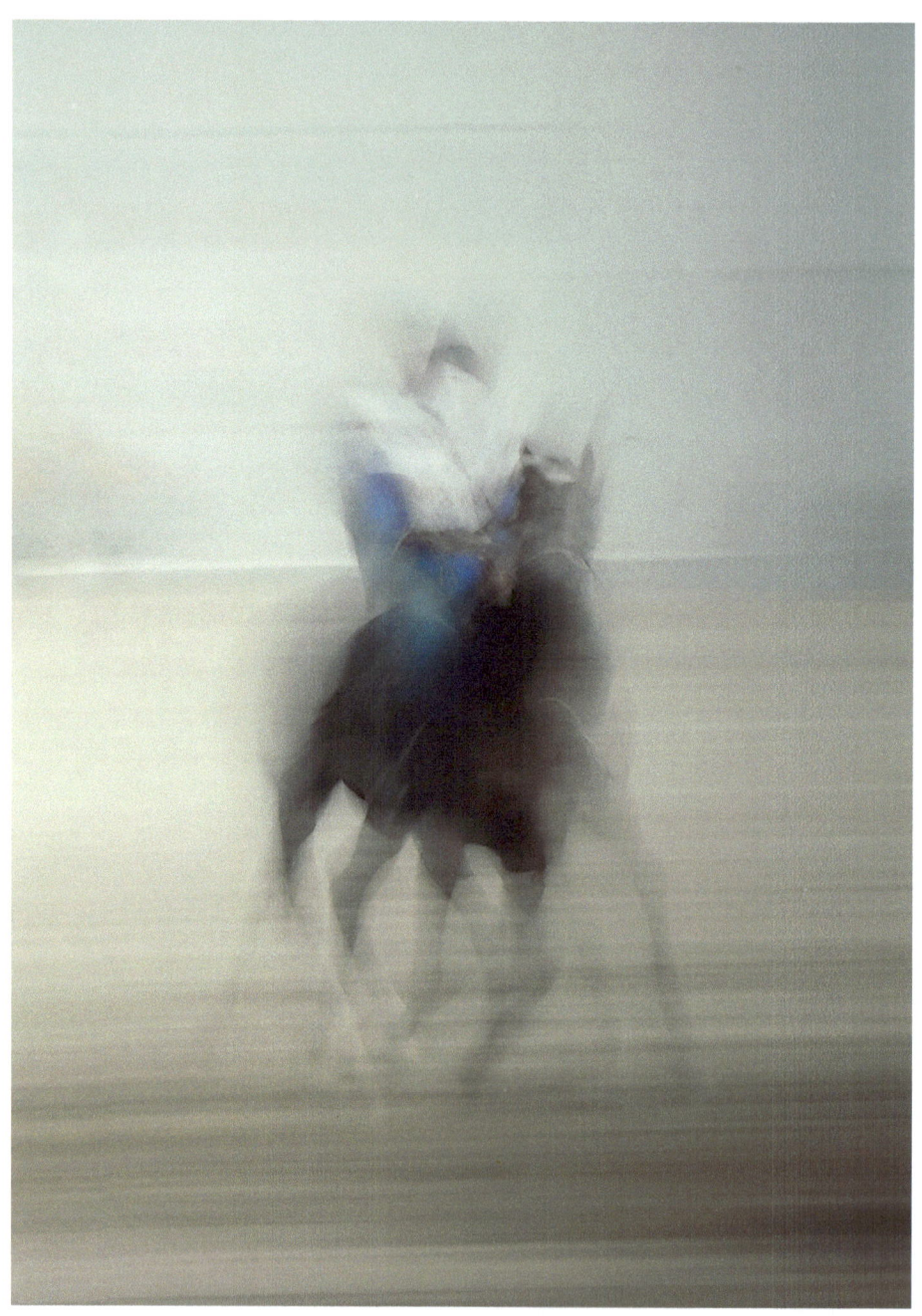

Return - This image was taken at the end of a long day of horse wrestling in the World Nomad Games in Kyrgyzstan, 2018.

A calm and peaceful moment for the horse and rider. 61.5"x45"

USD 5200

art-mine.com/artistpage/danny_johananoff.aspx

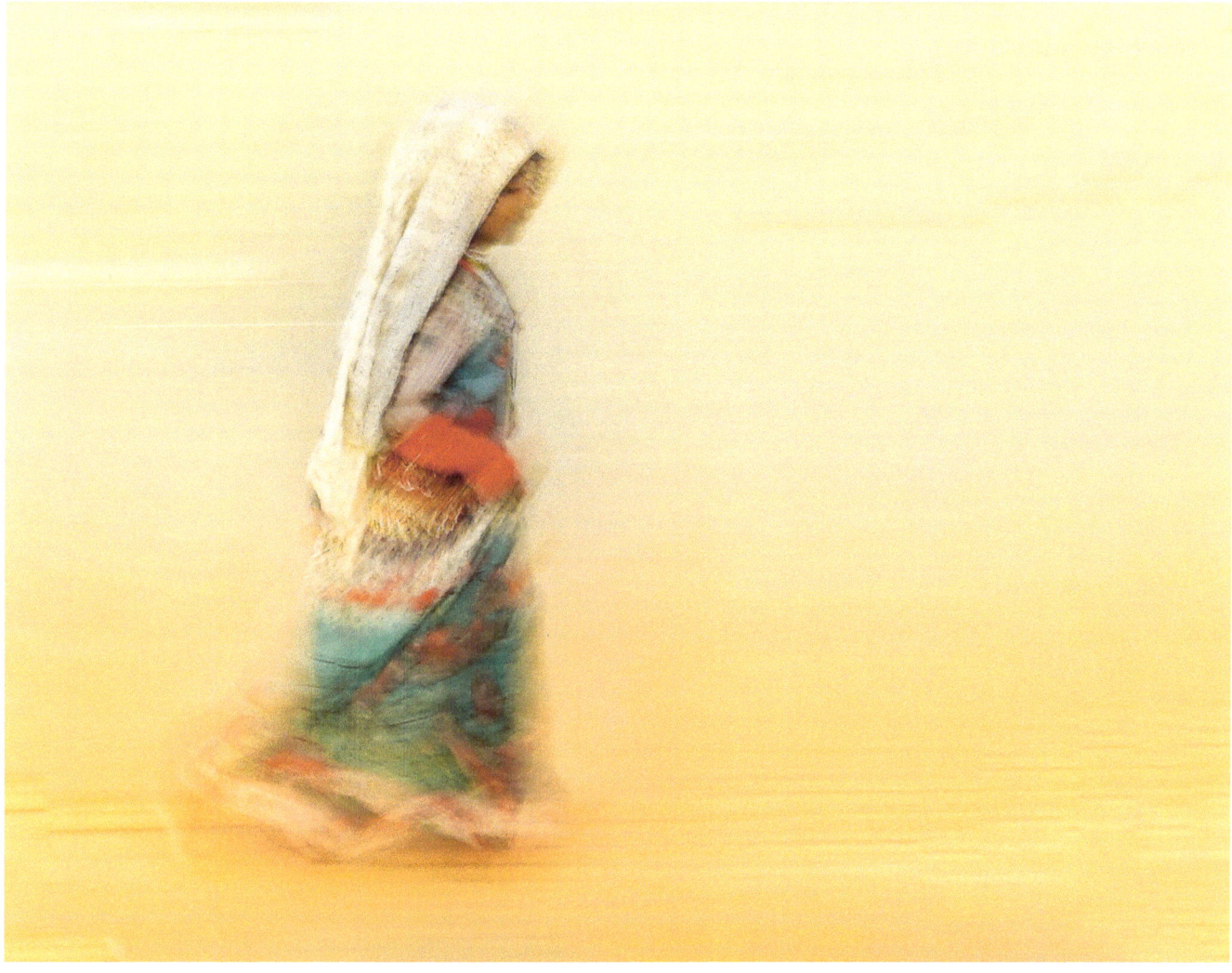

Girl in Dunes - This photo was taken in the dunes of west India. This Gypsy girl lives in a small village near Jaisalmer. The contrast but well blending of the colorful dress on the background of sandy dues is what attracted my eye. 28"x37"

USD 2600

Ludmila Budanov
キプロス | Cyprus

ロシア出身Ludmila Budanov氏は興味深い世界観を持っている。音楽を学び、音楽家になり、天職と感じてアーティストになったため、彼女の作品は音と色の融合と呼ばれている。作品には様々な色をふんだんに使うが、それは、人生を前向きにとらえ、喜びを他者と分かち合いたいと願う自身の姿勢を反映しているといえる。彼女はユニークで個人的な技法を使用しており、その方法は多くの専門家たちにとってもいまだ謎のままである。抽象絵画とは、写真のように現実を再現するためものではなく、見る者の想像力を掻き立たせ、自由に連想し、感情を目覚めさせるためのものであると考えている。

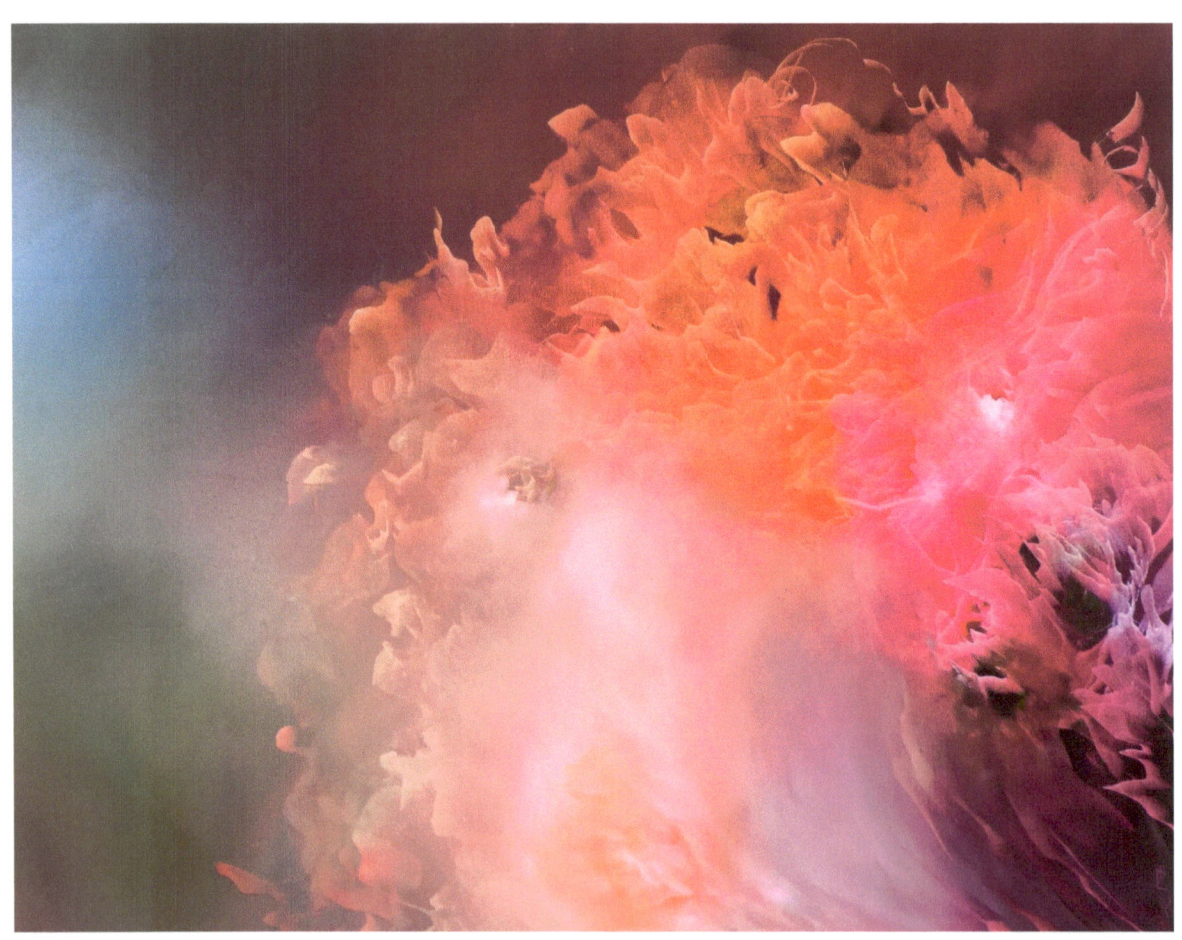

技術 | 絵画
価格帯 | USD 700 - USD 7000
販売レポート | USD 25000 [2018年] - USD 50000 [2019年]
有効な年数 | 10年

In the Clouds
Oil/canvas, 90x120 cm. 2019
USD 3000

ludmilabudanov.com

Ludmila Budanov is an author with an interesting vision of the world: was born in Russia and is a musician by education and an artist by vocation, which is why her work deserves to be called color-sounding. The paintings are full of color and this, most likely, reflects the attitude of the author, speaking about the positive perception of life and the willingness to share with others her joy. Budanov's technique is unique and personal and even for many professionals remains a mystery. The task of abstract paintings is not to reproduce reality with photographic precision, but to encourage the flight of fantasy, to let imagination flow, to awaken certain feelings and associations.

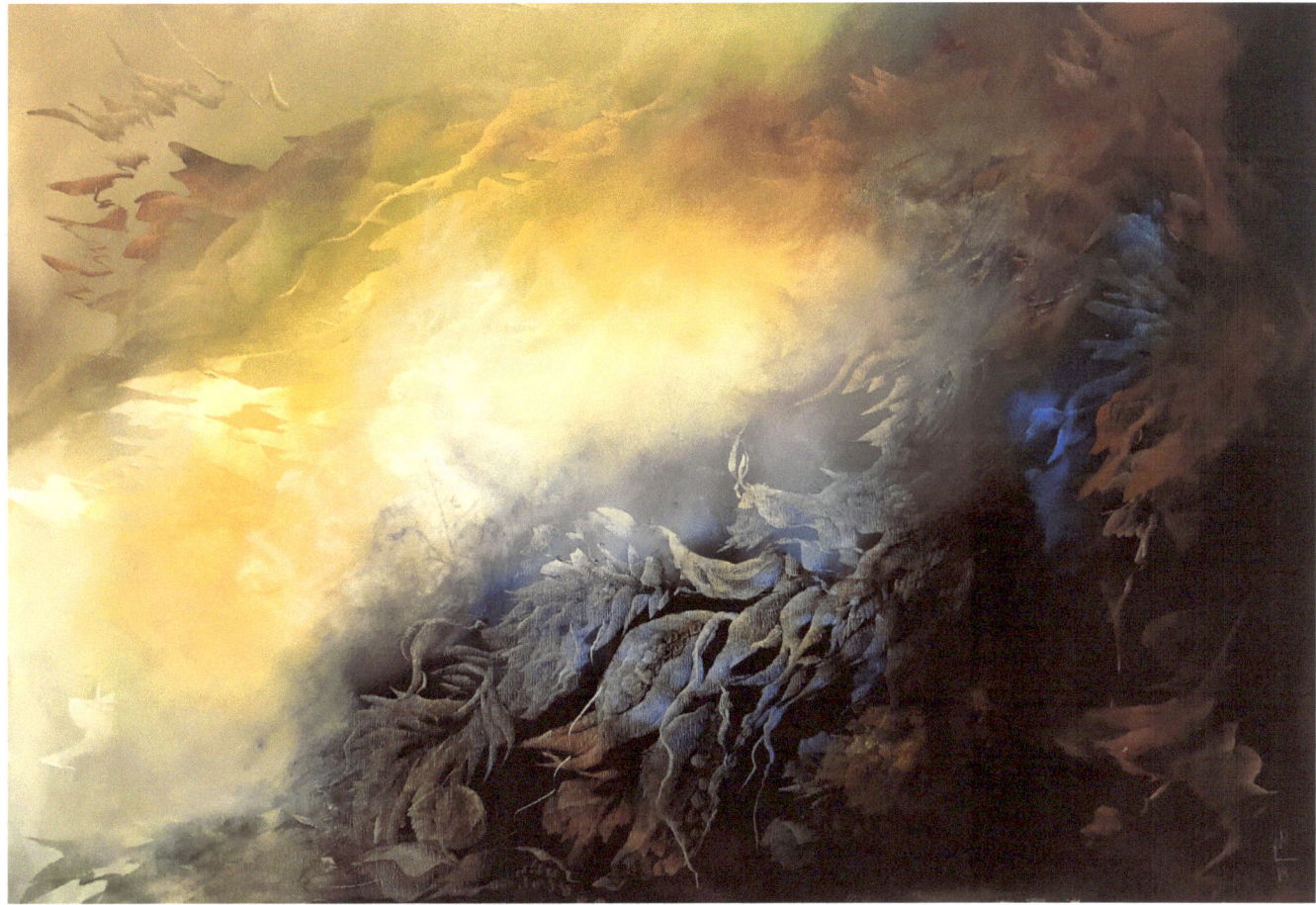

Technique | Painting
Price Range | USD 700 - USD 7000
Sales Report | USD 25000 (2018) - USD 30000 (2019)
Active Years | 10 years

The Streaming Light
Oil/canvas, 80x120 cm. 2019
USD 3500

Ludmila Budanov
キプロス | Cyprus

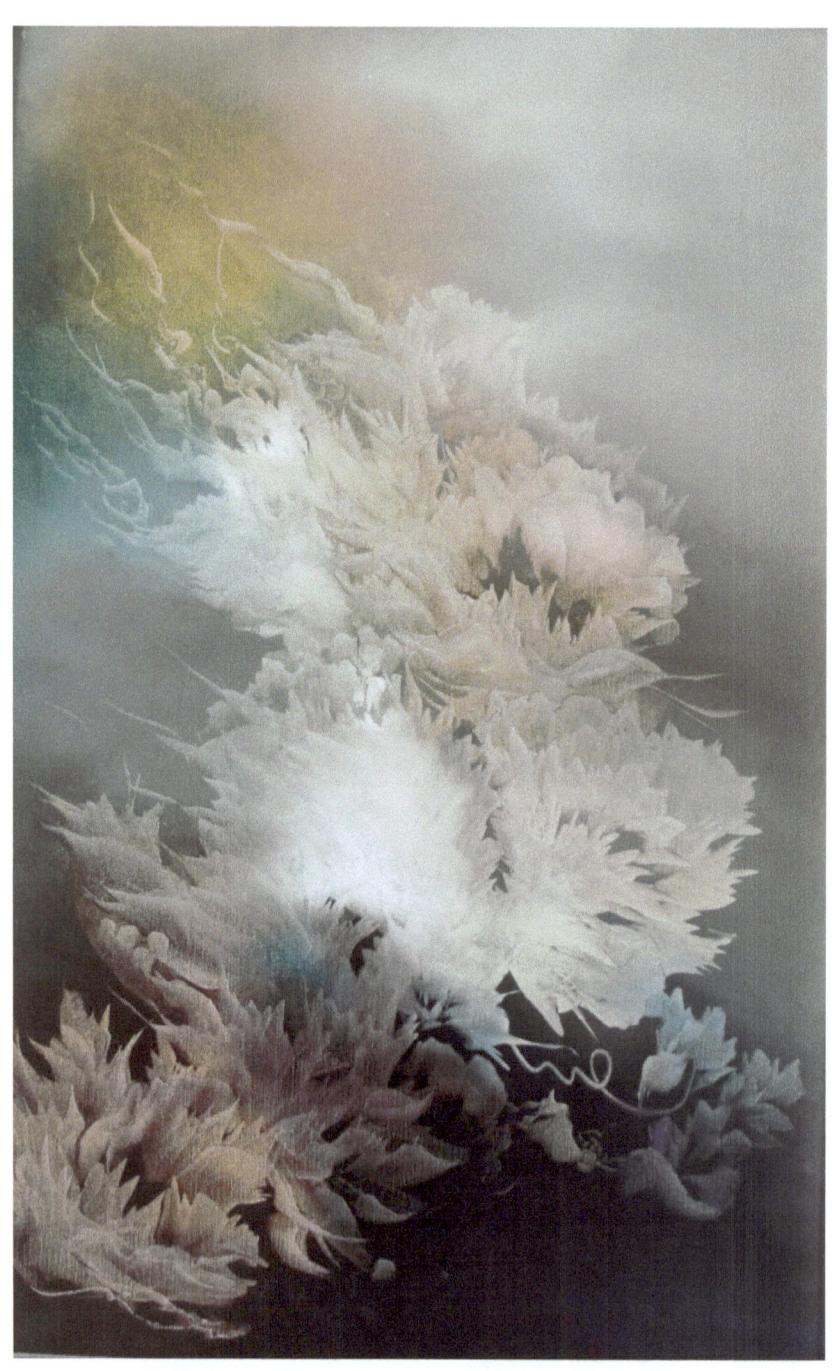

The Elegy
Oil/canvas, 90x60 cm. 2018
USD 1600

ludmilabudanov.com

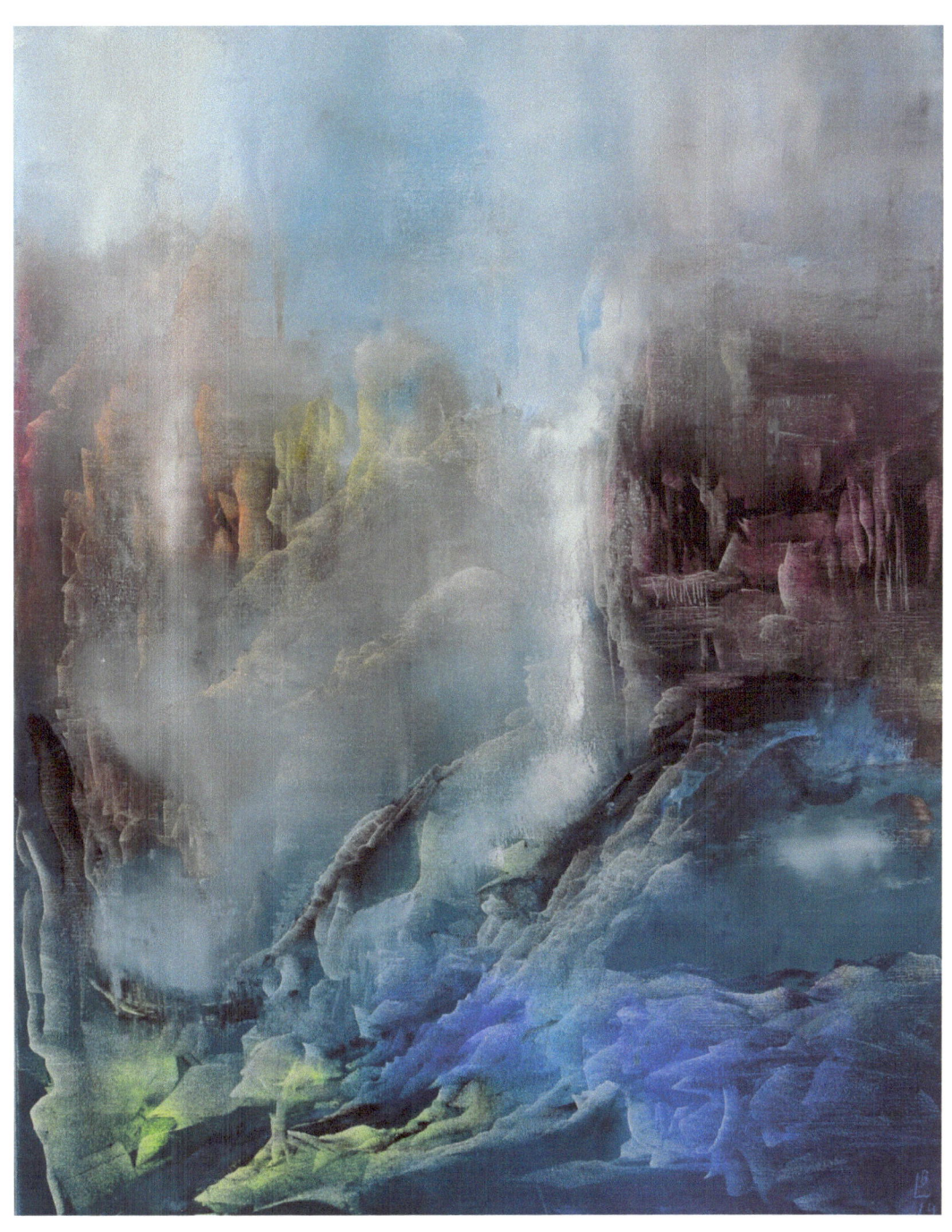

The Mirage
Oil/canvas, 100x80 cm. 2019
USD 2500

Francesco Ruspoli
イギリス | United Kingdom

自身にとってアートとは、現状に立ち向かい、人々の感情と精神を蘇らせ、改めて感化させるためのもので、それは必然的に現在世界で起こっている現状との闘いとなる。肝心なのは、アートとは何かというだけでなく、アートに何ができるか、また、何をすべきかである。最も憂うべきことは、儲けがすべてという世の中のシステムであり、それによって創造性や個人の表現の可能性を潰してしまっていると考えている。自身の中の創造性を見つけるのに長い時間がかかったが、その課程でこのような商業主義との闘いが多くあった。それは非常に強力で陰湿であり、気に入らないものを排除したり無視したりするものだとしている。

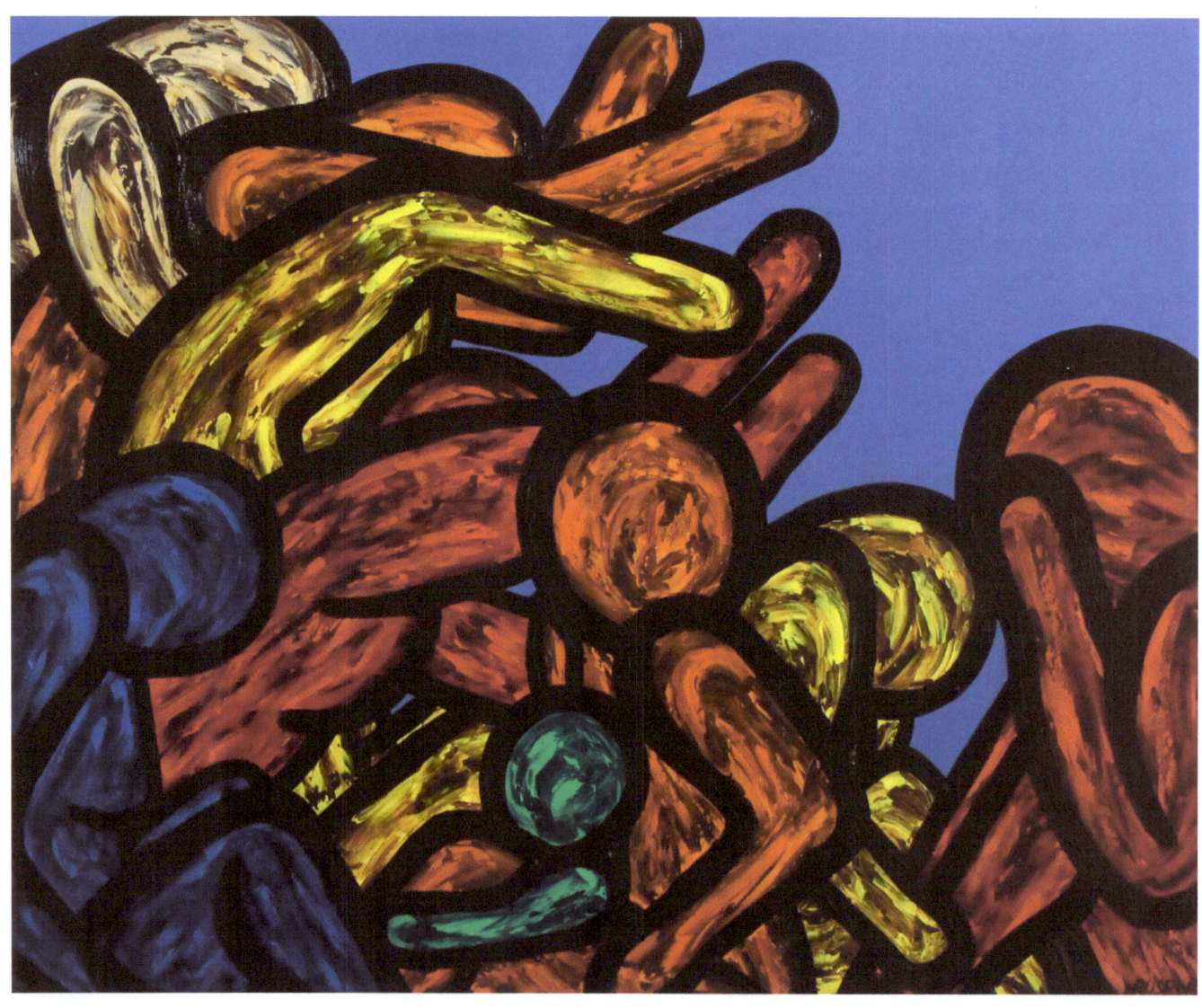

技術 | 絵画
価格帯 | 2000 US$ - 15000 US$
販売レポート | n/a US$ [2018年] - n/a US$ [2019年]
有効な年数 | 40年

Exhortation

USD 6400

francescoruspoliart.com

Born in 1958 in Paris from a British mother with a French background and a Belgian father with an Italian background, Ruspoli has presented his work in international art fairs and international galleries increasing worldwide exposure. He has been recipient of a number of important international awards and medals such as to mention a few: Eugene Fromentin Award and Gold Medal in France, Masters Award and Honorable Award in USA, Gold Medal in China, Honorary Award of Distinction and Honorable Award in UK, Silver Medal in Italy. Inspired by his surrounding Ruspoli moved towards a new way of working stimulated by the influences of artists such as Chaim Soutine, Georges Rouault, Henri Matisse, Edward Munch and Egon Schiele. Ruspoli art work places the human figures in an abstract environment supported by a vivid use of colours where subtle gradation and dramatic contrast express nuance of emotion and sensuous physicality. The work also expresses the direct sensation of lived experience through organic shapes and forms woven from flowing lines and the gaze of the viewer. You are invited to participate in a creative encounter with these elements constructing your own visual languages and meanings. Ruspoli is internationally awarded with some of his paintings in Museum's permanent collections.

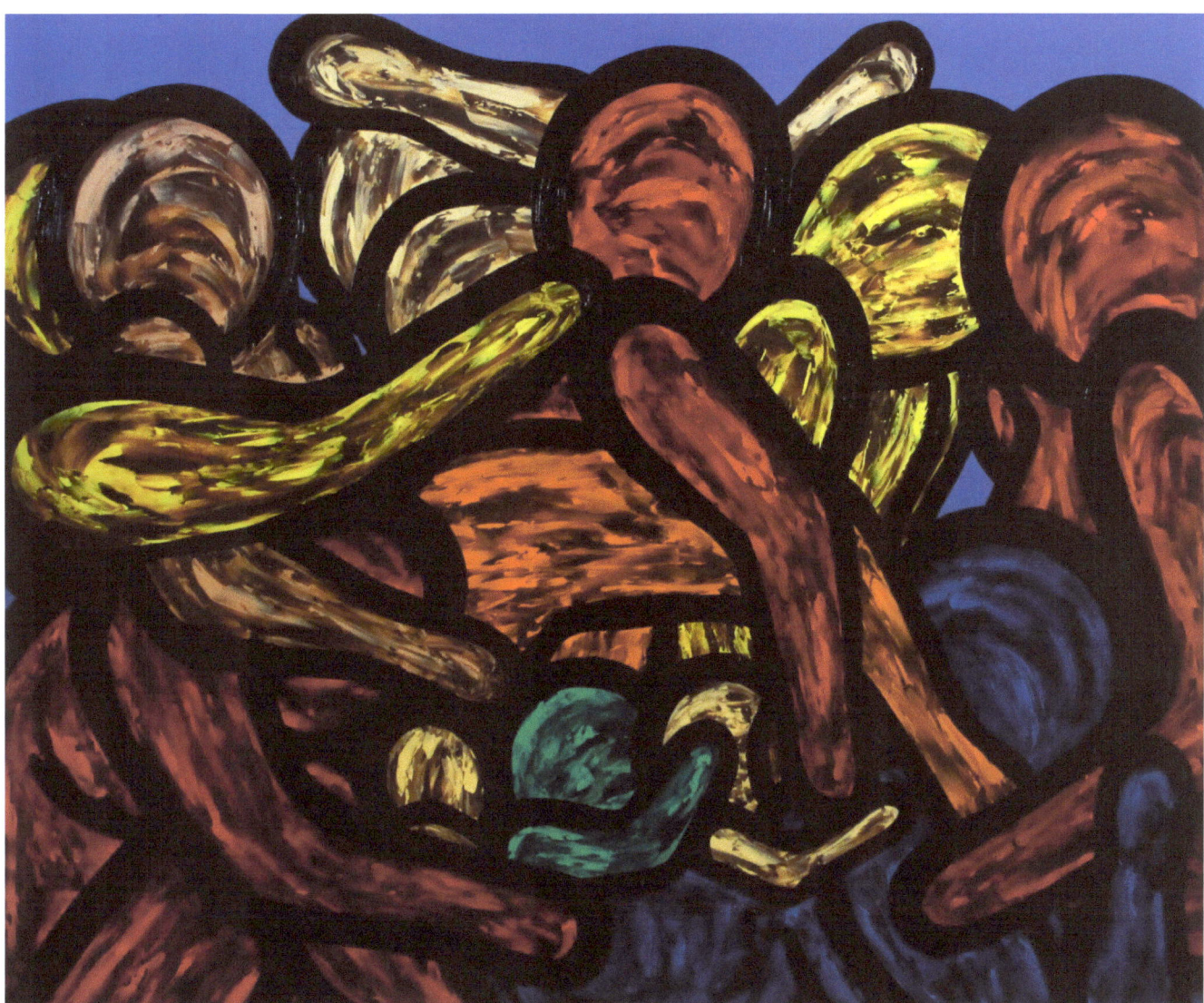

Technique | Painting
Price Range | 2000 US$ - 15000 US$
Sales Report | n/a US$ (2018) - n/a US$ (2019)
Active Years | 40 years

Life Ark
USD 6400

Francesco Ruspoli
イギリス | United Kingdom

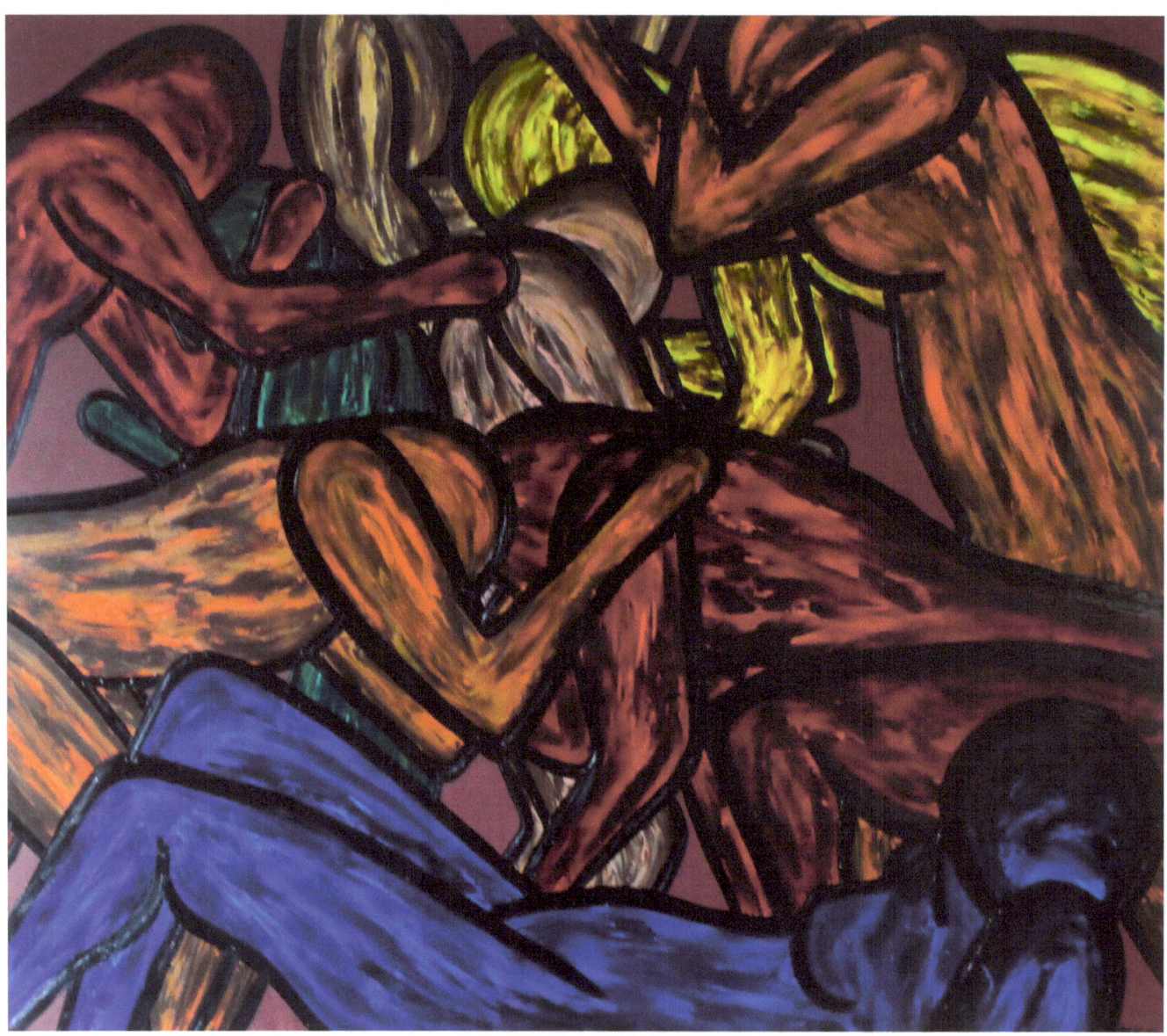

Reputation

USD 10000

francescoruspoliart.com

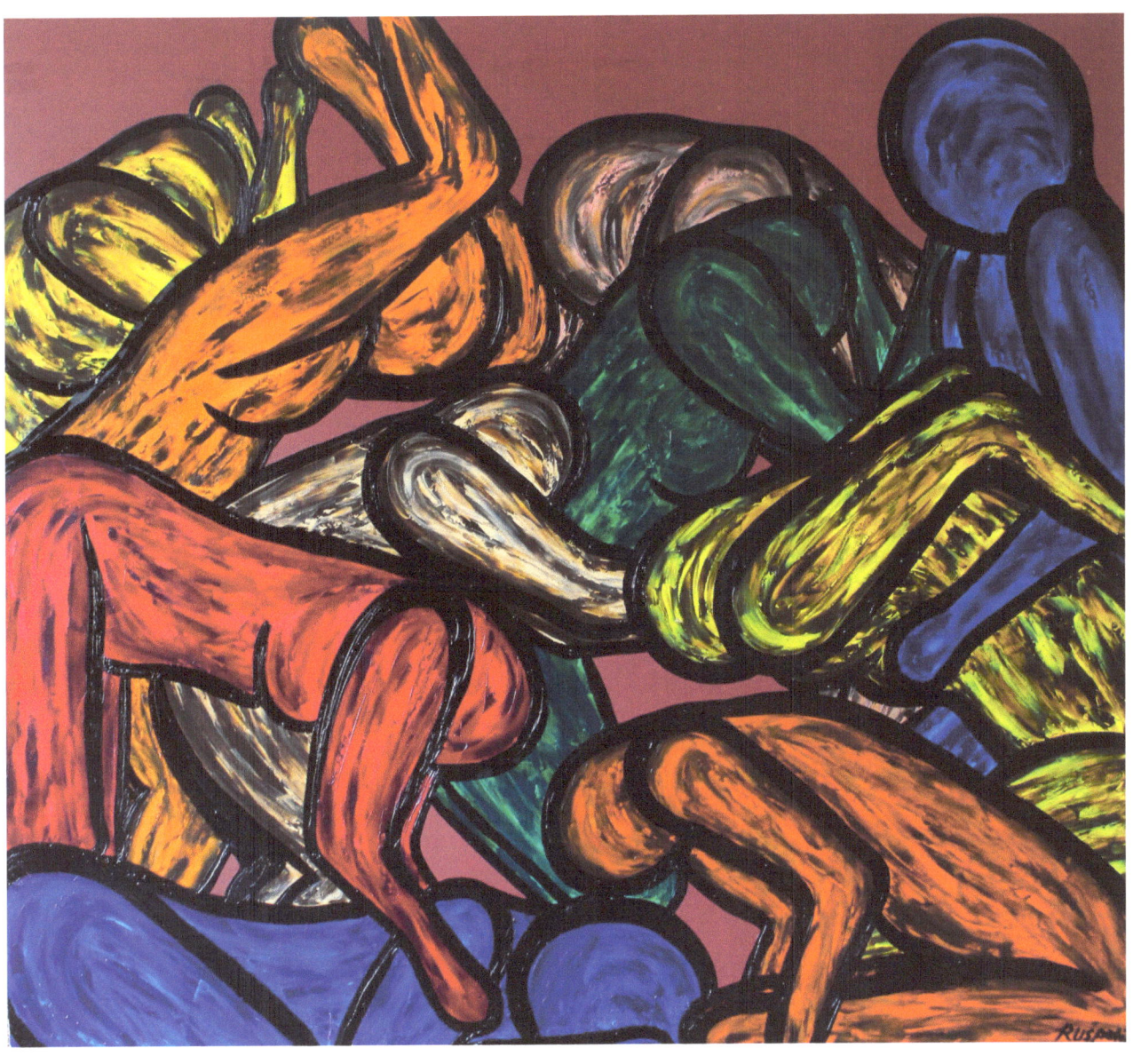

Sleeping Mother

USD 10000

Gro Folkan
ノルウェー | Norway

Gro Folkan氏は1949年生まれ。ノルウェー、オスロ出身で、現在はオスロとトロムセーを拠点にしている。National Art Academy in Osloでアートを学ぶ。ノルウェーをはじめとした海外の主要なギャラリーで計29回の個展を開催。多くの合同展覧会にも参加。彼女の作品はNorwegian National Gallery、the Museum of Contemporary Art in Oslo、the National Bank of Norway、国立大学、団体、国家機関などによって購入されている。隠された真実を思い起こさせるために何千年にもわたり西洋の人々に使用されたルーン文字のように、絵画は手段だと考えている。真の絵画とは、キャンバスに描かれた色や線ではなく、鑑賞者自身の心に浮かぶイメージである。

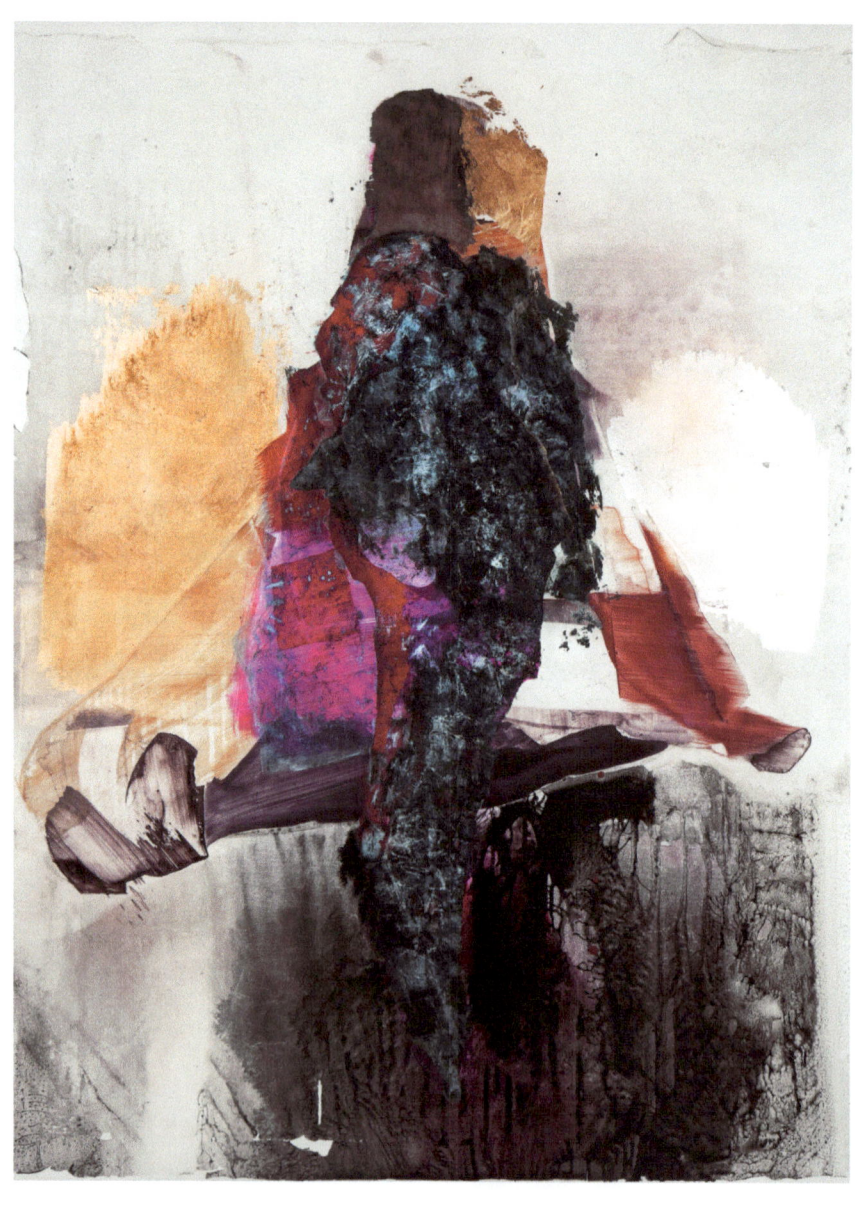

Freya. Acrylic, aluminium, copper, oxidized brass and copper, interference color, 160x120 cm, 2019

USD 13478

技術 | 絵画
価格帯 | 1347 US$ - 13478 US$
販売レポート | 22463,83 US$ [2018年] - 16847,87 US$ [2019年]
有効な年数 | 53年

grofolkan.no

Gro Folkan was born in 1949 in Oslo, Norway and lives between Oslo and Tromsoe. She studied art at the National Art Academy in Oslo. She has had 29 solo exhibitions of paintings in leading galleries in Norway and abroad, and has also taken part in numerous joint exhibitions. Her works have been purchased by the Norwegian National Gallery, the Museum of Contemporary Art in Oslo, the National Bank of Norway, national universities, institution and national offices.

FEMALE RUNES

My pictures are instruments, like runes, used for thousands of years by Northern peoples to invoke hidden aspects of reality. The real pictures, the images are not the lines and colors on my canvases, but the images coming into being in the mind of the onlooker.

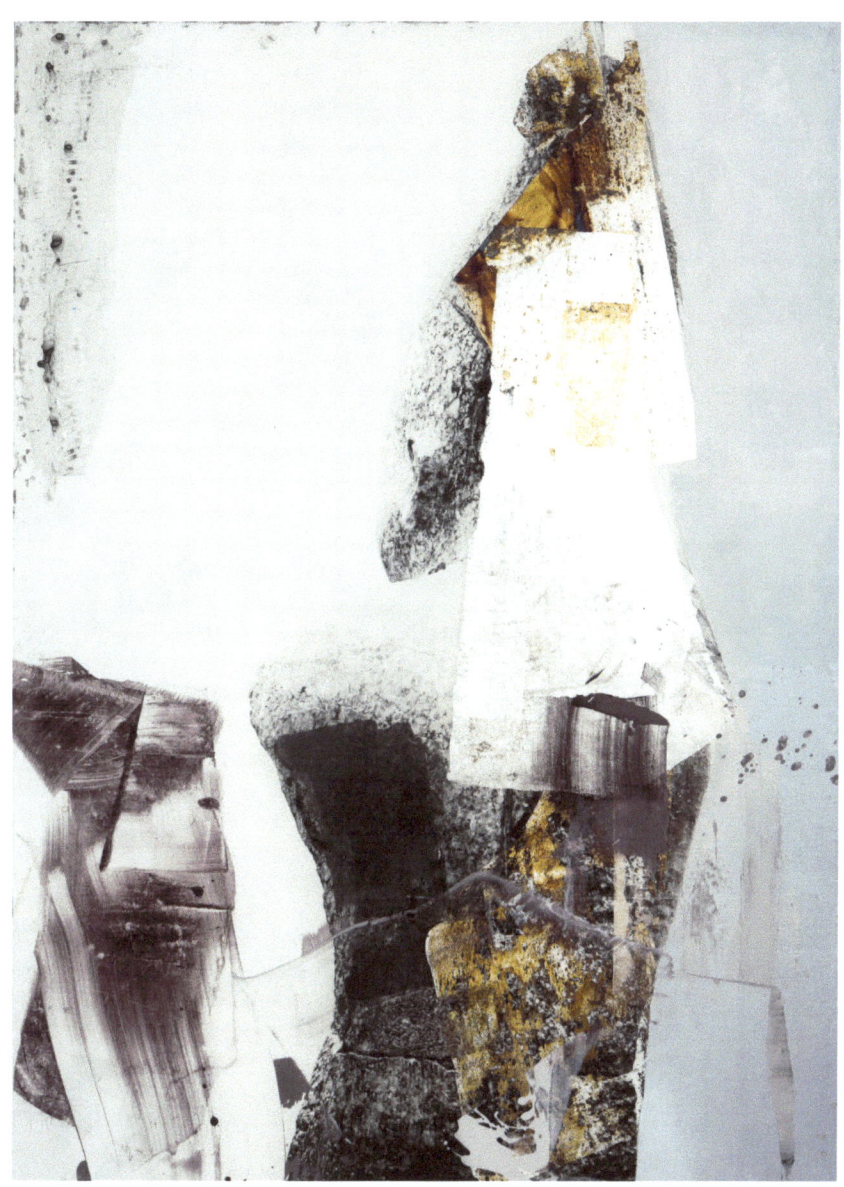

Technique | Painting
Price Range | 1347 US$ - 13478 US$
Sales Report | 22463,83 US$ (2018) - 16847,87 US$ (2019)
Active Years | 53 years

Inanna. Acrylic, oxidized silver, metal dust, interference color, 150x108 cm, 2017
USD 13478

Gro Folkan
ノルウェー | Norway

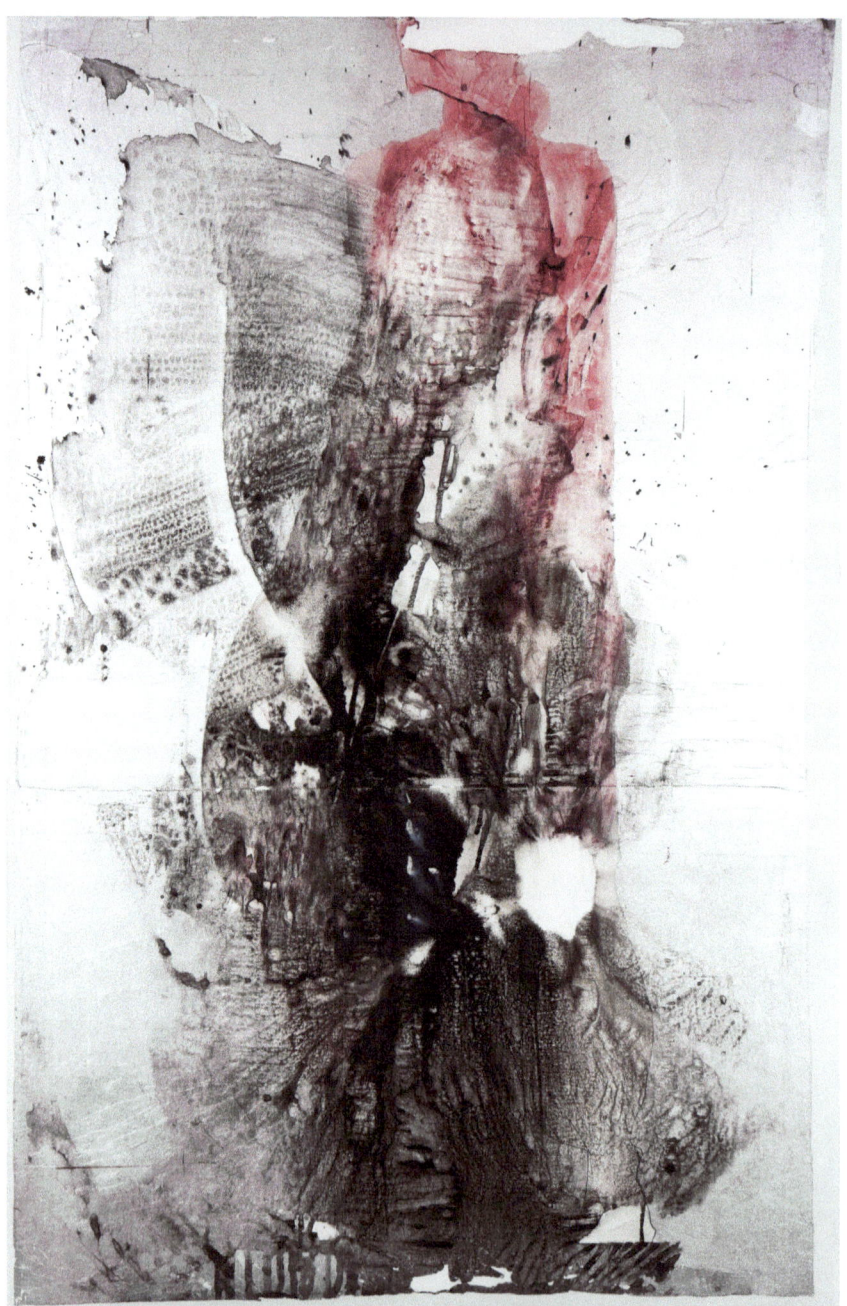

Lillith
Acrylic, aluminium, 150 x100 cm, 2017
USD 13478

grofolkan.no

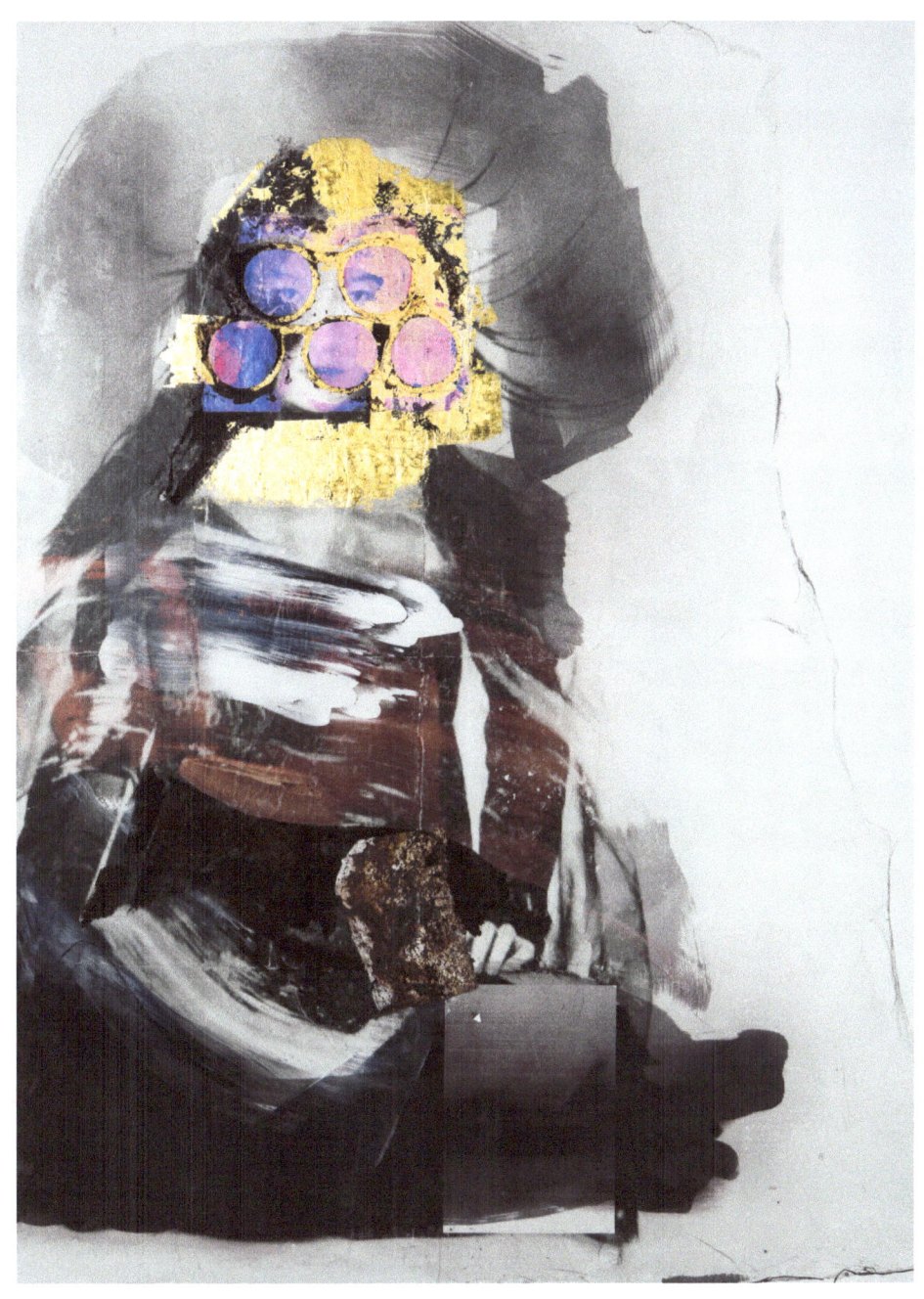

Groa, awakening. Acrylic, metal dust, photographic technique,
interference color, oxidized silver and brass, gold, 150 x110 cm, 2019
USD 13478

Hélène DeSerres
カナダ | Canada

絵画、彫刻、ジュエリー制作、写真など様々な媒体を使って色や形、質感を表現するマルチメディアアーティスト。異花受粉のようにそれぞれの技法がお互いを補い合っている。幼い頃から絵を描いたり色を塗ったりすることが好きだったが、アーティストになる夢をかなえたのは結婚し、子育てを終えた後だった。フィレンツェ、ニューヨーク、マイアミ、モントリオールなどで個展を開催。ヨーロッパ、アメリカで多くのグループ展に参加している。

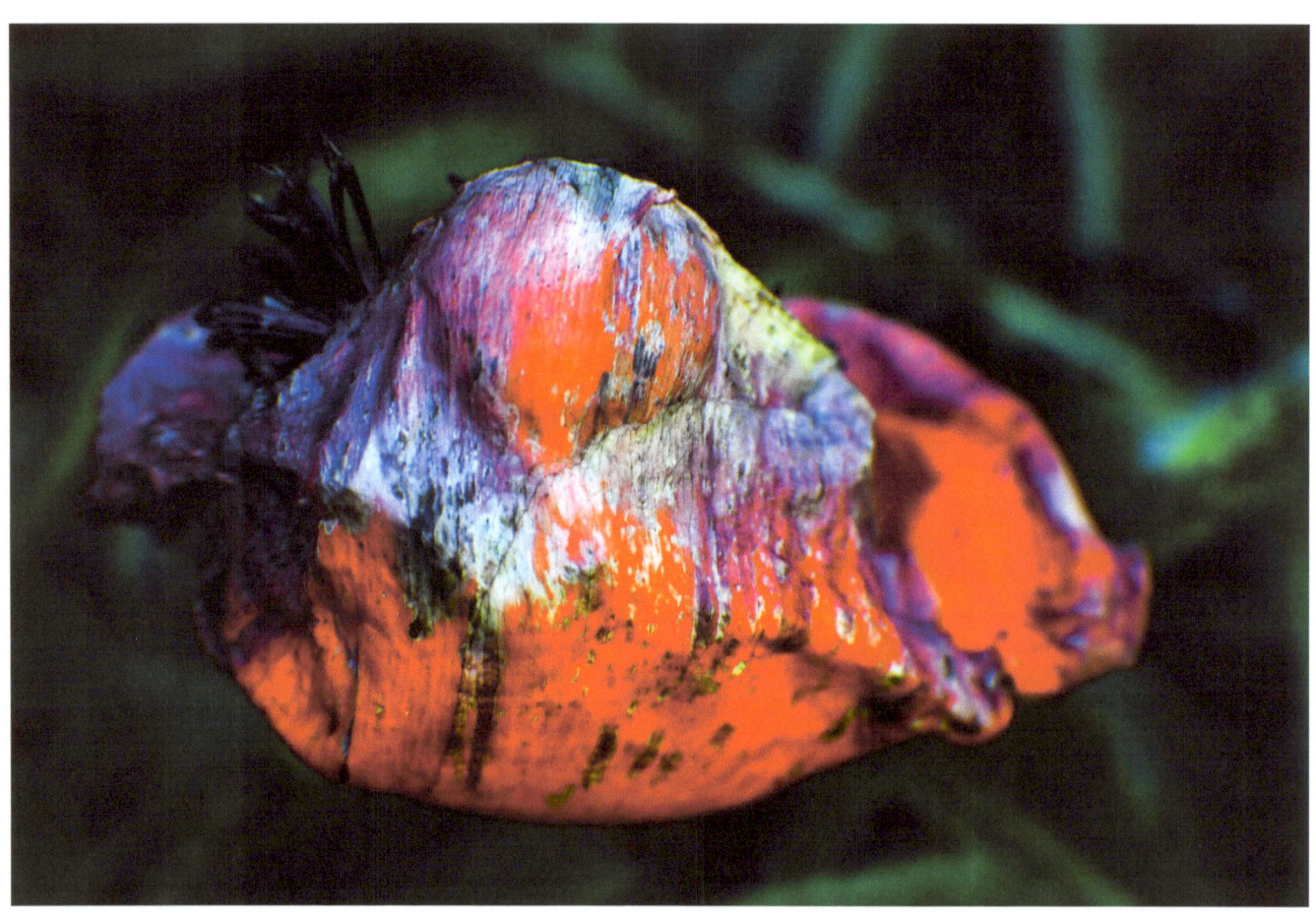

技術	写真
価格帯	1800 US$ - 寸法 US$
販売レポート	n/a US$ [2018年] - n/a US$ [2019年]
有効な年数	20年

Awakening
Photo 2019
Price Upon Request

helenedeserres.com

I am a multimedia artist who likes to explore colours, shapes, textures using various media such as painting, sculpting, making jewelry, doing photography. One technique feeds the other, like cross pollination. As a child I always loved drawing and colouring. After my studies, raising my family, I could finally realize my dream, to become a full time artist.I have had solo shows in Florence, Italy, NewYork City, Miami, Montreal, and numerous participation in group shows in Europe and America.

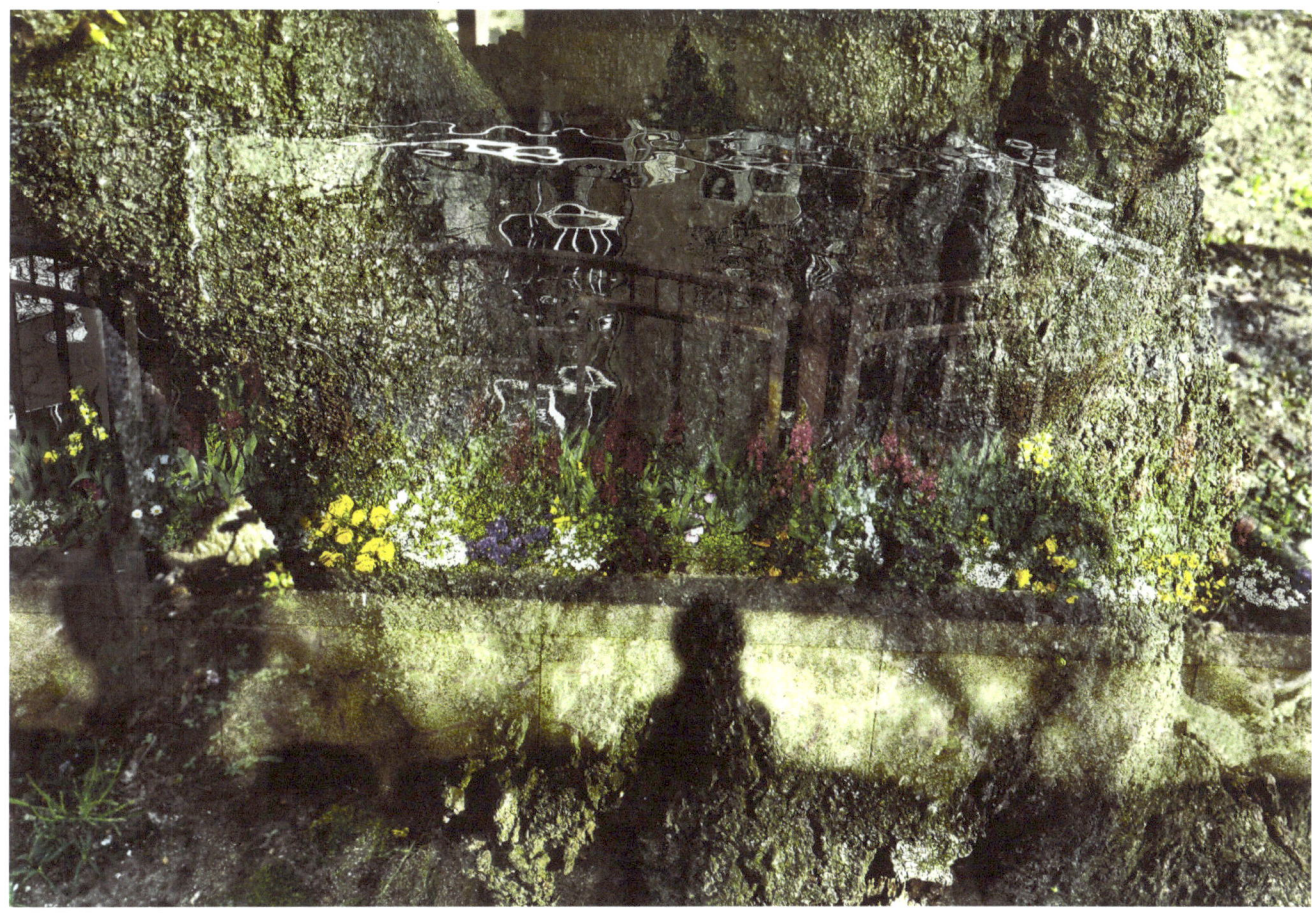

Technique | Photography
Price Range | 1800 US$ - depending size US$
Sales Report | n/a US$ (2018) - n/a US$ (2019)
Active Years | 20 years

My Shadow
Photo 2019
Price Upon Request

Hélène DeSerres
カナダ | Canada

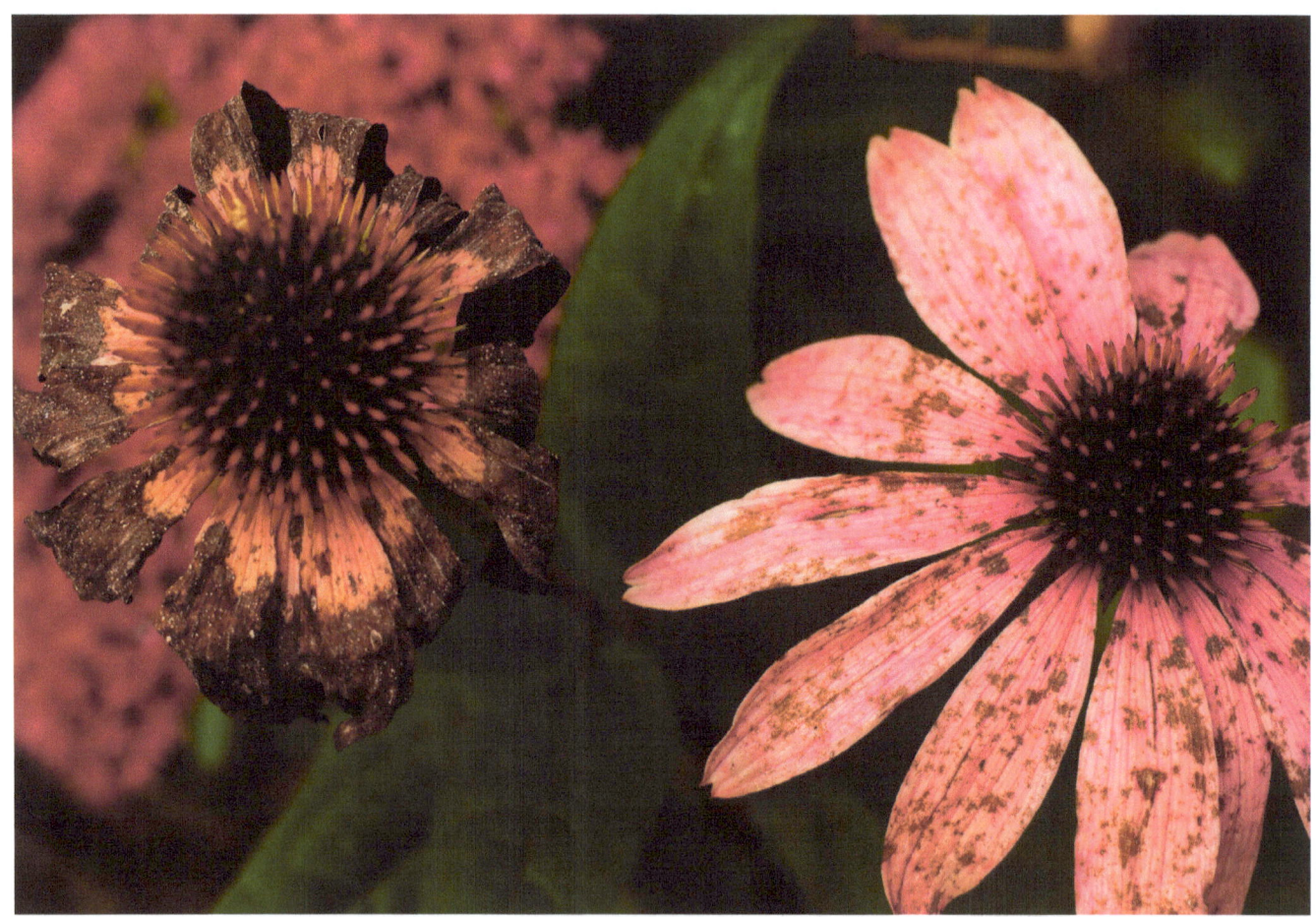

Sisters

Photo 2019

Price Upon Request

helenedeserres.com

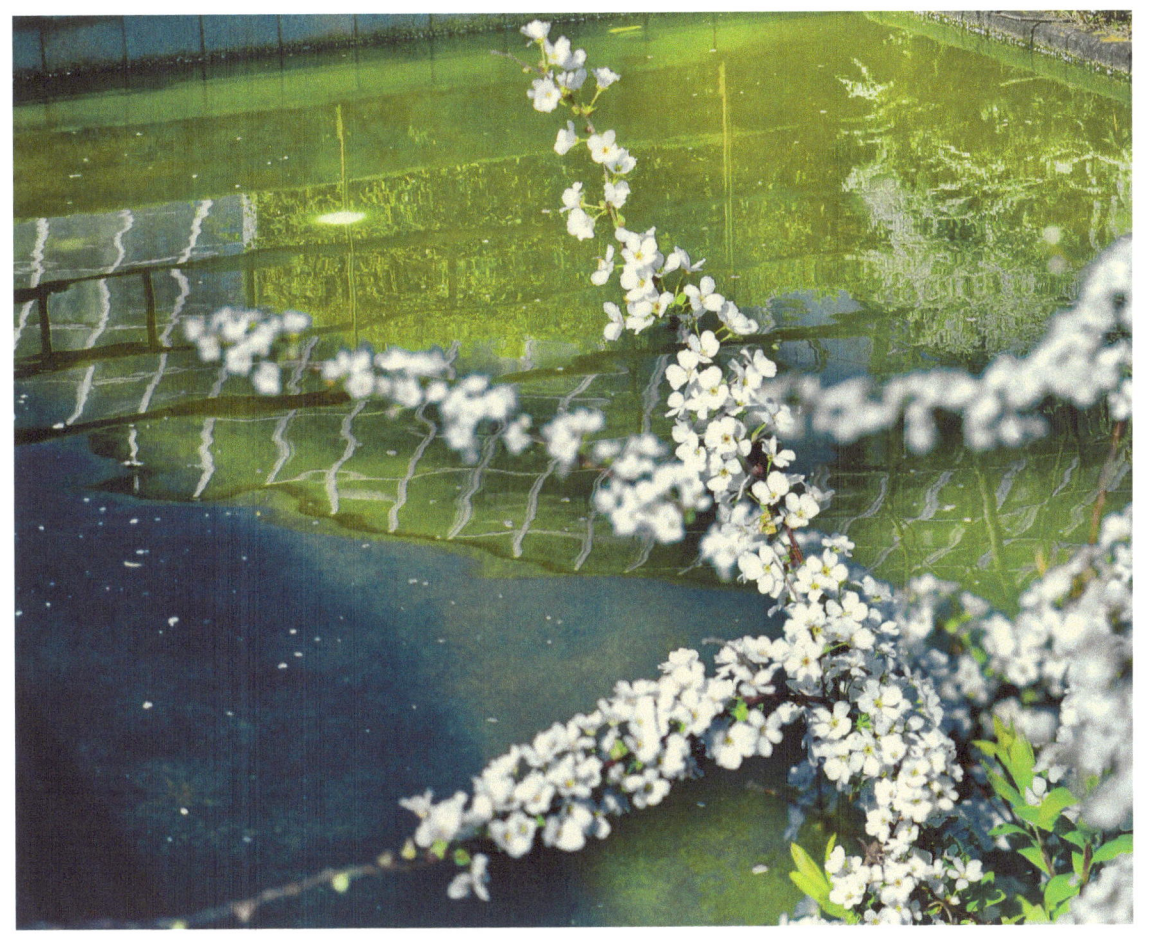

Serenity

Photo 2019

Price Upon Request

Karin Monschauer
スイス | Switzerland

Karin Monschauer氏は、コンピュータグラフィックスソフトを用いて様々な色と形状で埋め尽くされた世界を繰り広げ、彼女のデジタルアートは無限の解釈ができる抽象アート作品を生む。刺繍技術に魅了され、色と形の繋がりと交錯を具現化している。この方法論はアラビア語で「raqm」と呼ばれるもので、単数または複数の異なる色の糸を使用して生地に装飾デザインを施すことを可能にする。初めにデザインを手描きし、それからアートデザインプログラムを使用して幾何学的進化に富んだ抽象的なデザインに温色から寒色までの色調を組み合わせる。彼女は自身の純粋な想像力と古代と現代のアートの巨匠による自然と質感への明快な参照による描写を目に見える言葉で表現している。また、人が誰でも受け止め、たどる漠然とした道をデジタルで描いている。

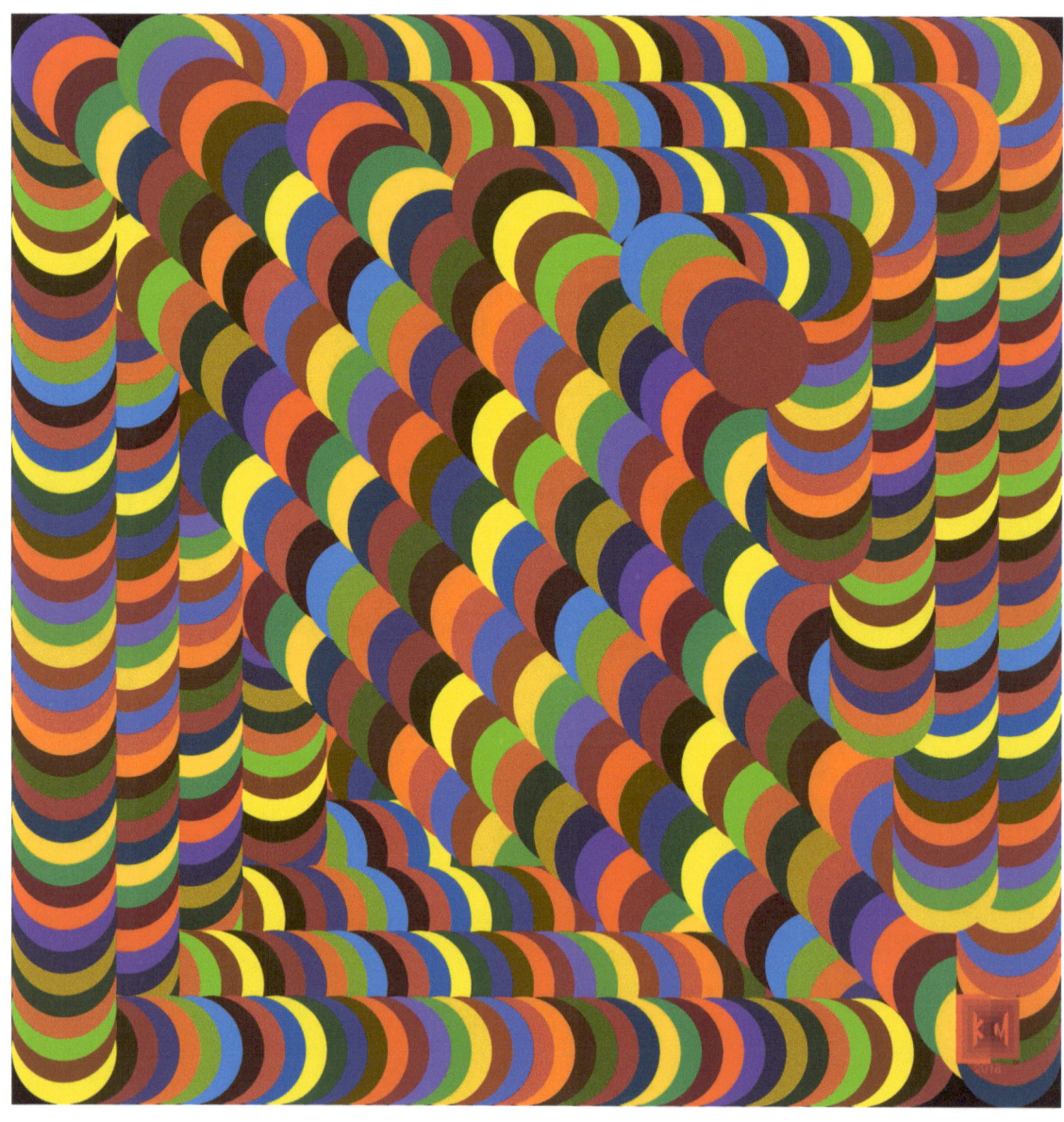

技術 | デジタルアート
価格帯 | 2300 US$ - 7700 US$
販売レポート | 10000 US$ [2018年] - 15000 US$ [2019年]
有効な年数 | 3年

Untitled

2018, 50x50 cm, Digital Art on Canvas

USD 2300

karinmonschauer.ch

Karin Monschauer creates worlds full of shapes and colors with computer graphics software. Her Digital Art creates abstractions of infinite interpretations. The embroidery technique has always fascinated her, allowing to externalize the connection and the interweaving of colors and shapes. This methodology, 'raqm' in Arabic, allows to create ornamental designs on fabric through the use of one or more threads of different colors. She draws on her intially manual skills and uses art design programs to plan abstractions rich in geometric evolutions connected in tonal ranges between hot and cold. Monschauer proposes visual languages characterized by pure imagination as well as explicit reference to nature and textures by ancient and modern masters. She digitally paints undefined tracks every human being interprets and follows.

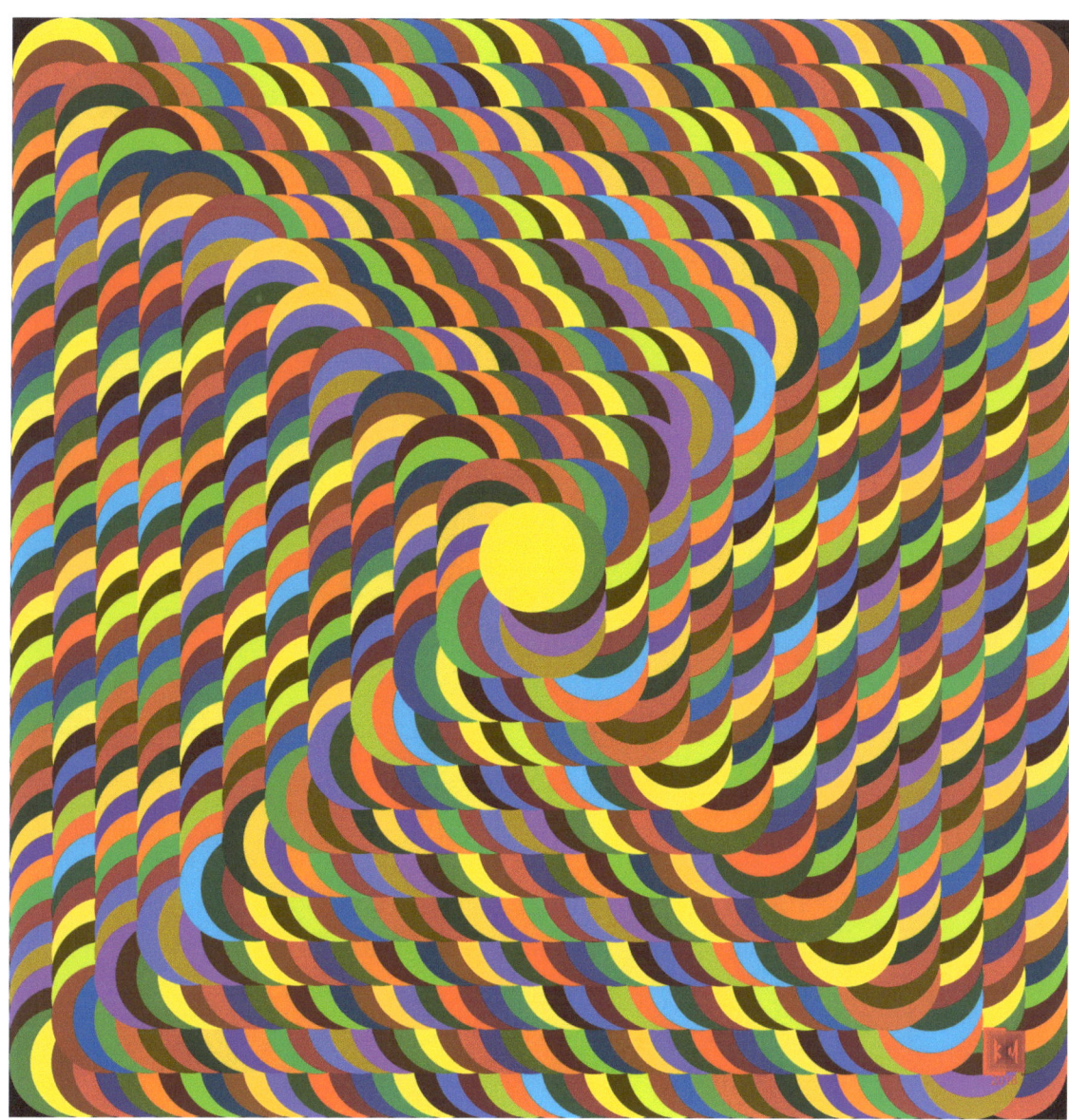

Technique | Digital Art
Price Range | 2300 US$ - 7700 US$
Sales Report | 10000 US$ (2018) - 15000 US$ (2019)
Active Years | 3 years

Untitled
2018, 50x50 cm, Digital Art on Canvas
USD 2300

Karin Monschauer
スイス | Switzerland

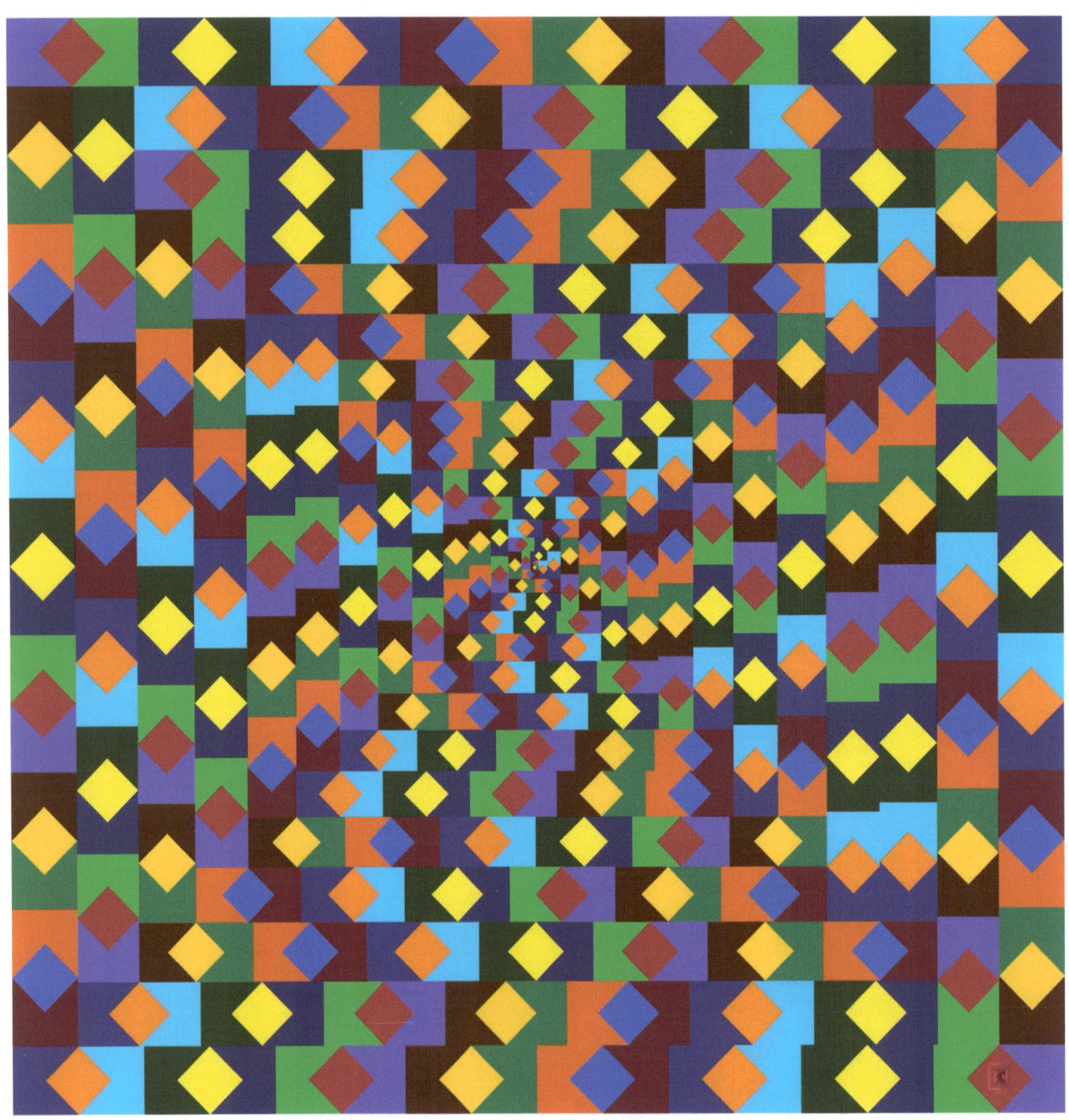

Ragnatela
2019, 96x96 cm, Digital Art on Canvas
USD 4300

karinmonschauer.ch

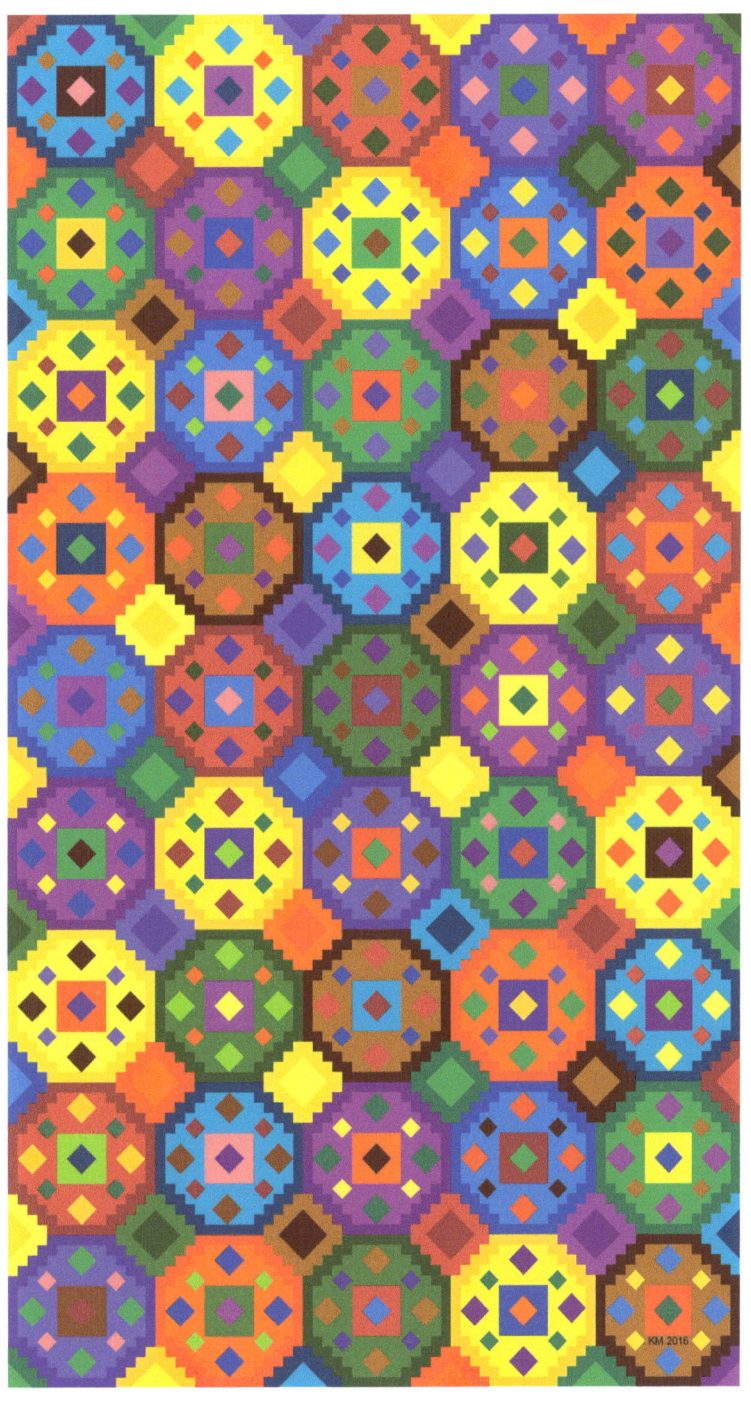

Augenweide

2016, 60x108 cm, Digital Art on Canvas

USD 3800

Edmund Ian Grant

ハンガリー | United States

Edmund Ian Grant氏は、世界的にコレクターがおり、受賞歴もある独学のアーティストである。過去30年間で、ロスアンゼルス、サンフランシスコ、ロンドン、ニューヨーク、パリなどのアメリカやヨーロッパの主要都市の多くの展示会に出展。The LA Art Show、Art Aspen、Art Monaco、Art Basel week のConcept Art Fair-Miamiをはじめとした一流の展示会にも出展している。また、the Leonardo Award絵画部門で優勝、the International Biennale of Chianciano 2015で最高名誉賞受賞など数々の受賞歴を持ち、最近ではthe London Art Biennale 2019の絵画部門で準グランプリを受賞した。作品は多くのカタログ、アートブック、また、世界的に有名な美術史家や、彼の作品を「パワフル」だと評価する美術評論家Edward Lucie-Smithなどによる論評などの出版物に収録されている。

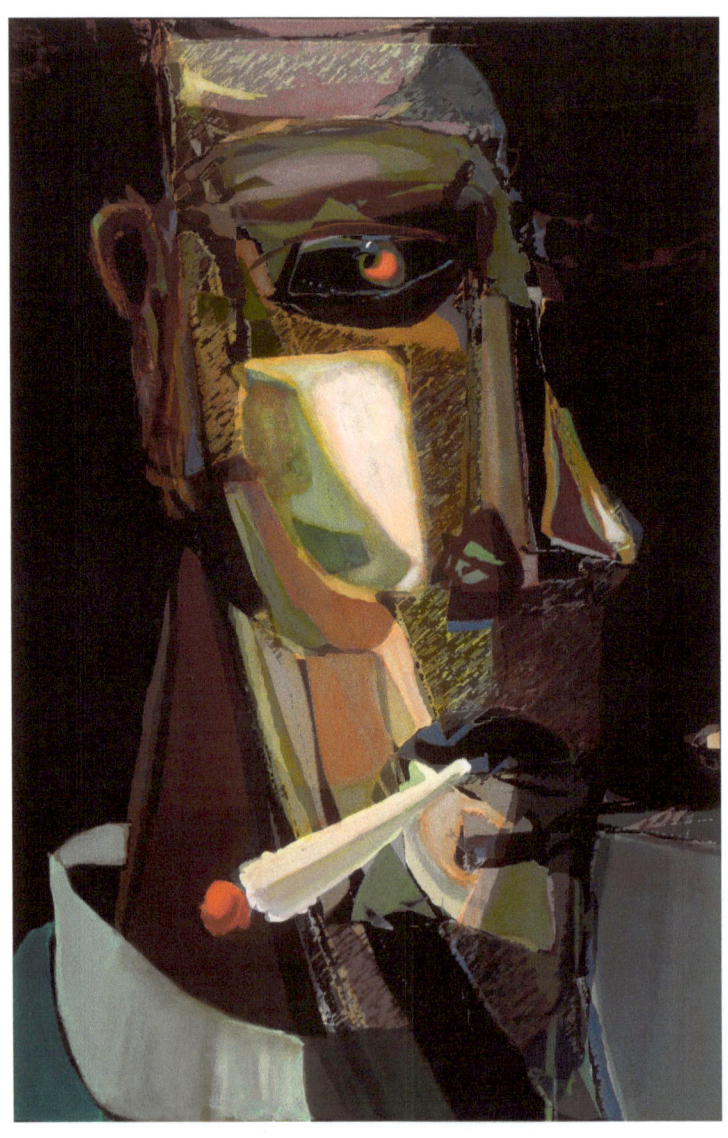

技術 | 絵画

価格帯 | 1500 US$ - 20000 US$

販売レポート | n/a US$ [2018年] - n/a US$ [2019年]

有効な年数 | 30年

Palookaville

Acrylic on canvas 60" x 40" (inches) 2014

Price Upon Request

edmundiangrant.com

Edmund Ian Grant is a self-taught, Internationally collected, award winning artist whose extensive exhibitions over the last 30 years include shows in major USA and European cities including Los Angeles, San Francisco, London, New York and Paris. He has exhibited at many prestigious art fairs including The LA Art Show, Art Aspen, Art Monaco and Concept Art Fair-Miami during Art Basel week. Among his numerous awards is the Leonardo Award, First Prize in Painting, the top honor at the International Biennale of Chianciano 2015 and most recently, Second Prize in Painting at the London Art Biennale 2019. His work is in numerous catalogues, art books and publications including a critical essay by world-renowned art historian and art critic Edward Lucie-Smith who calls his art "powerful".

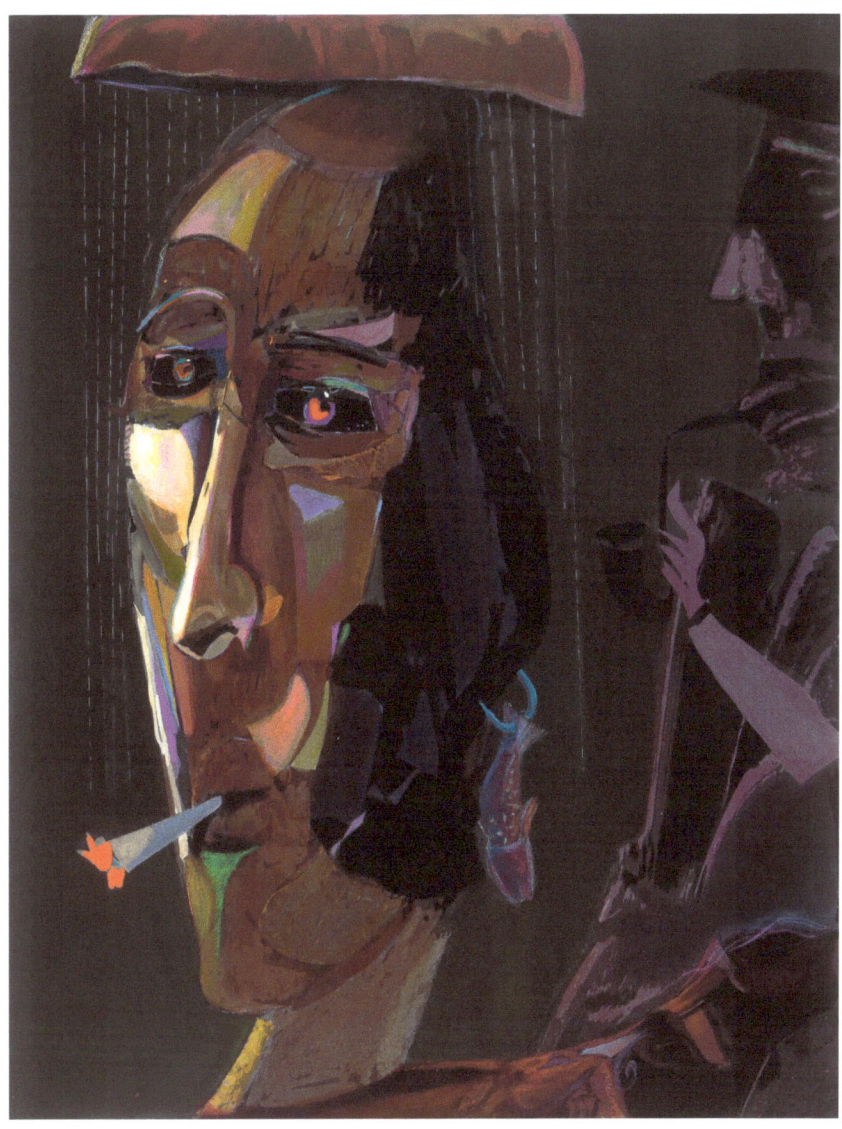

Technique | Painting
Price Range | 1500 US$ - 20000 US$
Sales Report | n/a US$ (2018) - n/a US$ (2019)
Active Years | 30 years

Here's That Rainy Day
Acrylic on canvas, 44.5" x 34.5'" (inches) 2016
Price Upon Request

Edmund Ian Grant
ハンガリー | United States

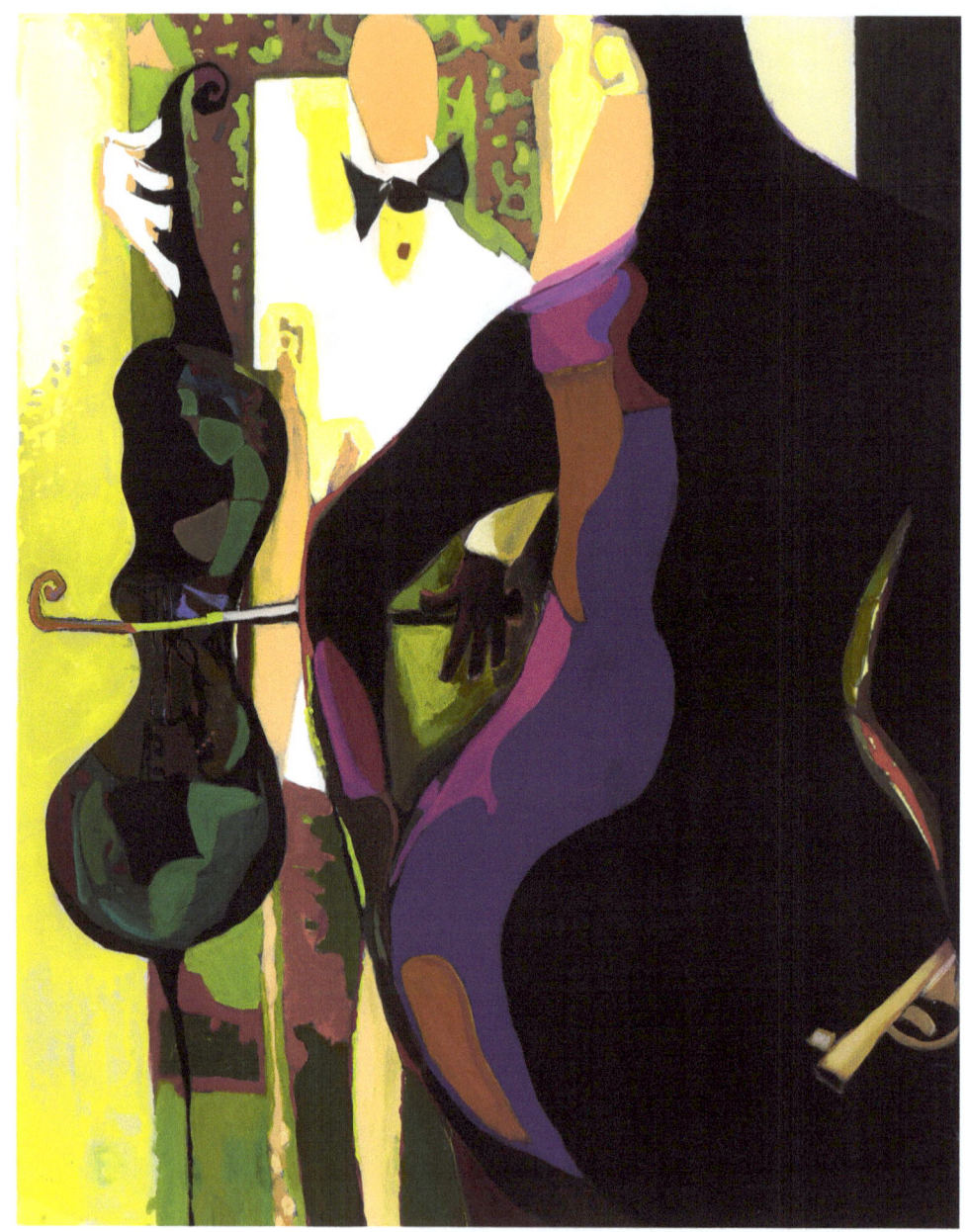

The Player

Acrylic on canvas, 54" x 43" (inches) 2018

Price Upon Request

edmundiangrant.com

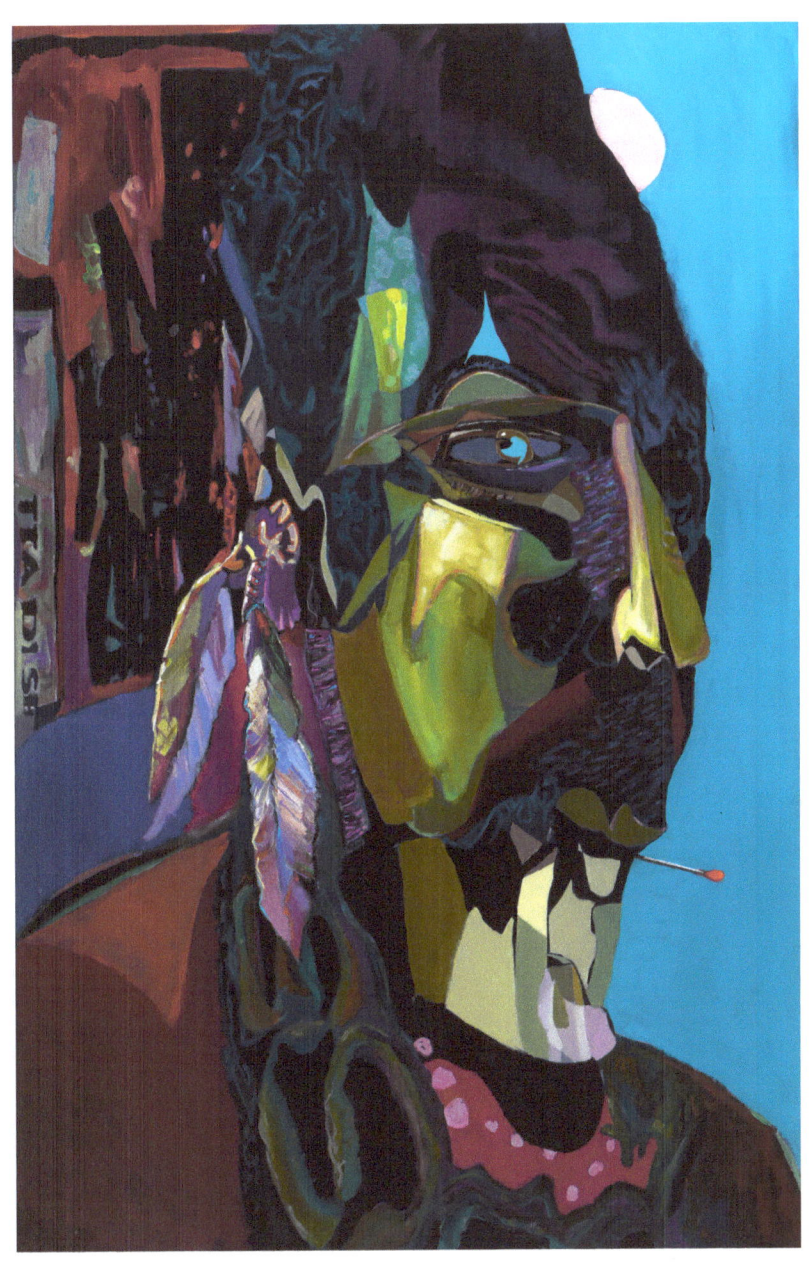

The Warrior
Acrylic on canvas, 60" x 40" (inches) 2019
Price Upon Request

Caspar Baum

シンガポール - ギリシャ | Singapore - Greece

Caspar Baum氏は、「"dynamic structuralism"(動的構造主義)」を表現する有名なドイツのアーティストグループの一員であり、作品の中の対象物や状況にも表現豊かな観点を持つ。過去30年間で、世界中のプライベートギャラリーや公的美術館などの様々な展覧会に数多く参加し、いくつもの意義深い個展も開催した。作品は光と対象物の構造から影響を受けており、影、イルミネーション、前面と裏面をいじりながら、幾層にもわけては組み立てなおし、静寂で繊細な世界の中で鑑賞者の新たな想像力を掻き立てる。多くの賞を受賞し、作品は世界中の公的機関やコレクターの代表コレクションとなっている。

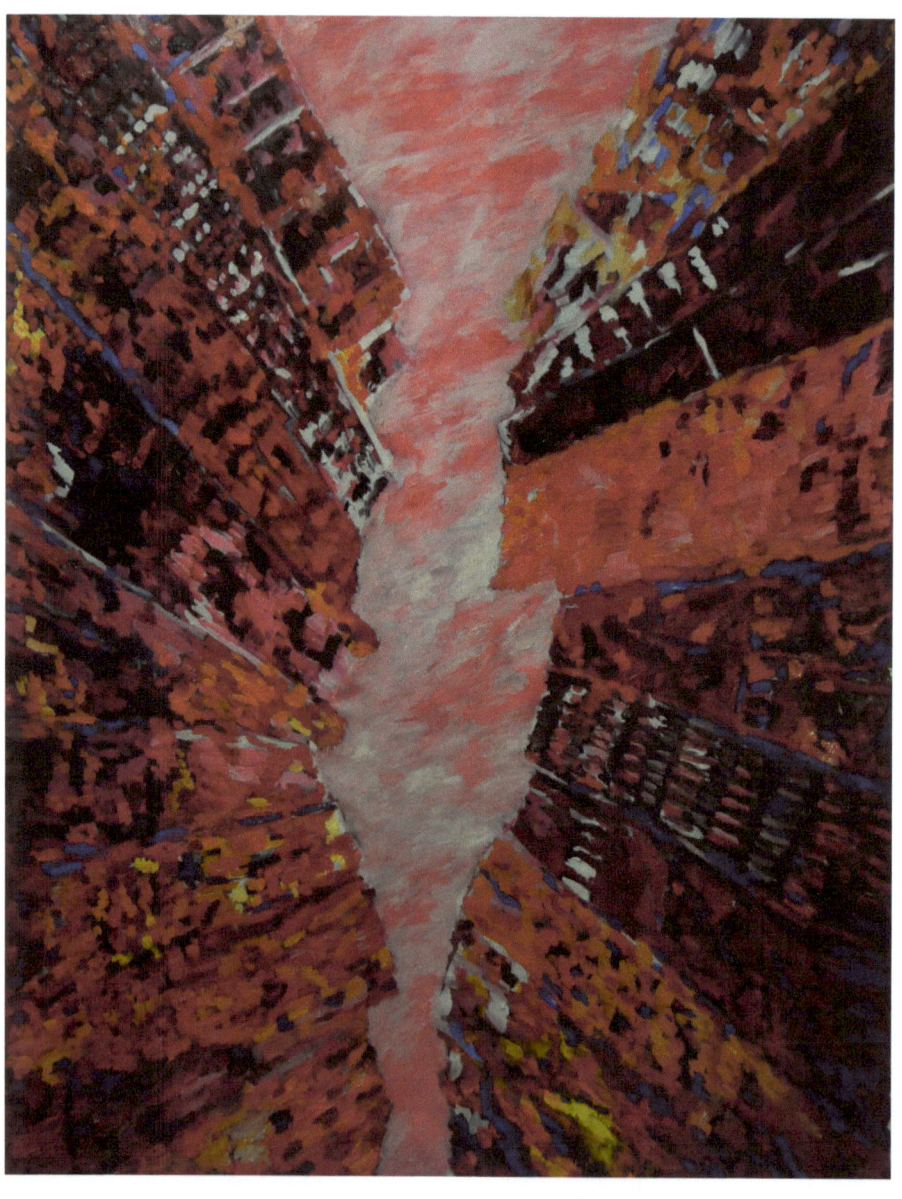

技術 | 絵画
価格帯 | 2000 US$ - 15000 US$
販売レポート | 70000 US$ [2018年] - 120000 US$ [2019年]
有効な年数 | 35年

New York
Oil on Canvas, 200 x 130 cm, 2019
USD 10000

casparbaum.com

Caspar Baum belongs to a well-known group of German artists representing "dynamic structuralism" as well as an expressive view on subjects and situations frozen into his paintings. He has frequently participated in various exhibitions in private galleries as well as public museums globally, between others also with some significant solo shows during the last three decades. His work is influenced by the light and structure of the objects. It plays with shadows and illumination, background and front, separates into layers and re-composes those to a new imagination taking the observer into a silent sensitive environment. Caspar Baum has received many awards and his works are represented in private and public collections around the globe.

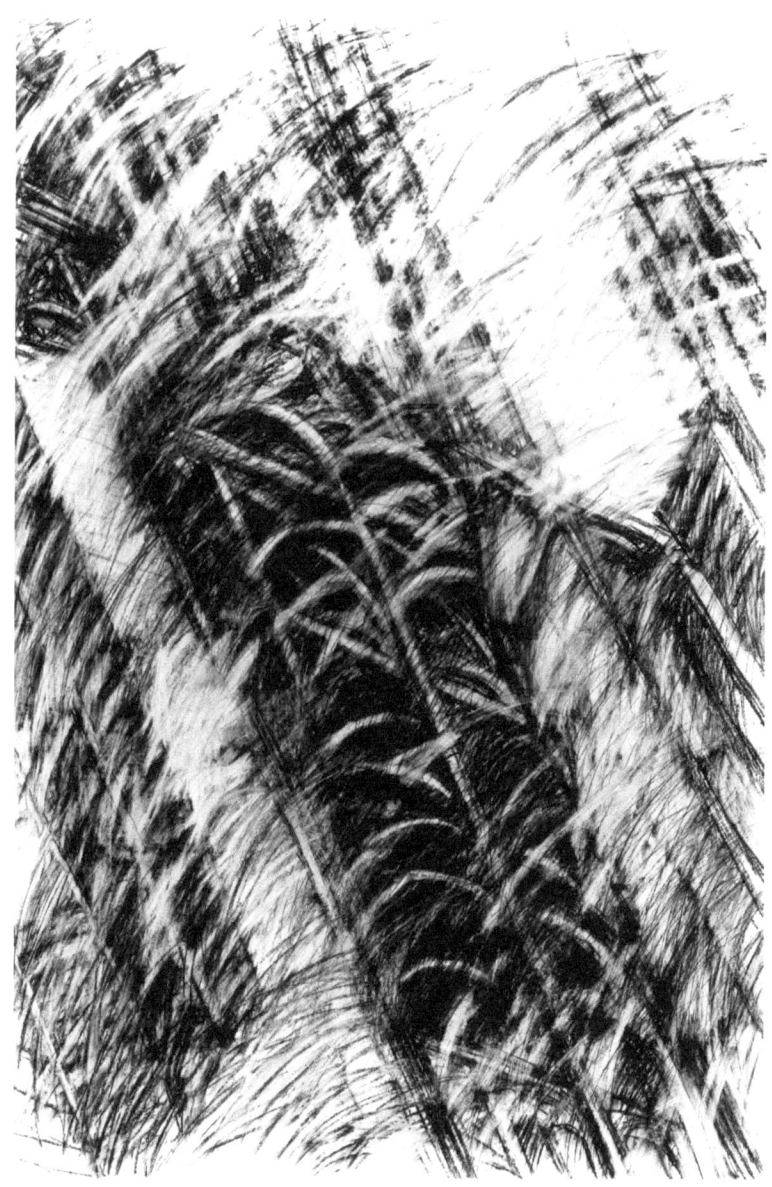

Technique | Painting
Price Range | 2000 US$ - 15000 US$
Sales Report | 70000 US$ (2018) - 120000 US$ (2019)
Active Years | 35 years

Gothic Board
Oil Crayon Pencil on Wood, 250 x 170 cm
USD 10000

Caspar Baum
シンガポール - ギリシャ | Singapore - Greece

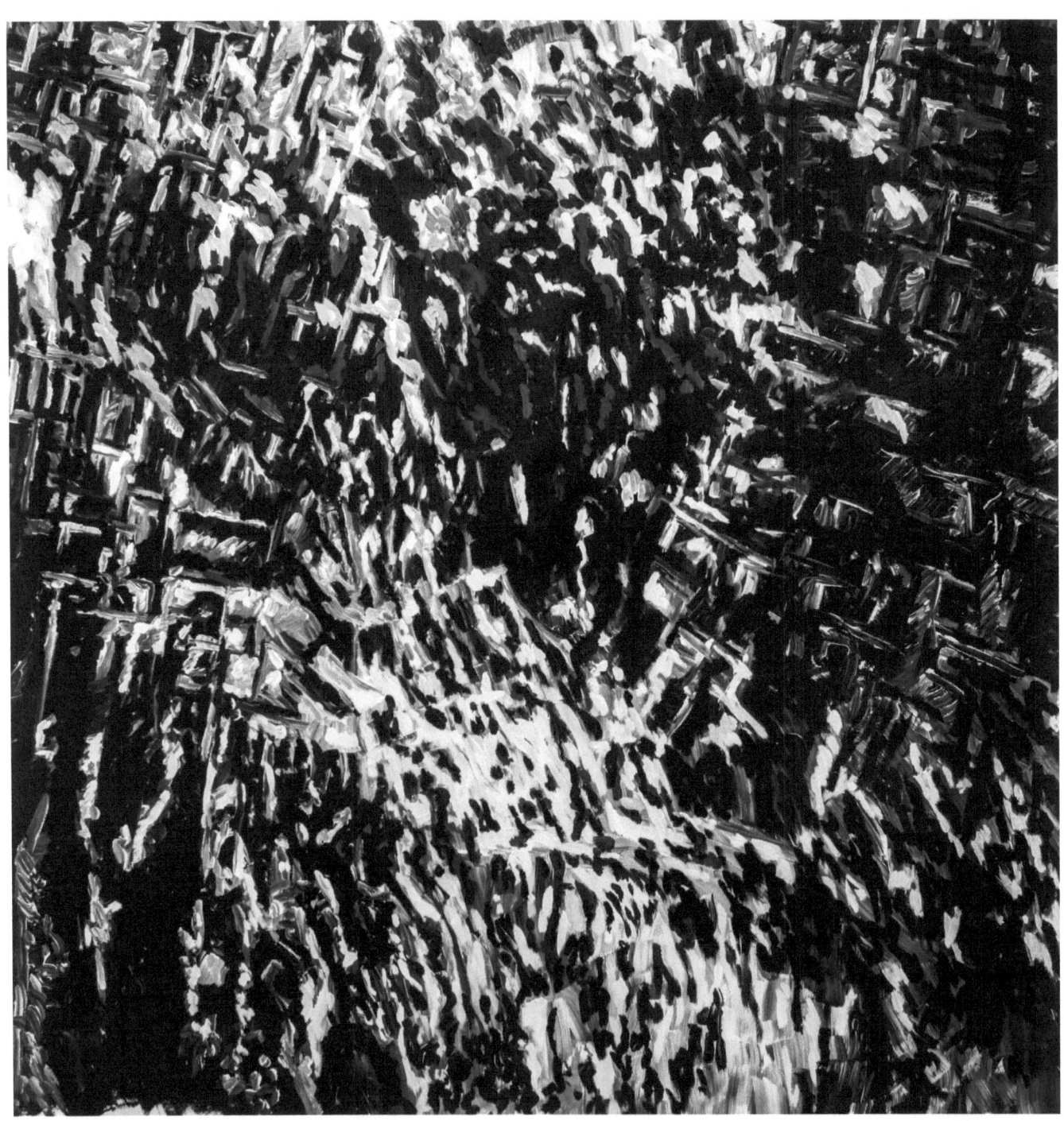

Night in the City

Oil on Canvas, 180 x 180 cm, 2018

USD 7000

casparbaum.com

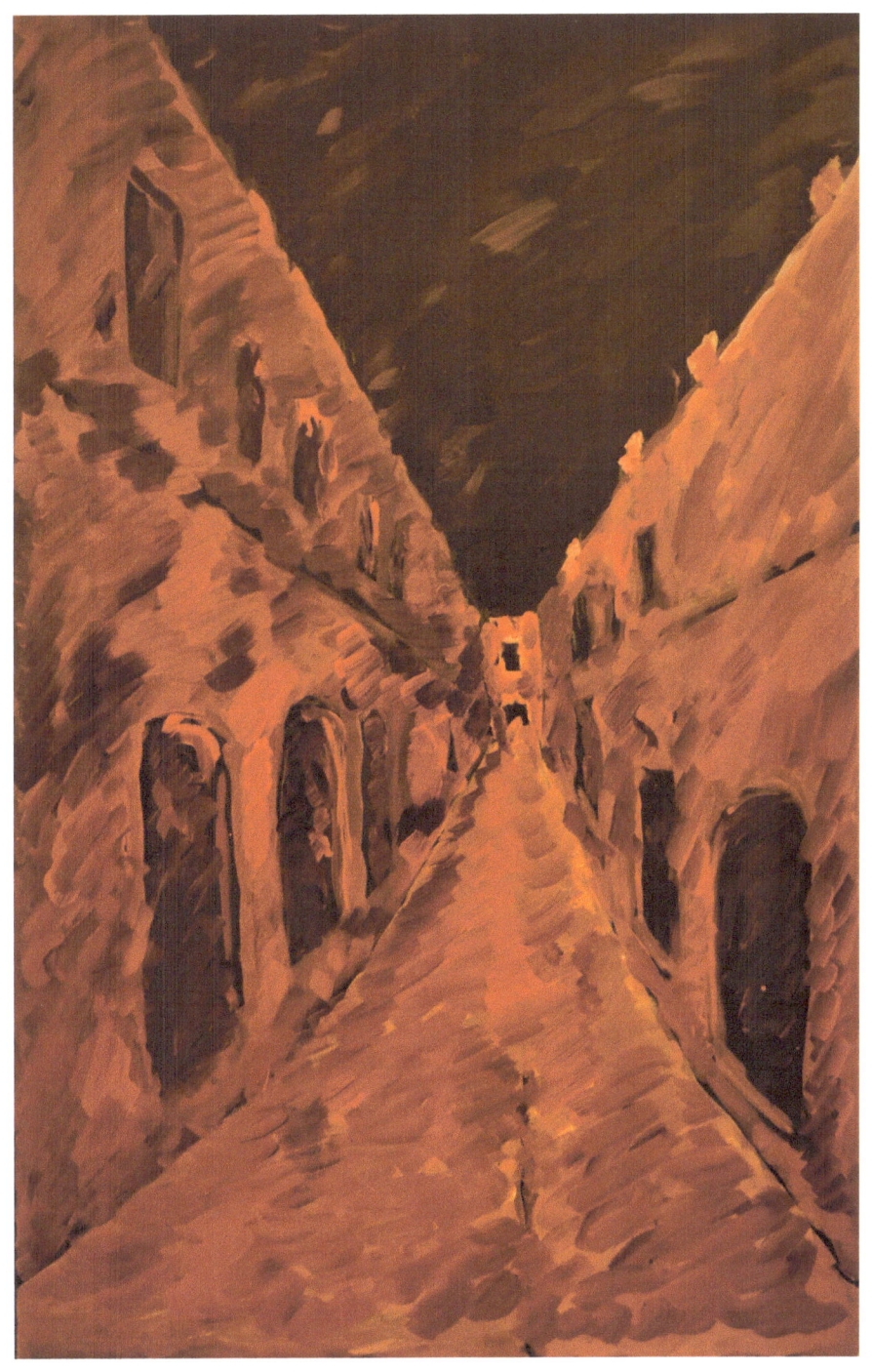

Rhodes Ipoton

Oil on Canvas, 70 x 50 cm, 2019

USD 1500

Bo Song
韓国 | South Korea

1968年韓国ソウル生まれ。雲中洞在住。幸いにも指導教授に才能を見出され、画家として活動を開始したのは2012年の夏、43歳の時だった。アメリカのOakland Universityを卒業後、韓国へ帰国しGraduate Art School at the Hongik and Dankookへ進学。2017年よりAgora GalleryとPaks Galleryの代表アーティストとなる。自身のアートを自然と人間の精神から発せられる見えないエネルギーというコンセプトで紹介。生けるものすべては美しさに溢れており、それは常に動きと変化があると考えている。油絵を始めたとき、キャンバスは彼にとっての「瞑想空間」となった。

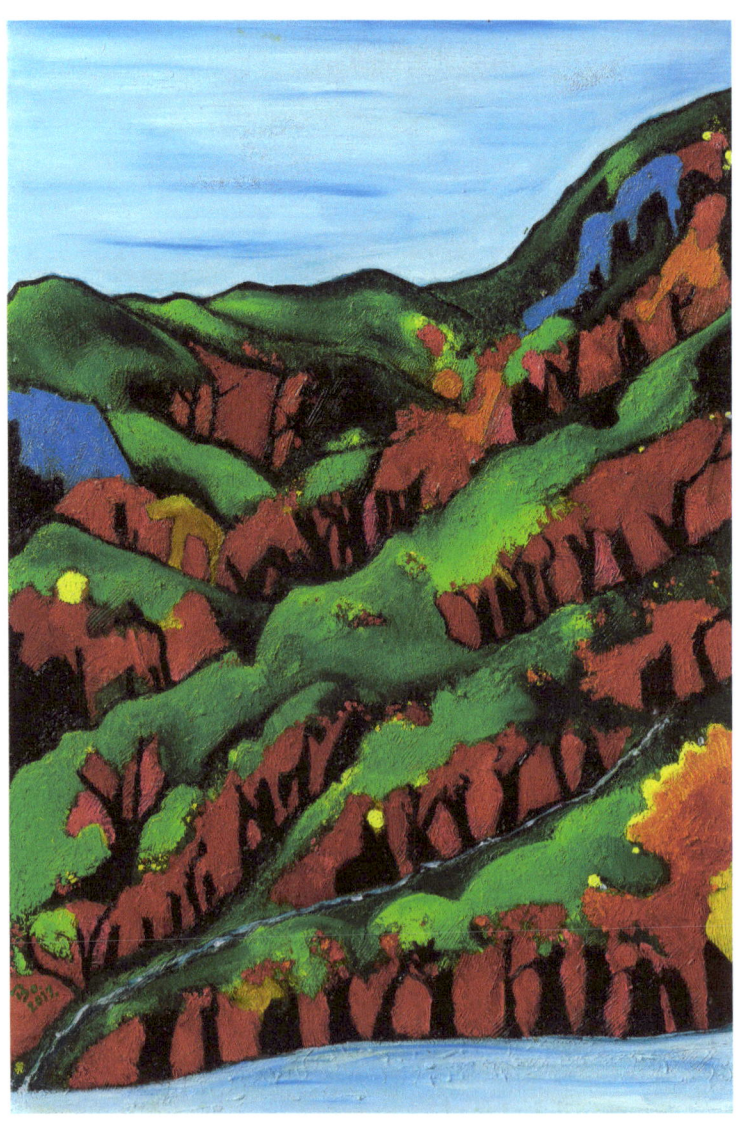

技術 | 絵画
価格帯 | 4000 US$ - 8000 US$
販売レポート | 3800 US$ [2018年] - 12000 US$ [2019年]
有効な年数 | -年

Climb a Mountain

USD 8000

bksong.com

I was born in 1968 at Seoul Korea. I am currently living and working in Unjung-dong, Korea. My journey as a painter began in the summer of 2012 at the humble age of 43, what was a delight let to discovery my talent and recognition by professors. After graduated from Oakland University, USA I returned to Korea and I continued to study in Graduate Art School at the Hongik and Dankook. Since 2017 I am represented artists from Agora Gallery and Paks Gallery. I showcase my art through the concept of invisible energy from nature and human spirits. Everything that is alive brims with beauty, and that which lives is ever moving and chaning. When I began oil painting, the canvas became "meditation" for me.

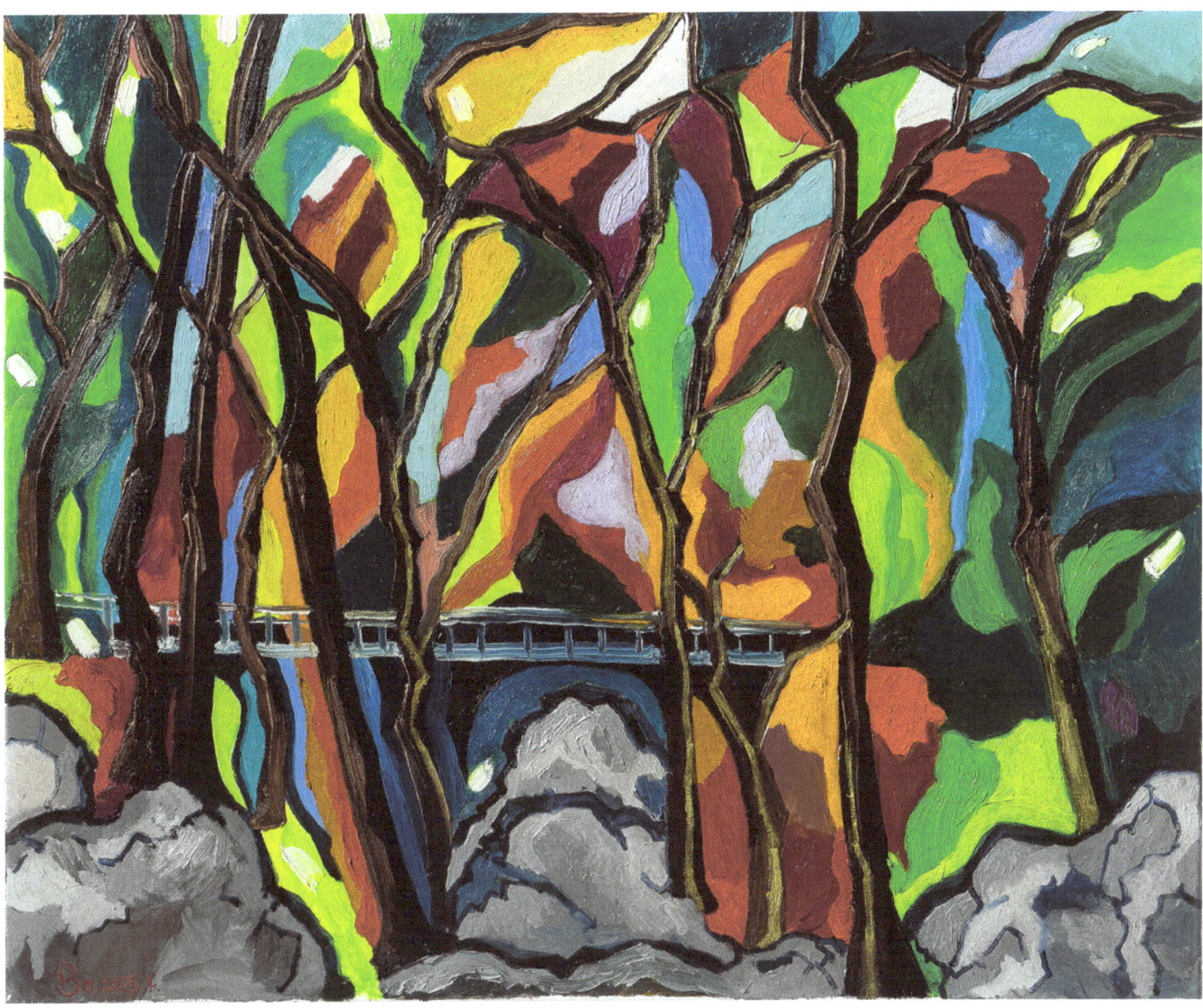

Technique | Painting
Price Range | 4000 US$ - 8000 US$
Sales Report | 3800 US$ (2018) - 12000 US$ (2019)
Active Years | - years

Korean Mountain

USD 5000

Bo Song

韓国 | South Korea

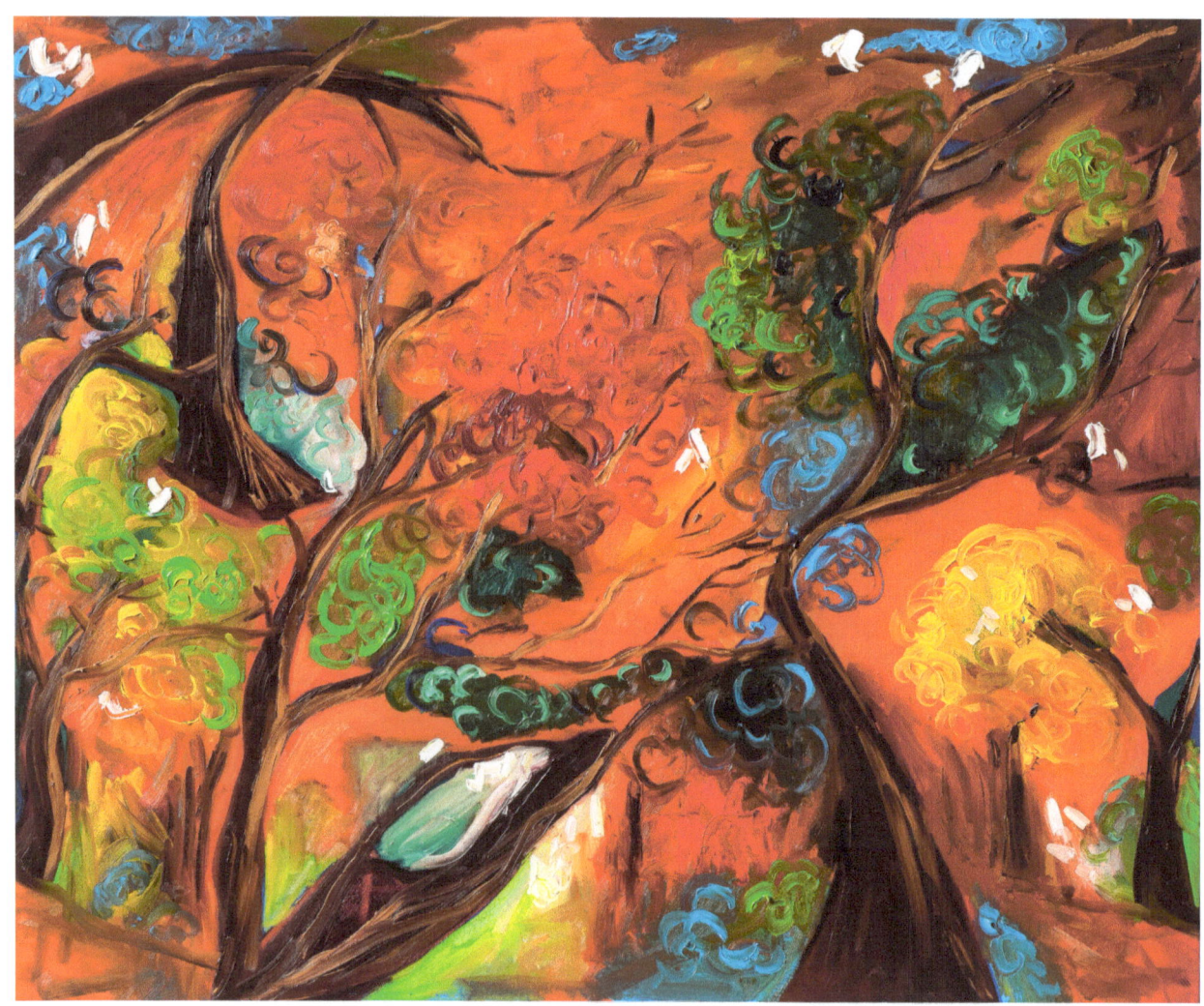

Vitality

USD 4000

bksong.com

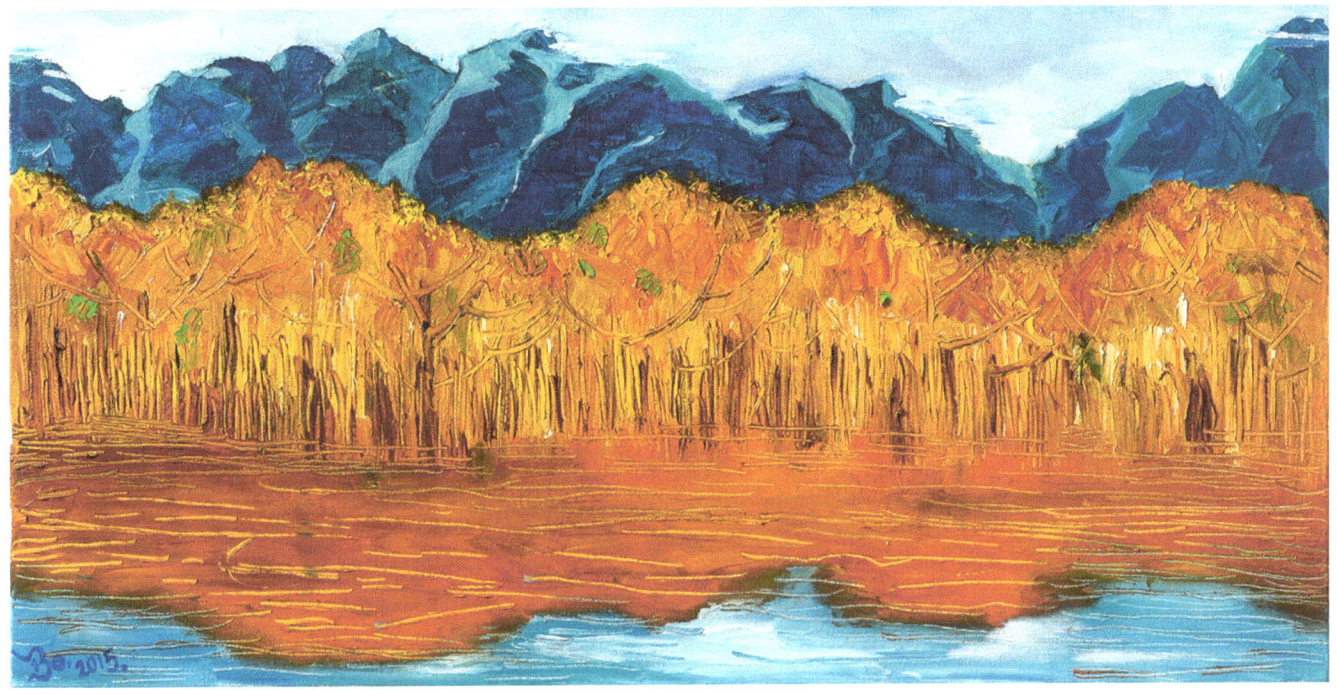

Autumn Season

USD 2700

August Vilella
スペイン | Spain

August Vilella氏はバルセロナ在住のアーティストである。油絵作品をシュールで直観的な手法を用いて制作する。このプロセスでは、事前にスケッチをしたり、アイデアを集めるということをせず、即興で潜在意識に直接形を与えようと試みている。その結果、作品に夢幻的なオーラ、不思議な魅力、隠喩的な意味あい、達観した言葉などが作品に織り込まれ、鑑賞者に評価されている。作品は極細筆、油絵具とニスを使用した非常に洗練された技法で描かれている。結果として、彼の作品には、非常に熟練した精巧な技法と、完全に直観に基づく即興で制作するスタイルという対照的なものが組み合わせられているのが興味深く、それはまるでジャズのような絵画である。

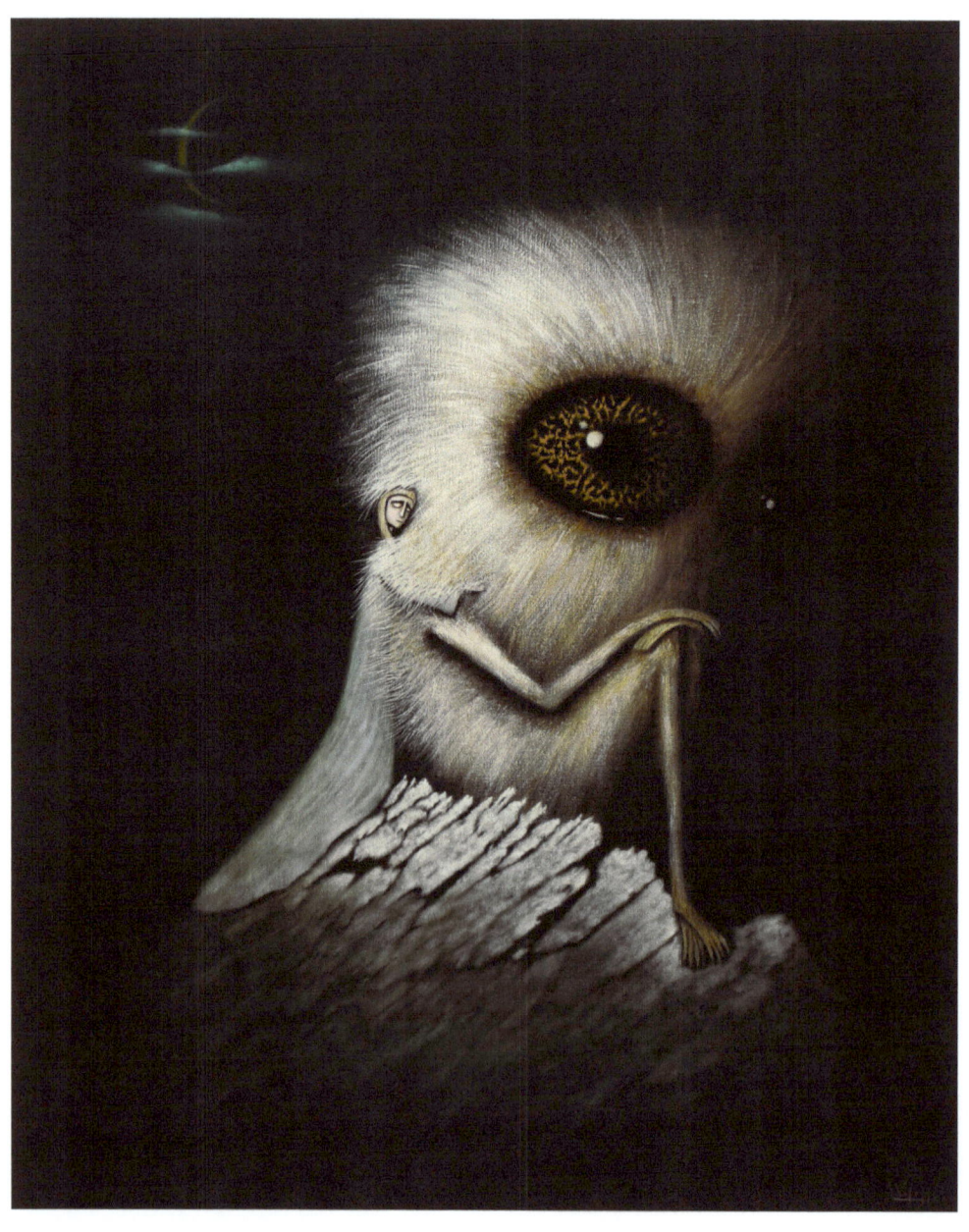

技術 | 絵画
価格帯 | USD 5500 - USD 60000
販売レポート | USD 165000 [2018年] - USD 225000 [2019年]
有効な年数 | 7年

Tenderness
Oil on canvas - 100x81cm - 2017
USD 22000

augustvilella.com

August Vilella is an artist based in Barcelona. He creates oil paintings by means of a surreal-intuitive method. Thanks to this process and without using any previous sketches or ideas, he tries to give shape to his subconscious mind. The result of this practice evokes a dreamlike aura and a magic, metaphoric, and even philosophical language, which invites the observing visitor to reflect. All this iconography is represented with a very refined technics using very small brushes and many slim layers of oil paint and varnish. In consequence, we can see in Vilella´s artworks a very curious contrast between a very technical and elaborated style, and a creative process that turns out to be completely intuitively improvised and unintentional… like a Jazz painting.

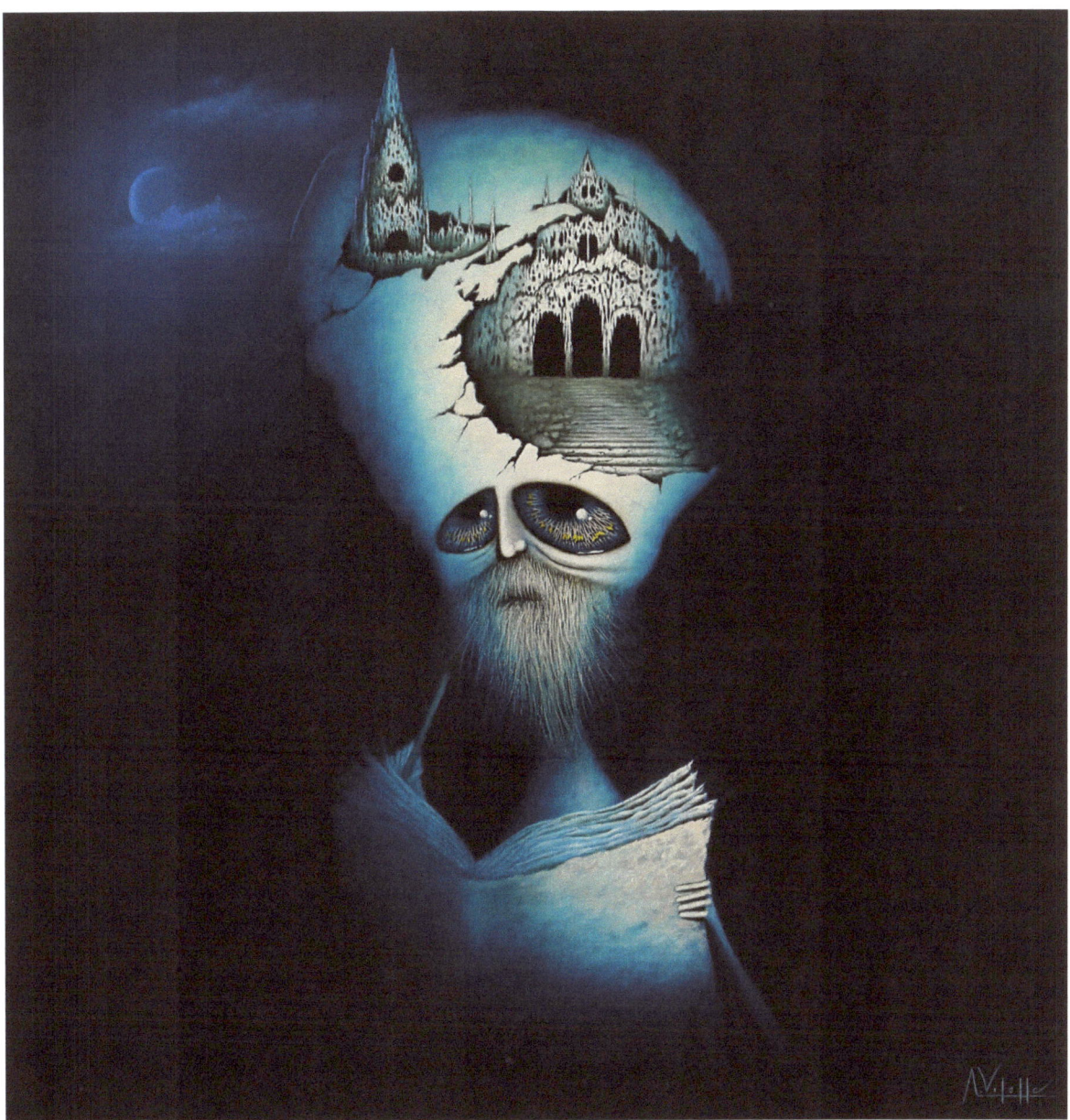

Technique | Painting
Price Range | USD 5500 - USD 60000
Sales Report | USD 165000 (2018) - USD 225000 (2019)
Active Years | 7 years

The Arquitect
Oil on canvas - 100x100cm - 2019
USD 25000

Claudia Mayer-Mallenau
オーストリア | Austria

私は心の底から楽しんでいるこれらの春の甘い朝のように、素晴らしい静寂が私の魂全体を所有しています。　私は一人で、私のような魂の至福のため
オーストリア人のClaudia　Mayer-Mallenau氏の描く大きく力強い肖像画は、人物の幾層もの内面を明らかにする確かな創作センスを示している。作品の視野とできばえは現代的であるが、伝統的なスタイルも守り、その人物のルーツや、世の中との関わり方を形成した感情的な経験などを作品に盛り込んでいる。それぞれの作品で、色、形、質感を巧みに組み合わせ、その強い表現者主義気質で作品の中に強い感情を導入している。

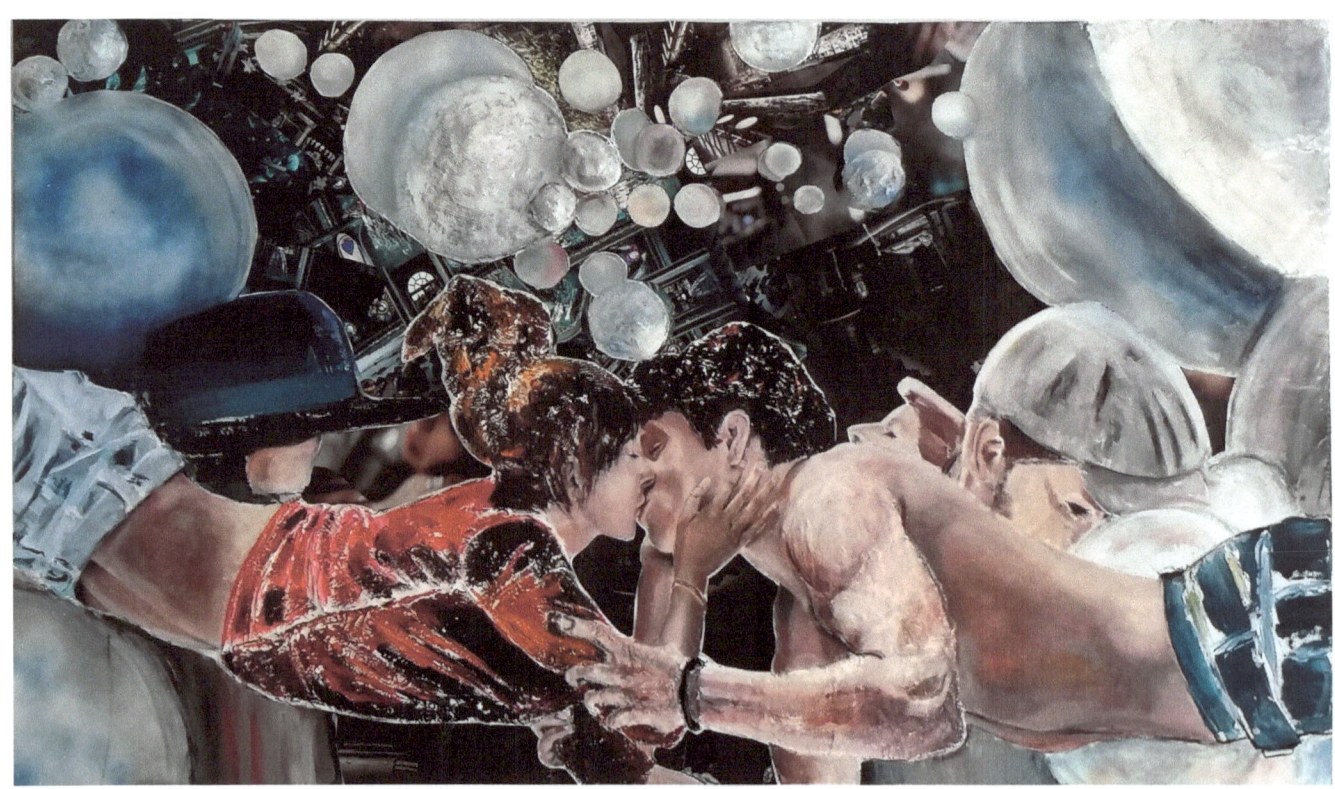

技術 | 絵画 - 混合メディア
価格帯 | USD 6000 - USD 12000
販売レポート | USD 13300 [2018年] - USD 27800 [2019年]
有効な年数 | 18年

Love Affairs III

12/2019, 3dimensional with plaster, collage, acrylic, resin, 45"x 63"

USD 11700

atelier-cmm.com

The large, powerful portraits of Austrian artist Claudia Mayer-Mallenau present a solid sense of composition with an almost unsettling ability to reveal the many internal layers of the subject. While her images are modern in scope and execution, she adheres to tradition whereby a portrait tells a story, such as where the person has come from or the emotional experiences that have shaped their interaction with the world. In each work, she masterfully combines color, form, and texture with a decidedly expressionist bent to convey strong emotions.

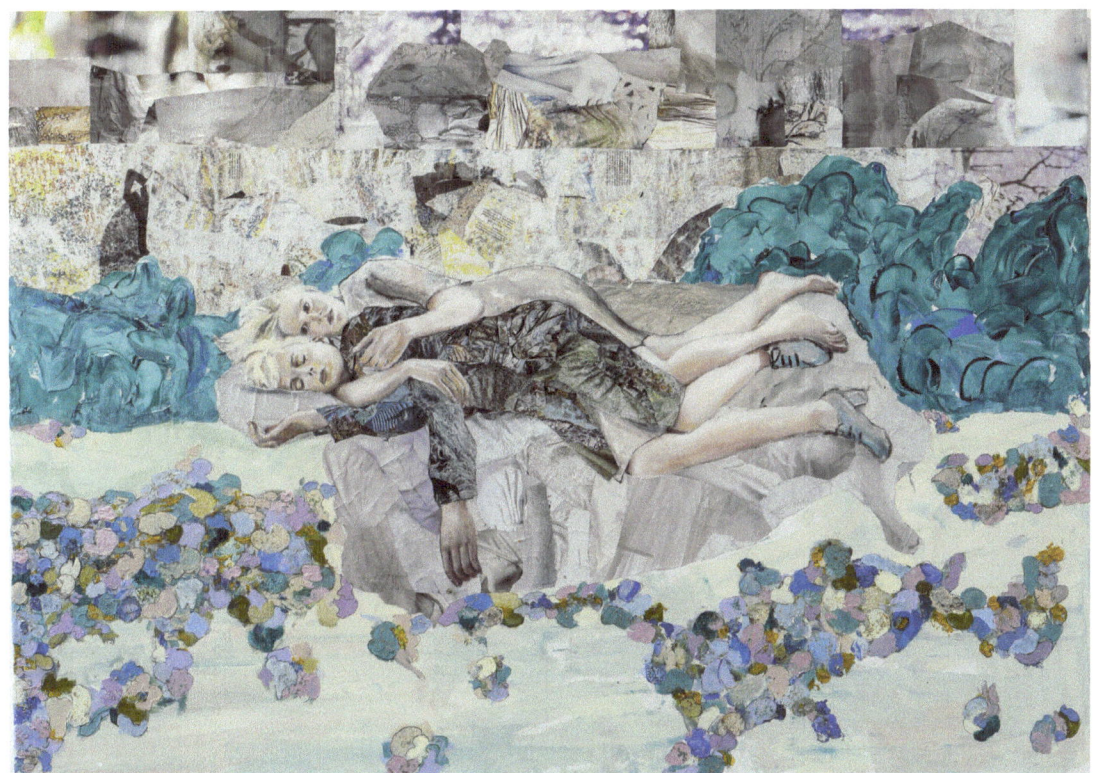

Technique | Painting - Mixed Media
Price Range | USD 6000 - USD 12000
Sales Report | USD 13300 (2018) - USD 27800 (2019)
Active Years | 18 years

Love Affairs I
4/2019, collage, acrylic, 45"x63"
USD 10580

Mayuko Ono Gray
ハンガリー | United States

Mayuko Ono Gray氏はテキサス在住のアーティストで、作品の主なスタイルはグラファイトドローイングである。日本で生まれ、幼少期は伝統的な書道を学び、10代で古典洋画を学ぶ。高校卒業後アメリカへ移住。2007年にthe University of Houston main campusでMFA（美術学修士号）を取得。現在はテキサスのCollege of the Mainlandで芸術の非常勤教授兼アートギャラリー・ディレクターとして勤務している。作品はヒューストンのHooks-Epstein galleriesやメキシコ、オアハカのGaleria 910で展示されており、過去には東京やオアハカなど、国際的に展示されている。

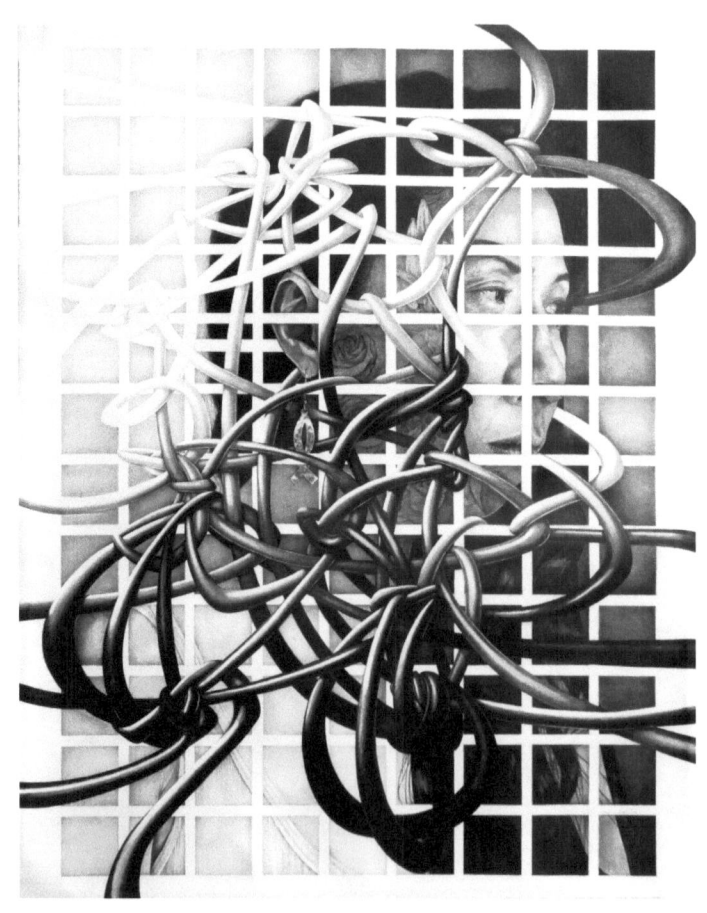

技術 | 描画
価格帯 | USD n/a - USD n/a
販売レポート | USD n/a [2018年] - USD n/a [2019年]
有効な年数 | 13年

となりの花はあかい - The rose is always redder next door. 41" x 33"
For purchase inquiries please contact Hooks-Epstein galleries at
www.hooksepsteingalleries.com and/or yvonne@hooksepsteingalleries.com

mayukoonogray.com

Mayuko Ono Gray is a Texas based artist whose main medium is graphite drawing. Born in Japan, she was trained in traditional Japanese calligraphy in her young childhood; later in her teenage she was trained in classical Western drawing. After graduating from high school in Japan, she moved to the U.S. She earned her MFA in painting from the University of Houston main campus in 2007. Currently she works as adjunct professor of Art and the Art Gallery director for the College of the Mainland in Texas City, TX. Her works are represented by Hooks-Epstein galleries in Houston TX and Galeria 910 in Oaxaca Mexico, and her works have been exhibited internationally in Tokyo Japan and Oaxaca Mexico.

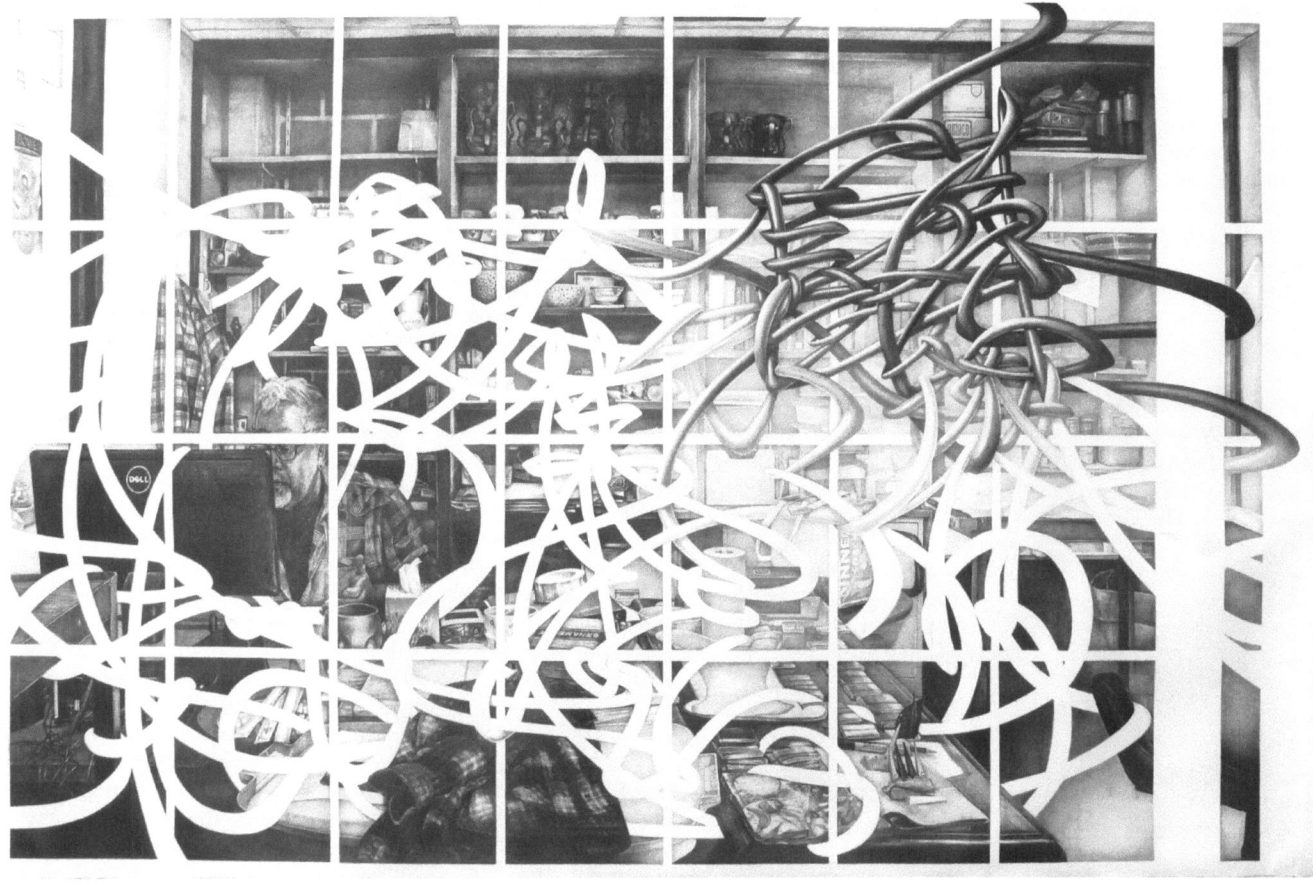

Technique | Drawing
Price Range | USD n/a - USD n/a
Sales Report | USD n/a (2018) - USD n/a (2019)
Active Years | 13 years

芸術は長く人生は短し - Art is long, Life is short (George). 41" x 65"

For purchase inquiries please contact Hooks-Epstein galleries at hooksepsteingalleries.com and/or yvonne@hooksepsteingalleries.com

Formento & Formento ArtYard Gallery
ハンガリー | United States

Formento & Formentoの二人は、フィクションと現実、明瞭さと曖昧さの境界線をぼかしたロマンチックで独創的な写真作品で知られている。彼らの作品は場所に対する思い入れが際立っており、その雰囲気と感触の魅力を映し出している。アメリカ、ヨーロッパ、キューバ、メキシコ、インド、日本などで、写真とフィルムへの溢れる情熱と互いへの永遠の愛を融合させた作品を展示している。

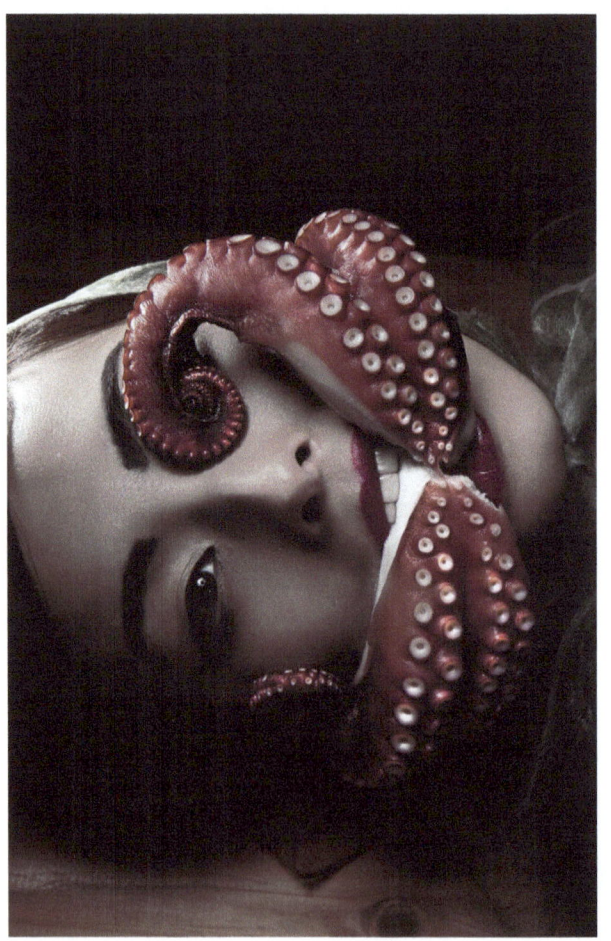

技術 | 写真
価格帯 | USD 3000 - USD 15000
販売レポート | USD 50000 [2018年] - USD 100000 [2019年]
有効な年数 | 15年

Mai VI
Photography 40x60". 2013. Edition 4 of 7 Signed, studio stamped verso.
USD 12000

artyardgallery.de

Formento & Formento known for their romantic and inventive photography that blur the lines of fiction and reality, clarity and ambiguity. Their style reveals a fascination with mood and texture where a sense of place figures prominently. From America, Europe, Cuba, Mexico, India to Japan they blend fervent passion for photography and film with a lasting love for one another.

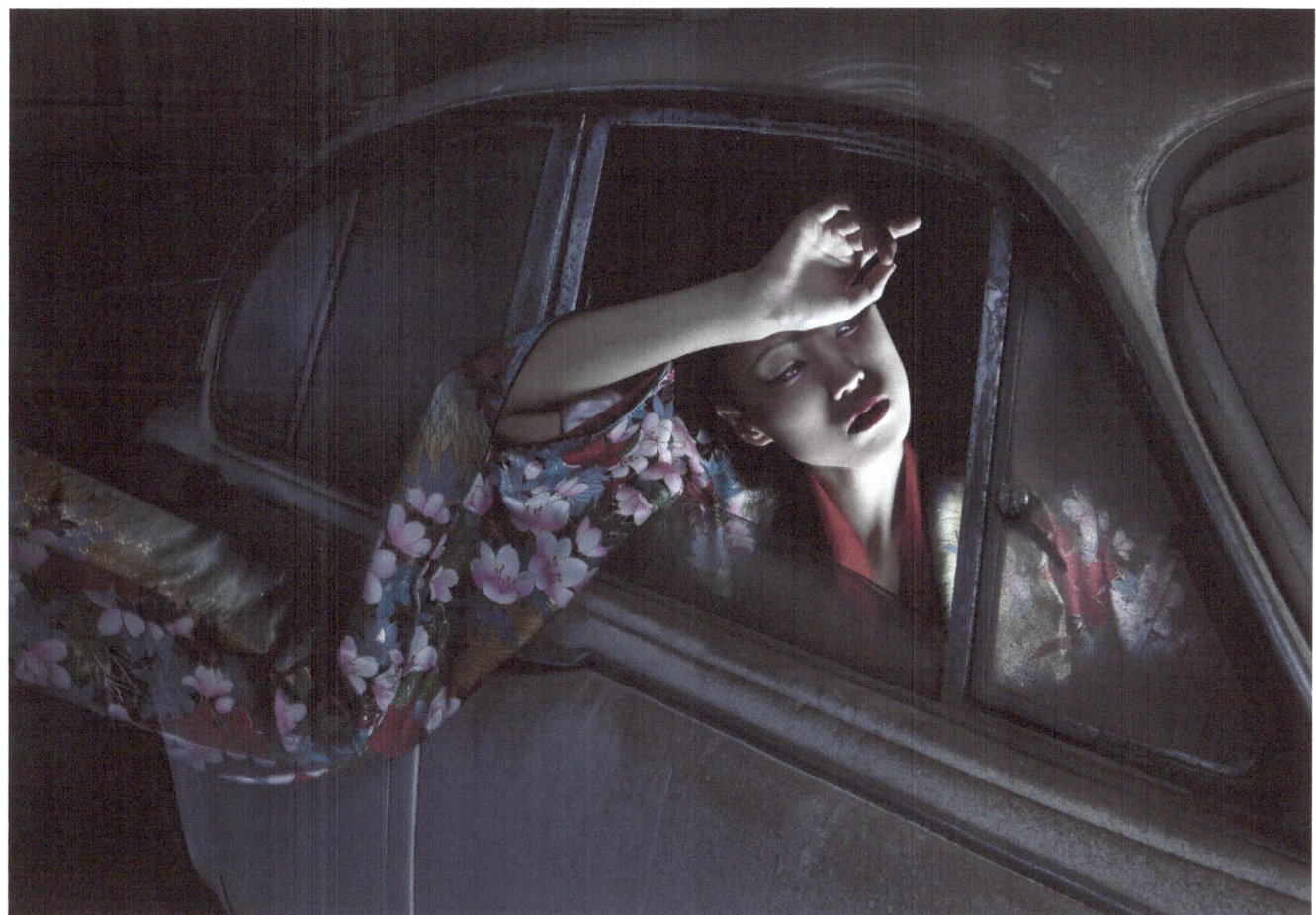

Technique | Photography
Price Range | USD 3000 - USD 15000
Sales Report | USD 50000 (2018) - USD 100000 (2019)
Active Years | 15 years

Yuka V

Photography 40x60". 2013. Edition 3 of 7 Signed, studio stamped verso.

USD 12000

Haruka Harada
日本 | Japan

Haruka氏は日本人ミクストメディアアーティスト兼デザイナーである。神奈川県出身、東京在住。ニューヨークとマイアミでアートを学ぶ。力強く挑発的な作品で、強く美しく、セクシーな女性を表現しており、官能的な女性の唇は彼女の定番スタイルである。作品には人々と音楽からのインスピレーションが反映されている。彼女の作品は東京、ニューヨーク、マイアミで非常に貴重なコレクションとして位置付けられている。

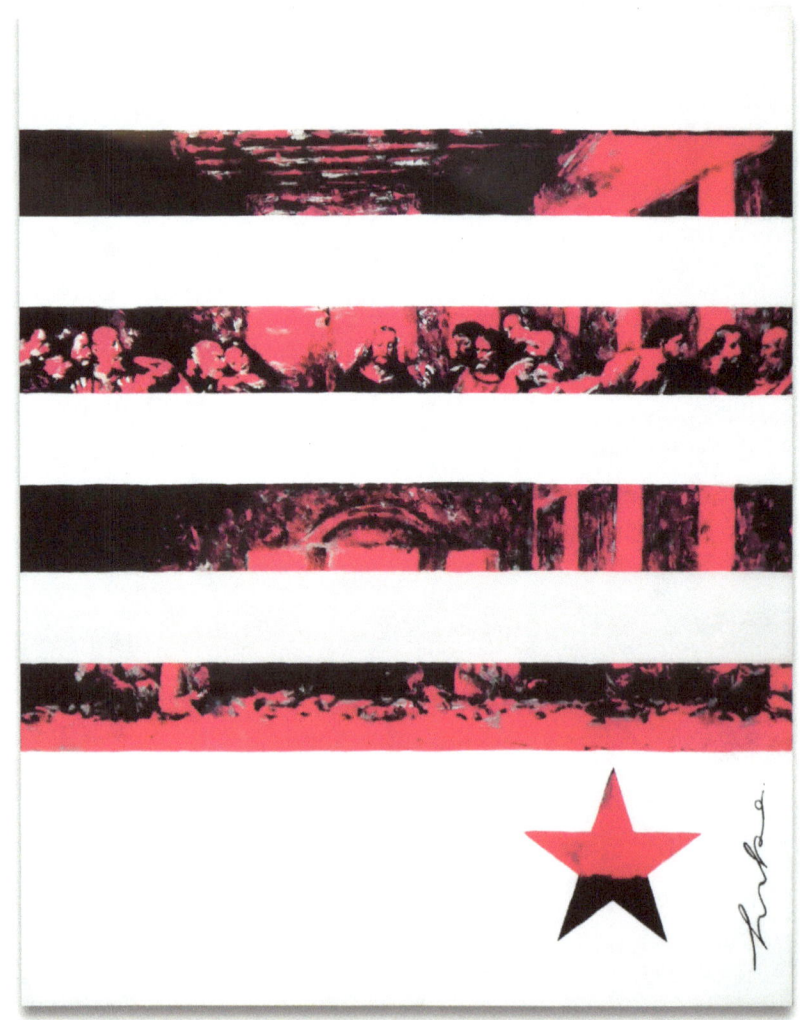

技術 | 絵画 - 混合メディア
価格帯 | USD 800 - USD 20000
販売レポート | USD n/a [2018年] - USD n/a [2019年]
有効な年数 | - 年

The Last supper 2019
Mixed media on woodpanel / 1000 x 803 mm
USD 8000

hrkartgallery.com

Haruka is a japanese mixed-media artist and designer. Born and raised in Kanagawa and based in Tokyo, Japan. She studied art in New York and Miami. Her work is powerful and provocative, it portraits strong, beautiful and sexy women; sensual women lips are her style staple. Haruka's inspiration comes from people and music. Her artwork is in very important collections in Tokyo, New York and Miami.

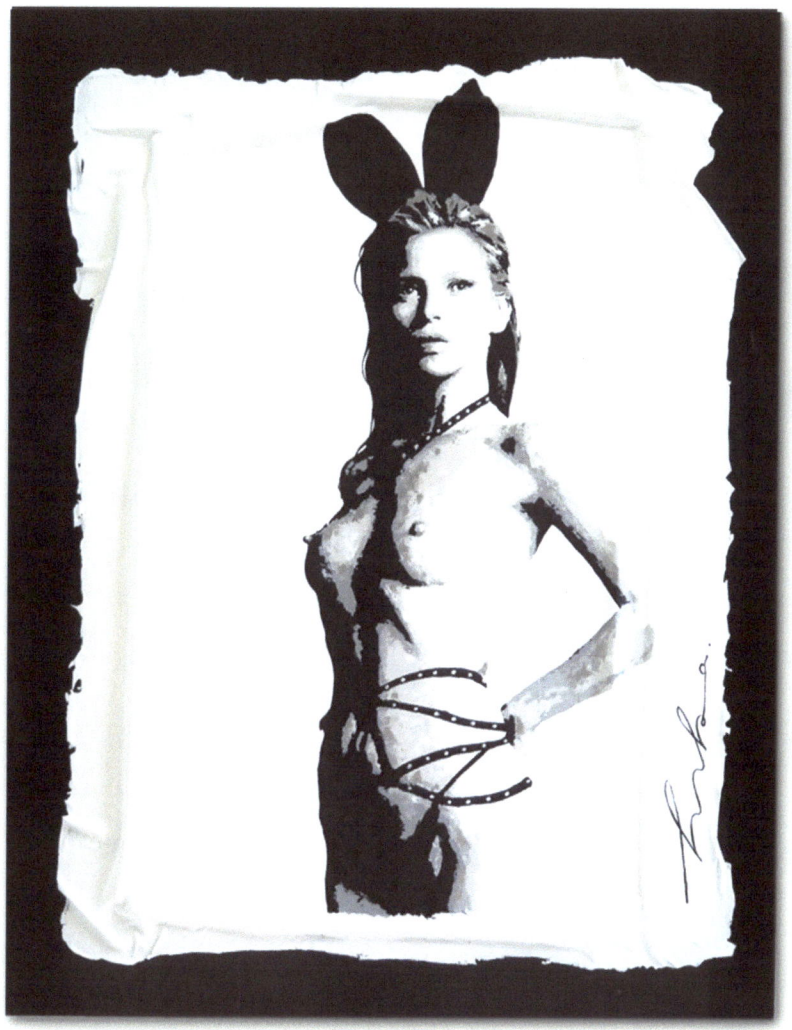

Technique | Painting - Mixed Media
Price Range | USD 800 - USD 20000
Sales Report | USD n/a (2018) - USD n/a (2019)
Active Years | - years

P. BOY Kate
Mixed media on woodpanel / 1000 x 803 mm
USD 8000

Peter Snopix
イギリス | United Kingdom

何かを創造的に表現しようと考えたときに、お金になるかどうかというのは一切気にしていない。誰にとっても創作活動は自分の想像力を発揮する究極の冒険だと考えている。だから、誰かに自分が作ったものを買ってもらえるのは、大変な偉業であり、経歴に花を添えてくれるものである。ここにある画像は自身の最新のデジタル作品である。過去の絵画作品や自身についての詳細な経歴についてのお問合せは、以下のメールアドレスへご連絡ください。
snopixx@hotmail.com

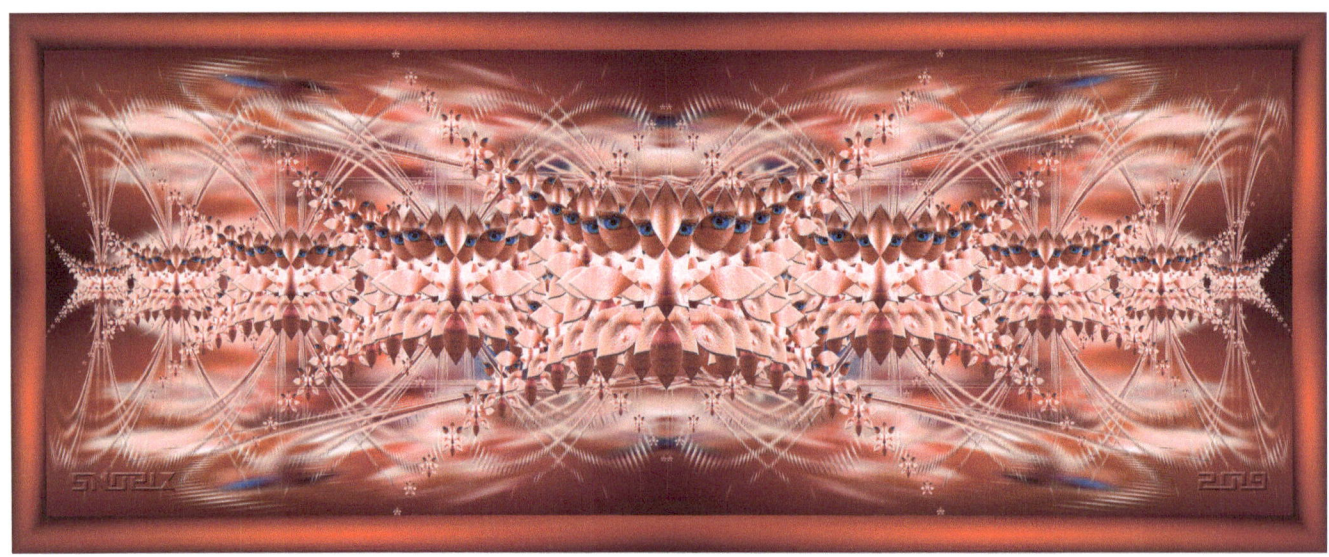

技術 | デジタルアート
価格帯 | USD n/a - USD n/a
販売レポート | USD n/a [2018年] - USD n/a [2019年]
有効な年数 | +40年

X Plode I 2 2019 Digital
300 Fine Art Canvas Print Unmounted
Price Upon Request

snopix.co.uk

When I first had the idea to try to express myself creatively the thought of payment was the furthest thing form my mind. For me it was the idea of the ultimate adventure for anyone to undertake into one's own imagination! So when someone does offer you money for something that only exists because you crated it, then that must be the ultimate achievement for a person. And the cherry on top of anyone's career! The images here and at my website are my most recent digital works, if you would like to see my earlier painted works or you need more details about me, then please email me at snopixx@hotmail.com

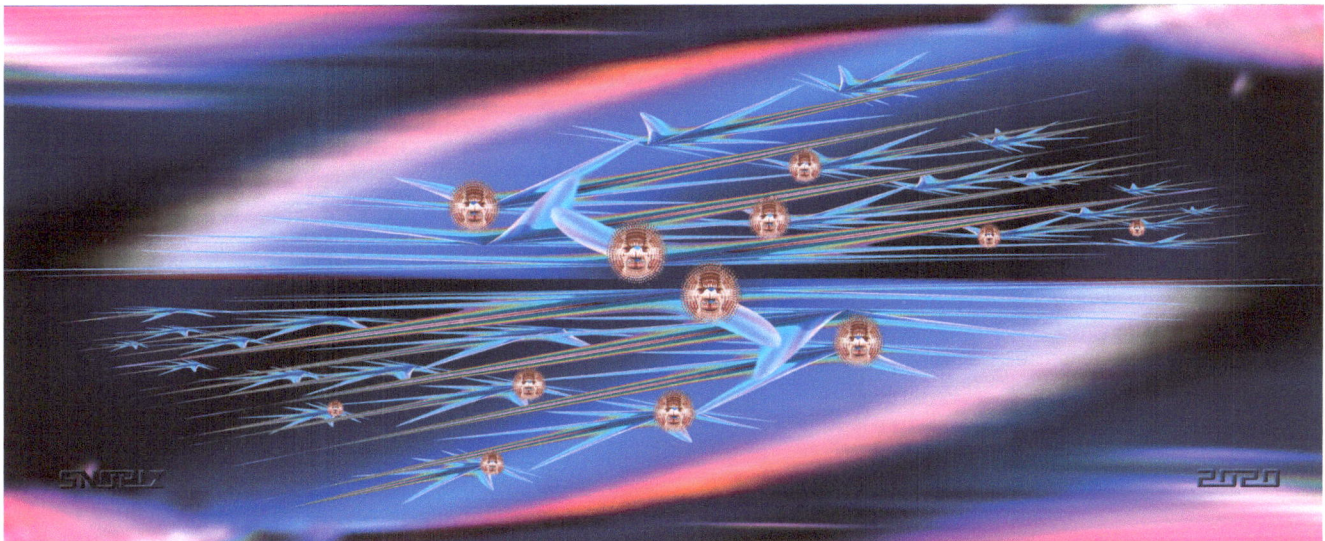

Technique | Digital Art
Price Range | USD n/a - USD n/a
Sales Report | USD n/a (2018) - USD n/a (2019)
Active Years | +40 years

Encounter 3 2020 Digital
300 Fine Art Canvas Print Unmounted
Price Upon Request

Maria Linares Freire
イギリス | United Kingdom

創作活動を始めた頃から、絡み合って一体化する宇宙、自然にひそむ幾何学の美しさ、多次元など、私たちが気づかなかった神秘的なものから常にインスピレーションを得ている。作品には幾何学、形象、象徴主義、未来派、精神性、科学などが融合されている。魅惑的な空間での平和な風景の表現、ストーリー性を持たせた作品、絵画、壁画、写真、デジタルアートを通じての愛のメッセージの発信などの方法で創作活動をおこなっている。作品制作の際には、初めに巻尺、定規、コンパスなどを使って作品のストーリーとバランスの合うサイズを調べ、その後、アクリル絵具を何層にも重ねながら意識を3次元の世界へ移行させる。作品にエネルギーを与え、鑑賞者を魅了するためにメタリックカラーを使い、光沢をつける効果も加えている。

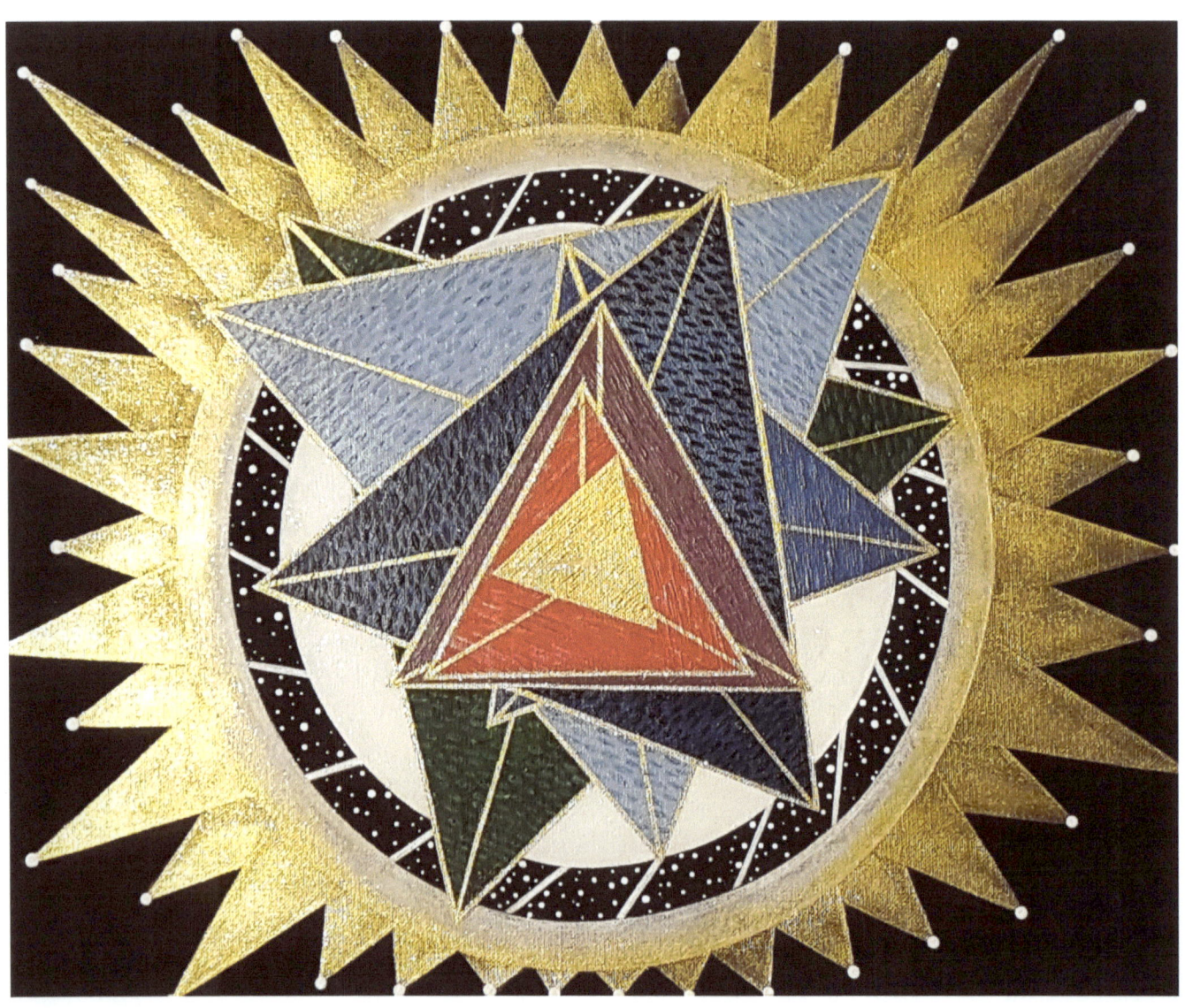

技術 | 絵画 - 混合メディア - 写真 - 壁画
価格帯 | USD 600 - USD 5000
販売レポート | USD 3000 [2018年] - USD 5370 [2019年]
有効な年数 | 5年

Cosmos
40.5x51 cm. Acrylic on canvas
USD 2800

marialinaresfreire.net

The united and entangled universe, the geometrical qualities hidden in nature and the multiple dimensions that our senses can't perceive have been a constant stream of inspiration since the beginning of my visionary creative period. My works are a combination of geometry, figuration, symbolism, futurism, spirituality and science.Showing peaceful landscapes from magical places, story telling with images, sending a message of love throughout fine arts, murals, photography of digital arts. The first stage of any of my paintings involves measures, rulers and compass in the search of a mathematical balance with a story to tell. Afterwards comes the multiple layering of acrylics transporting the mind to a tridimensional experience. To transmit energy and mesmerise the viewer I use metallic colours and shimmering effects.

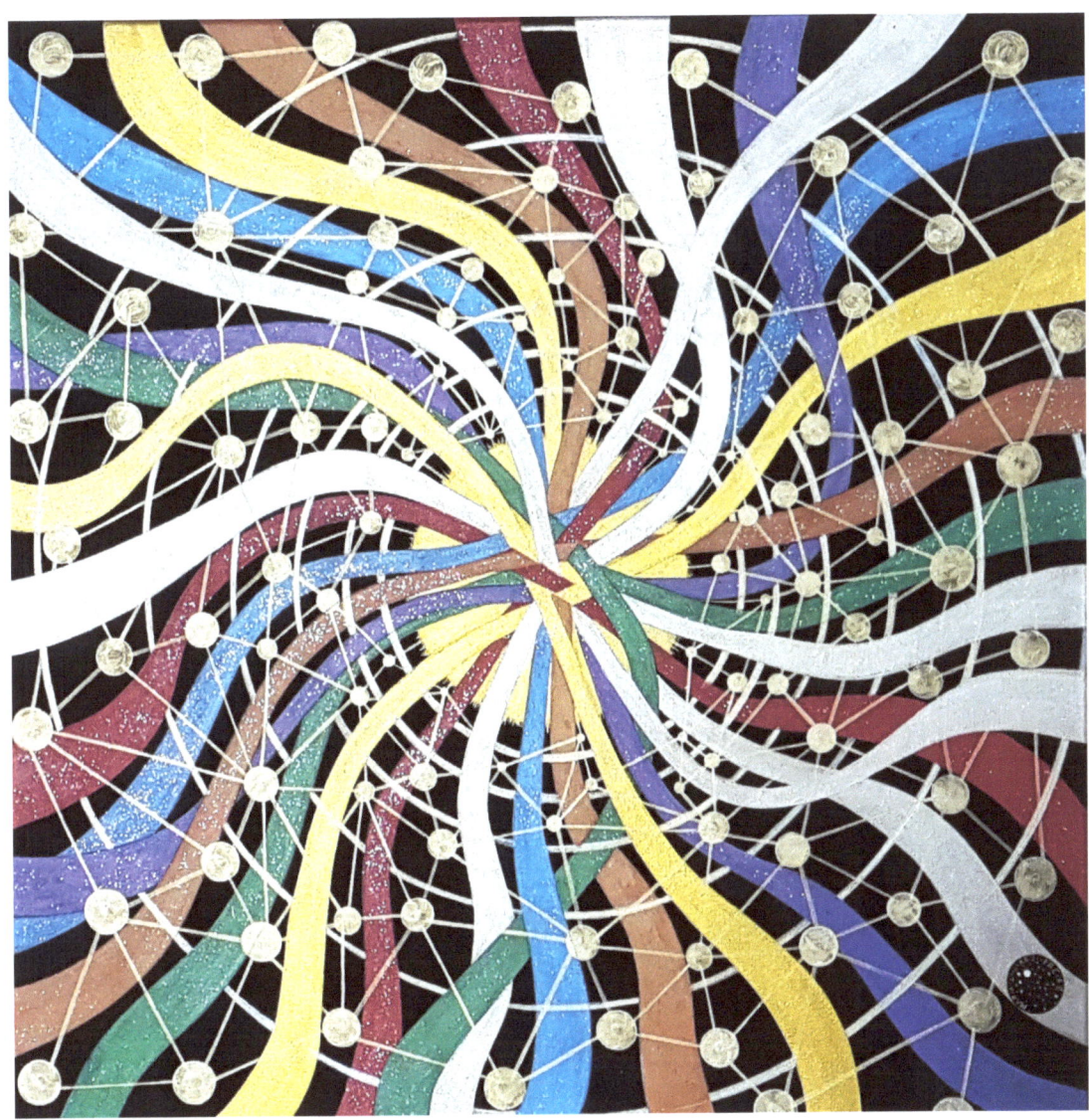

Technique | Painting - Mixed Media - Photography - Muralism
Price Range | USD 600 - USD 5000
Sales Report | USD 3000 (2018) - USD 5370 (2019)
Active Years | 5 years

The Mind
Acrylic and mixed media on cotton canvas. 60x60 cm
USD 2500

Chan Suk On
香港 | Hong Kong

香港理工大学卒業写真デザイン学部写真デザイン科卒業。香港中文大学芸術学修士号取得。編集者、写真家、そしてアーティストである。イメージ作り、インスタレーション、執筆活動などを好む。彼女の活動は、ドキュメンタリー写真からコンセプチュアルアートにわたり、その作品は「アート・マニュアル」と呼ばれる。アートに説明は必要だろうか？部屋から選んだ何気ないものも作品になり得る。時が経ってカメラの分厚い使用説明書は時代遅れとなり、カメラの様式も常に更新されていく。彫刻のフォームも色々と変えてみる。文章は順不同で写真撮影について書かれている。

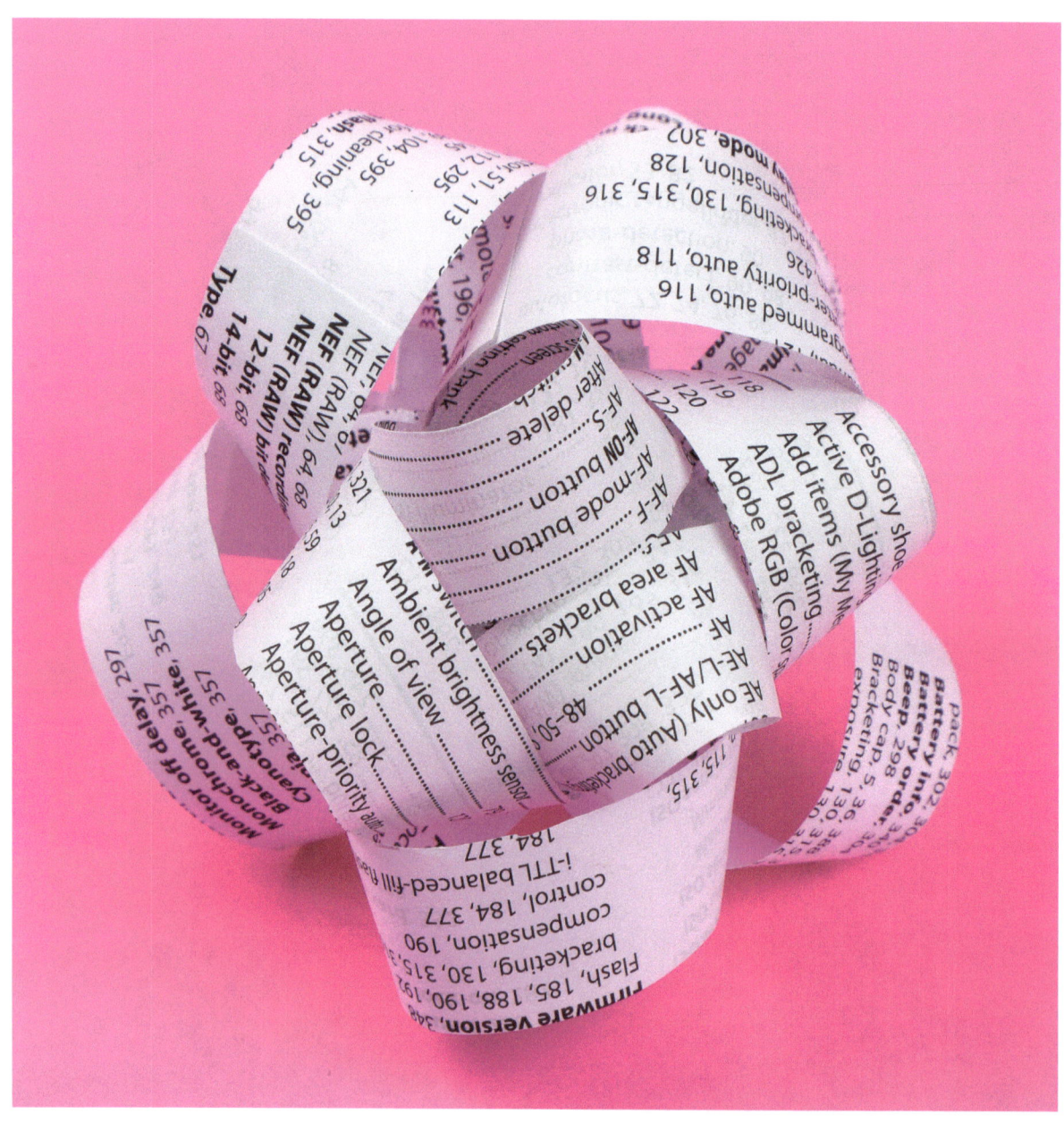

技術	写真
価格帯	USD 400 - USD 1000
販売レポート	USD n/a [2018年] - USD n/a [2019年]
有効な年数	2年

Art Manual
50x50 cm (variable size)
USD 450

httpschansukon.com

Chan Suk On graduated from the Hong Kong Polytechnic University with a Bachelor of Photographic Design. She gained her Masters of Arts in Fine Arts at the Chinese University of Hong Kong. On is an editor, photographer and artist. She likes to create images, installations and writing. Her journey is going from documentary photography to conceptual art. My artwork is called Art Manual. Does art need to be explained? I picked up the sundries in the room. Time passed, the thick camera manual was outdated, and the camera model was constantly updated. I tried to fold different sculptural forms. The texts were about photography randomly distributed.

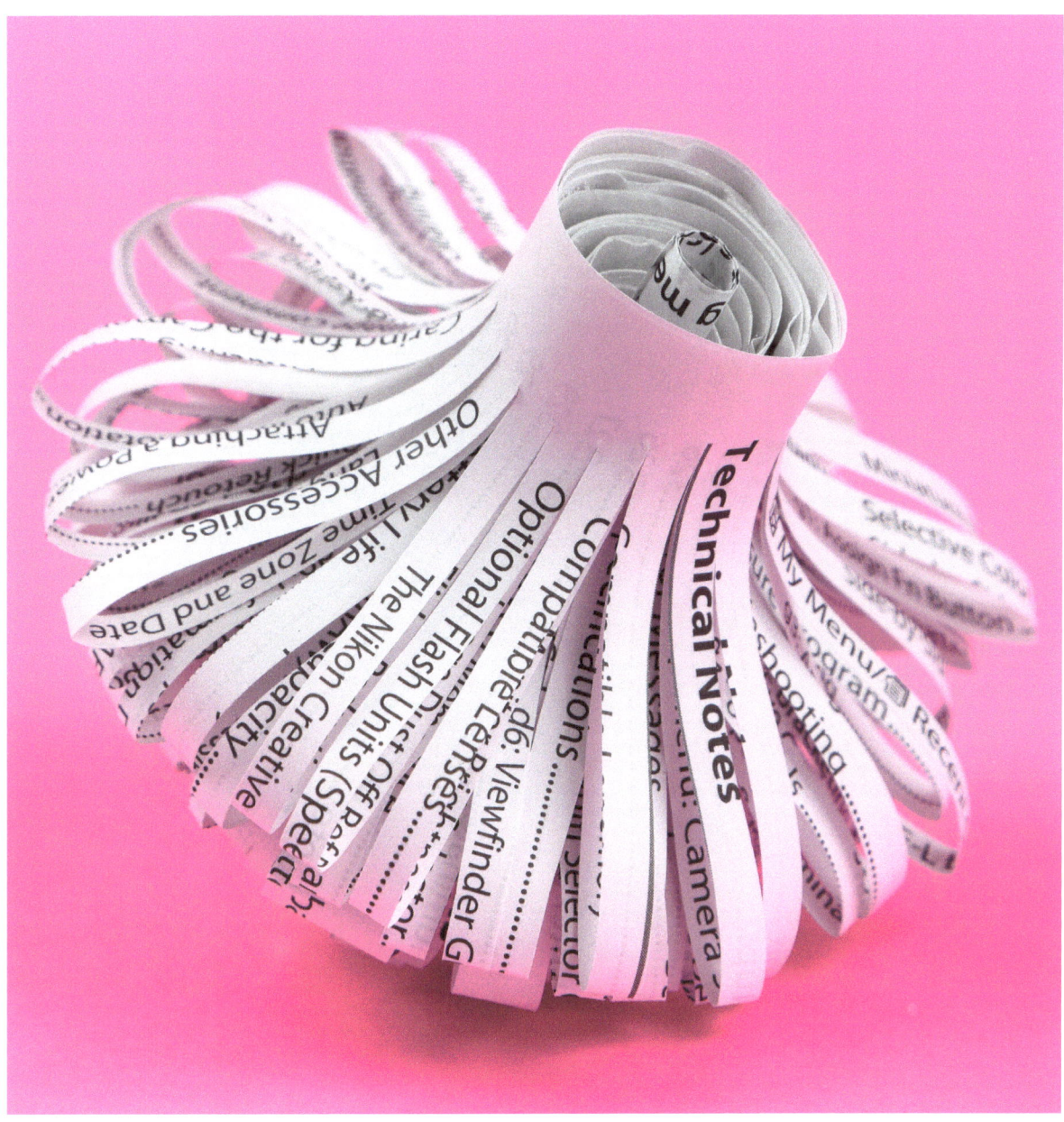

Technique | Photography
Price Range | USD 400 - USD 1000
Sales Report | USD n/a (2018) - USD n/a (2019)
Active Years | 2 years

Art Manual
50x50 cm (variable size)
USD 450

Marina Koraki

ギリシャ | Greece

Marina Koraki氏はChronis Botsoglou 教授の指導のもと、2006年にアテネのSchool of Fine Arts of Athensを卒業。その後、ミラノのAcademia di Belle Arti di Breraでモザイク、ステンドグラス、デジタルアート、舞台美術を学ぶ。2002年よりギリシャ、キプロス、イタリア、アメリカなどで個展開催やグループ展への参加をおこなっている。

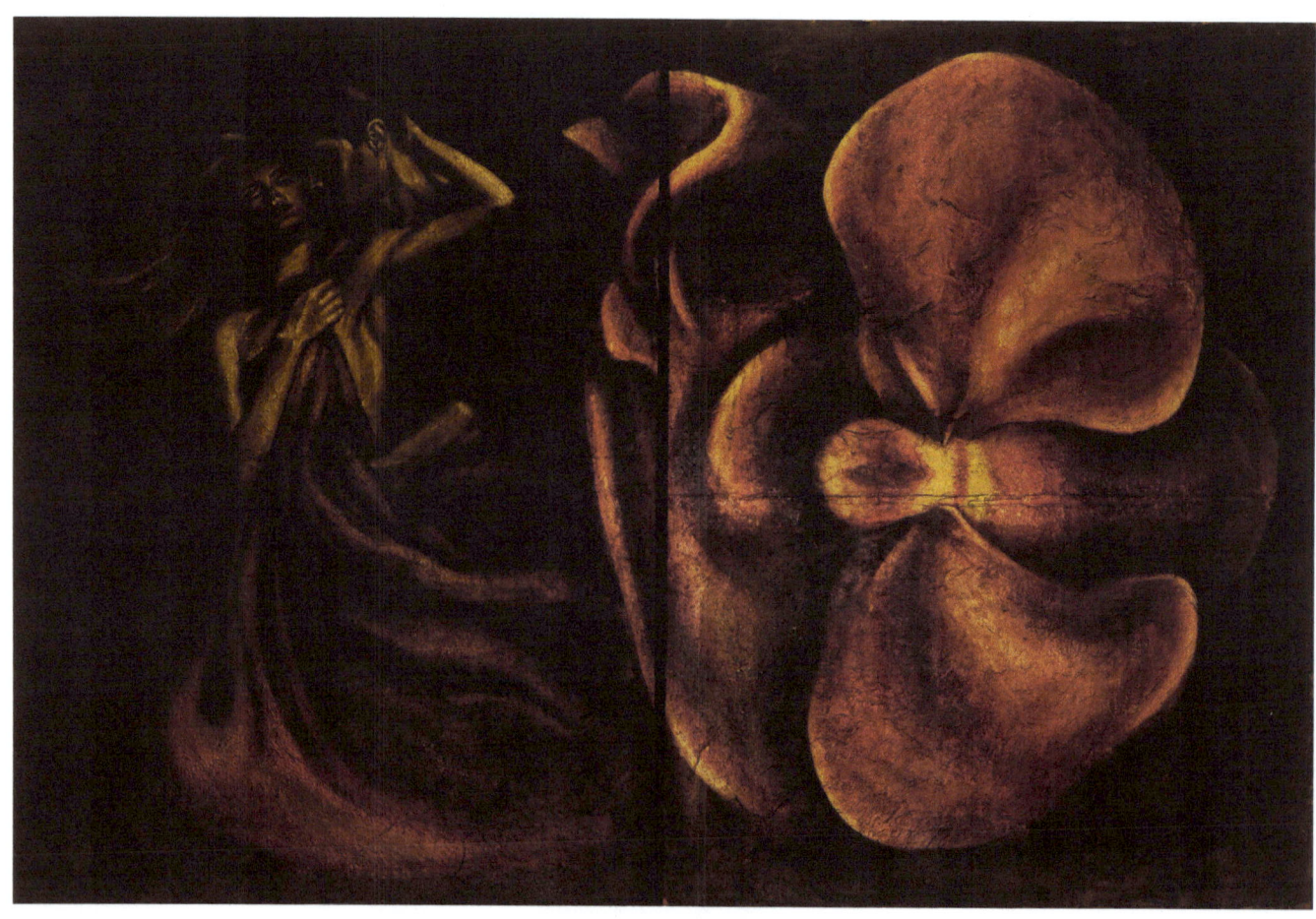

技術 | 絵画
価格帯 | USD 3000 - USD 20000
販売レポート | USD 18000 [2018年] - USD 16000 [2019年]
有効な年数 | 16年

Diptych-Persephone & Adonis
{2x(120x90)cm} - Mixed media on canvas
USD 18700

marinakoraki.com

Marina Koraki graduated from the School of Fine Arts of Athens in 2006, supervised by Chronis Botsoglou. She further studied the arts of mosaic, stained glass as well as digital arts and scenography in Academia di Belle Arti di Brera in Milan. Since 2002 she has participated in group and personal exhibitions in Greece, Cyprus, Italy and USA.

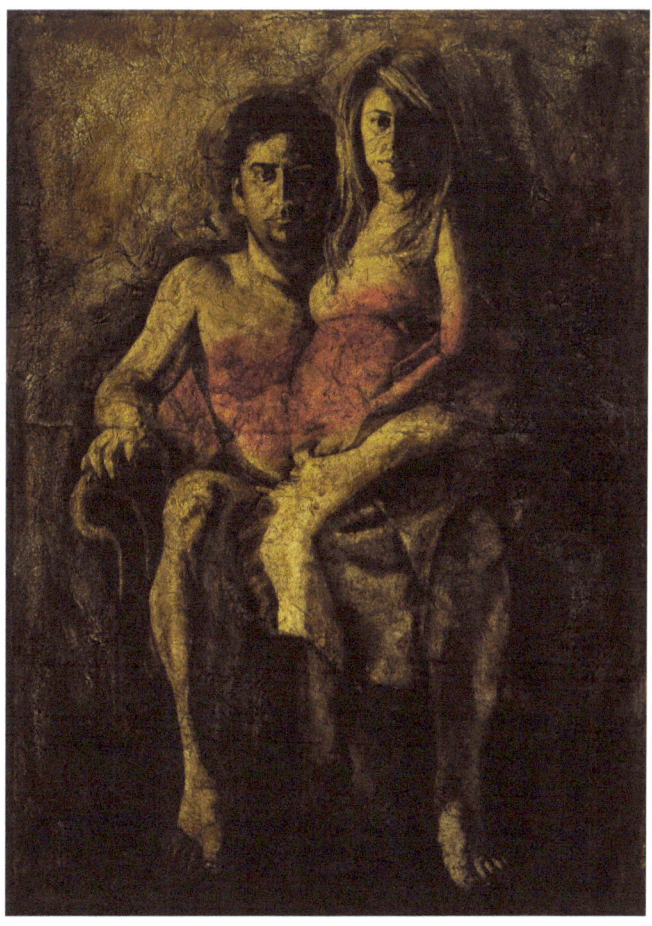

Technique | Painting
Price Range | USD 3000 - USD 20000
Sales Report | USD 18000 (2018) - USD 16000 (2019)
Active Years | 16 years

Uranus & Gaia
(120x90) cm - Mixed media on canvas
USD 17100

Howard Harris
ハンガリー | United States

Howard Harris氏は、アメリカとヨーロッパで活動するアメリカ人アーティストである。大学では芸術とデザインを専攻。米国の特許取得済みの工程を用いて作品を加工している。彼は、視覚的な印象は絶えず変化するものであり、目に見えるものはその時の心理状態や、光、色、動きや空間の組み合せを反映していると考えている。その立体的な写真は、動的性質と隠された複雑さによって知覚体験を再現している。作品にはアルミとアクリル版に印刷された単一画像を使用しているが、結果として、見る角度、絶え間なく変化する光の角度、鑑賞者の経験値や心理状態などが作用して、画像が立体的、流動的に見えるという視覚現象を生み出している。

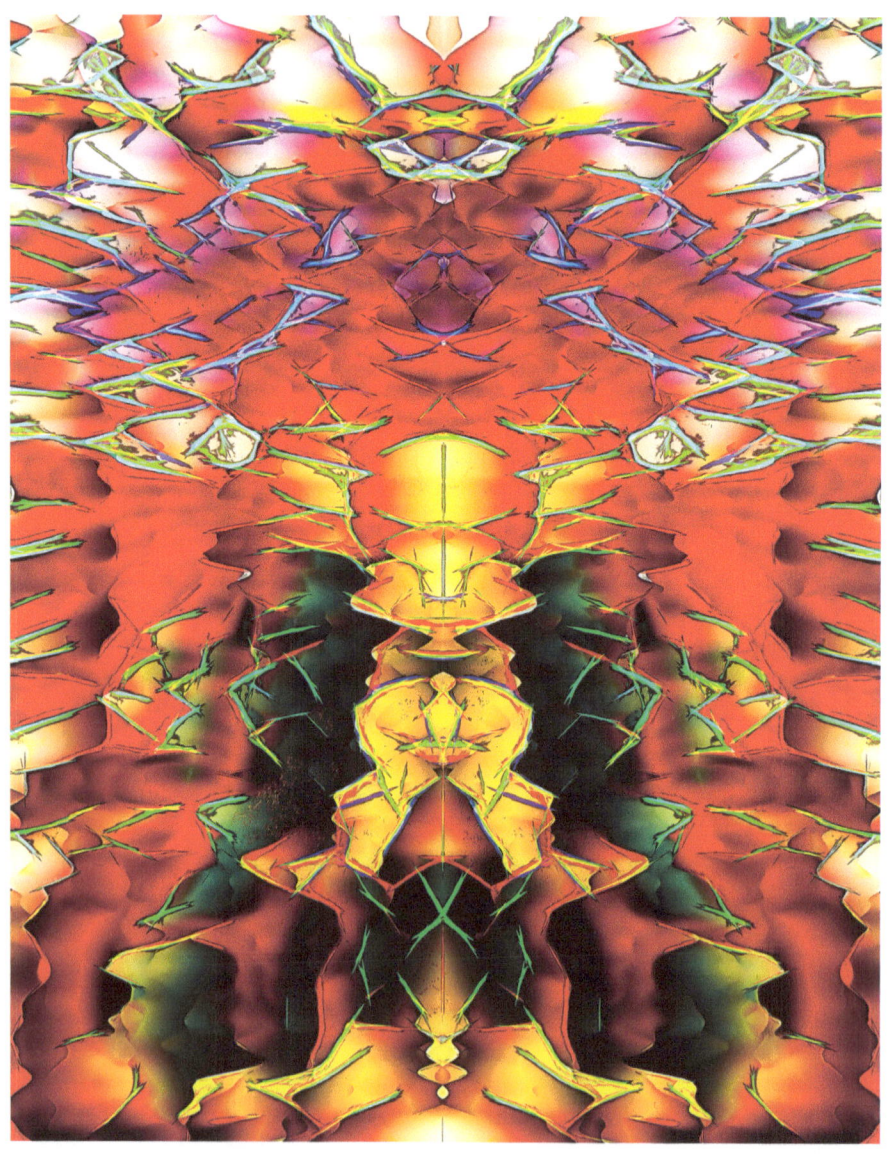

技術 | 写真
価格帯 | USD 1000 - USD 5000
販売レポート | USD n/a [2018年] - USD n/a [2019年]
有効な年数 | 5年

Battle Cloth
USD 3800

3038379721

Mr. Harris is a US artist that shows across the US and Europe. His degrees are both in Fine Arts and Design. He uses a US Patented process to enhance the image. Mr. Harris believes that visual reality is an ever-shifting experience. What one sees reflects our emotional state and a synthesis of light, color, movement, and space. His dimensional photographs recreate the perceptual experience, with its dynamic nature and hidden complexities. He uses a single image printed on aluminum and acrylic. The resulting visual phenomenon infuses the image with a sense of dimensionality, and fluidity affected by the viewing angle and ever-changing light and the viewer's experience and emotion.

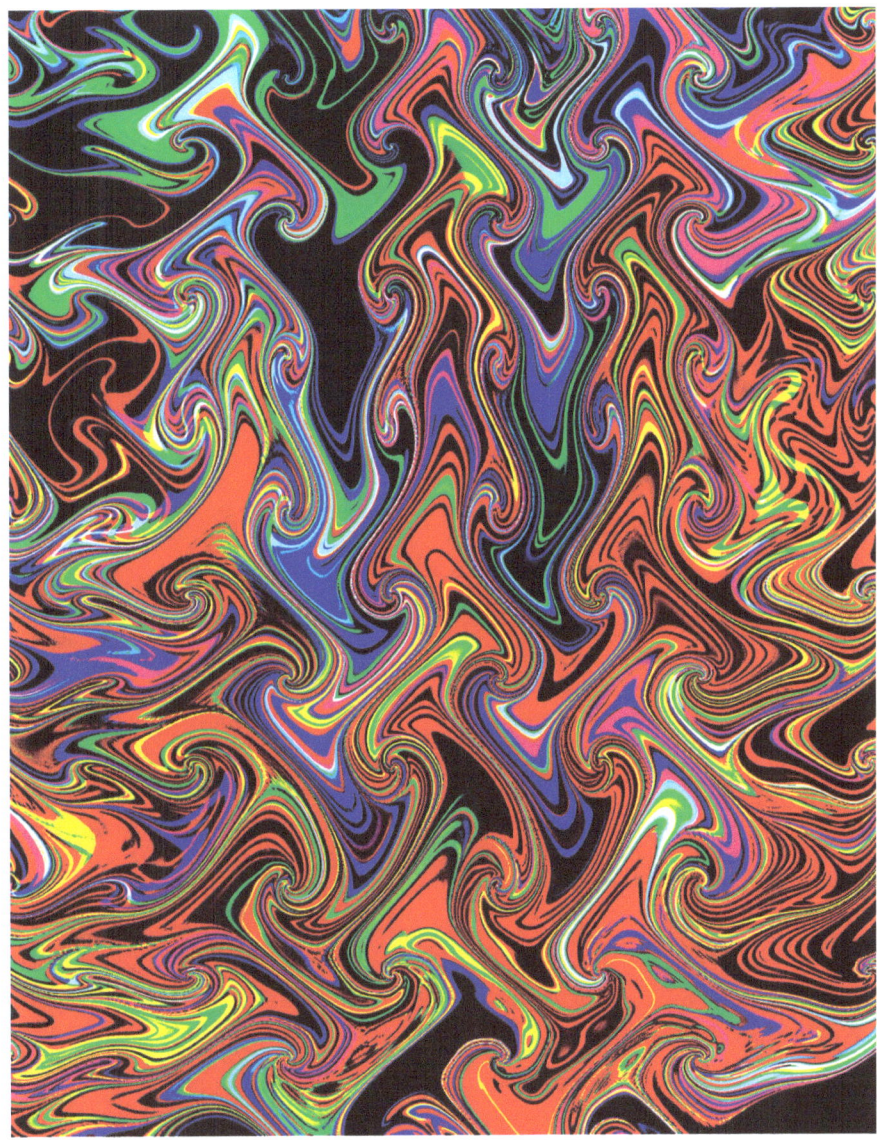

Technique | Photography
Price Range | USD 1000 - USD 5000
Sales Report | USD n/a (2018) - USD n/a (2019)
Active Years | 5 years

Elephant Dance

USD 3800

Herbert Hermans
オランダ | Netherlands

Herbert Hermans氏は1947年5月12日オランダ、フォールブルグ出身で現在はロッテルダム在住。オランダのDutch Art School SKVR in Rotterdamでアートを学ぶ。オランダ、フランス、ドイツ、ポルトガル、オーストリアで12の個展を開催し、オランダ、イギリス、イタリア、スペイン、アメリカ、中国で計56のグループ展に出展。彼の作品は多く国の公的機関や個人コレクターに所有されている。オランダの「Painting of the year」では2014、2016、2018、2019年の4度ノミネートされ、2020年1月にはthe Artavita 35th online contestで優勝し、the World of Art Artist of the Year 2020 Awardも受賞している。

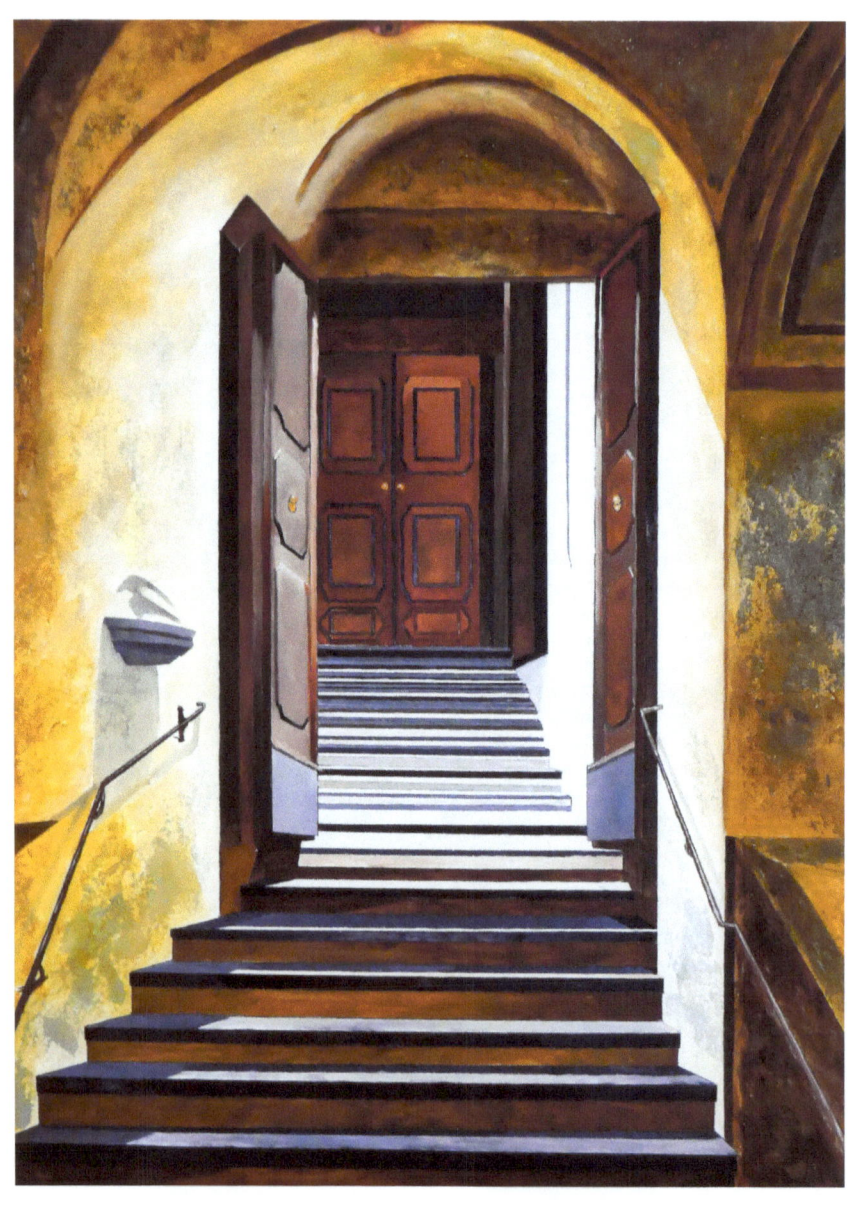

技術 | 絵画
価格帯 | USD 350 - USD 7000
販売レポート | USD 350 [2018年] - USD 1250 [2019年]
有効な年数 | 35年

Escape from the Crypt

Oil on canvas, 60 x 80 cm, 2019

USD 2950

kunstinzicht.nl/portfolio-en/werk/berthermans/index.html

Herbert Hermans (May, 12, 1947 Netherlands). Was born in Voorburg in The Netherlands (Europe) and lives now in Rotterdam. He studied at the Dutch Art School SKVR in Rotterdam in The Netherlands. He has had 12 solo exhibitions in The Netherlands, France, Germany, Portugal and Austria and 56 group participations in The Netherlands, The United Kingdom, Italy, Spain, the USA and China. His work belong to private and public collections in many countries. Herbert is an awarded artist and was 4 times nominated in 2014, 2016, 2018 and 2019 for the Dutch award 'Painting of the year'. In January 2020 he won the Artavita 35th online contest and , the World of Art Artist of the Year 2020 Award.

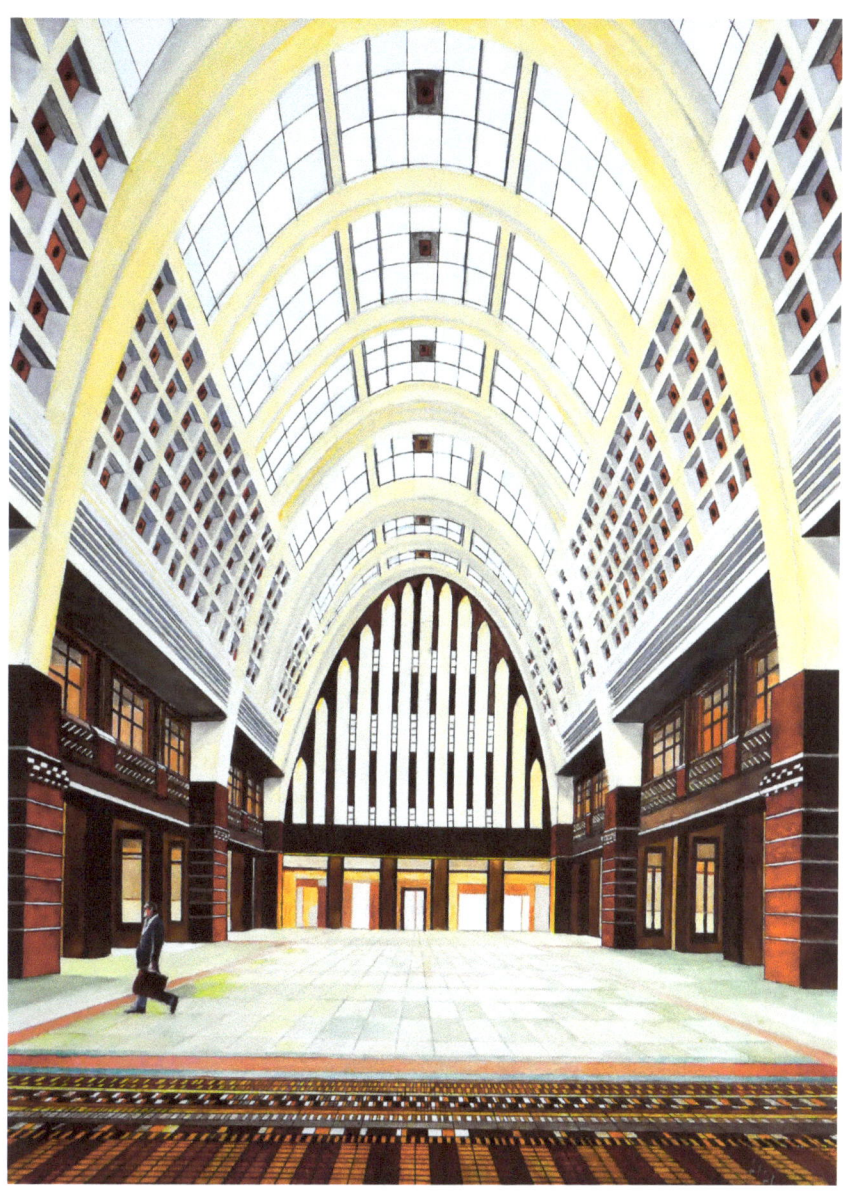

Technique | Painting
Price Range | USD 350 - USD 7000
Sales Report | USD 350 (2018) - USD 1250 (2019)
Active Years | 35 years

The Last Civil Servant
Oil on canvas, 60 x 80 cm, 2019
USD 2925

Betty Collier
オーストラリア | Australia

オーストラリア出身の受賞歴のある画家、彫刻家、そしてイラストレーターであるBetty Collier氏は、これまでにオーストラリア、イタリア、アメリカで作品を展示。作品はオーストラリア、ビクトリア州のFederation Universityにも保存されている。また、作品はDespina Tunberg, Australian Art Edit監修の「WORLD WIDE ART BOOKS」の2018、2019、2010年版、フィレンツェ・ビエンナーレの2011、2015年版、2018年から2020年にかけての「ART TOUR INTERNATIONAL MAGAZINES」のうちの数冊に収録されている。作品では、人と自然の姿を平面と立体で展開している。自然と、特に彫刻の中でより様々な価値を見出す彫り方と空間認識を示すオーガニックフォームとの調和の取れた解釈に重点を当てている。ペン、インク、水彩絵具、モノプリント、彫刻用の木と石、青銅の模型用ワックス、溶接鋼板など実に様々なツールを使用する。

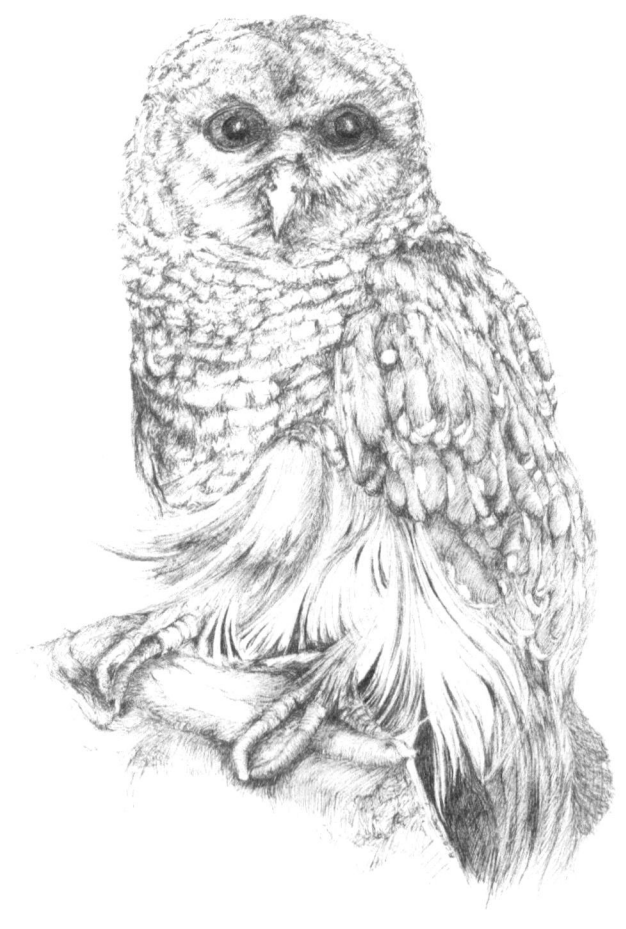

技術 | 図 - 彫刻
価格帯 | USD 1000 - USD 4750
販売レポート | USD 2500 [2018年] - USD 4000 [2019年]
有効な年数 | 50年

Barred Owl
Ink on Cotton Rag, h58cm x w42cm, Unframed
USD 750

bettycollier.com

Australian award winning painter, sculptor and illustrator, Betty has exhibited in Australia, Italy and the USA. Her artwork is at Federation University, Victoria, Australia and in private collections. Betty is published in several WORLD WIDE ART BOOKS Curated by Despina Tunberg, Australian Art Edit, editions 2018, 2019 2020. Florence Biennale Editions 2011 & 2015, and several ART TOUR INTERNATIONAL MAGAZINES 2018 – 2020. Betty`s art evolves around nature and the human figure in 2 & 3 Dimensions. There is an emphasis on harmonious interpretations of nature and organic forms showing undercutting and spatial awareness which leads to greater variations in values, especially in sculpture. Media includes pen and ink, watercolour, mono – prints, carving wood and stone, modelling wax for bronze, welding sheet steel.

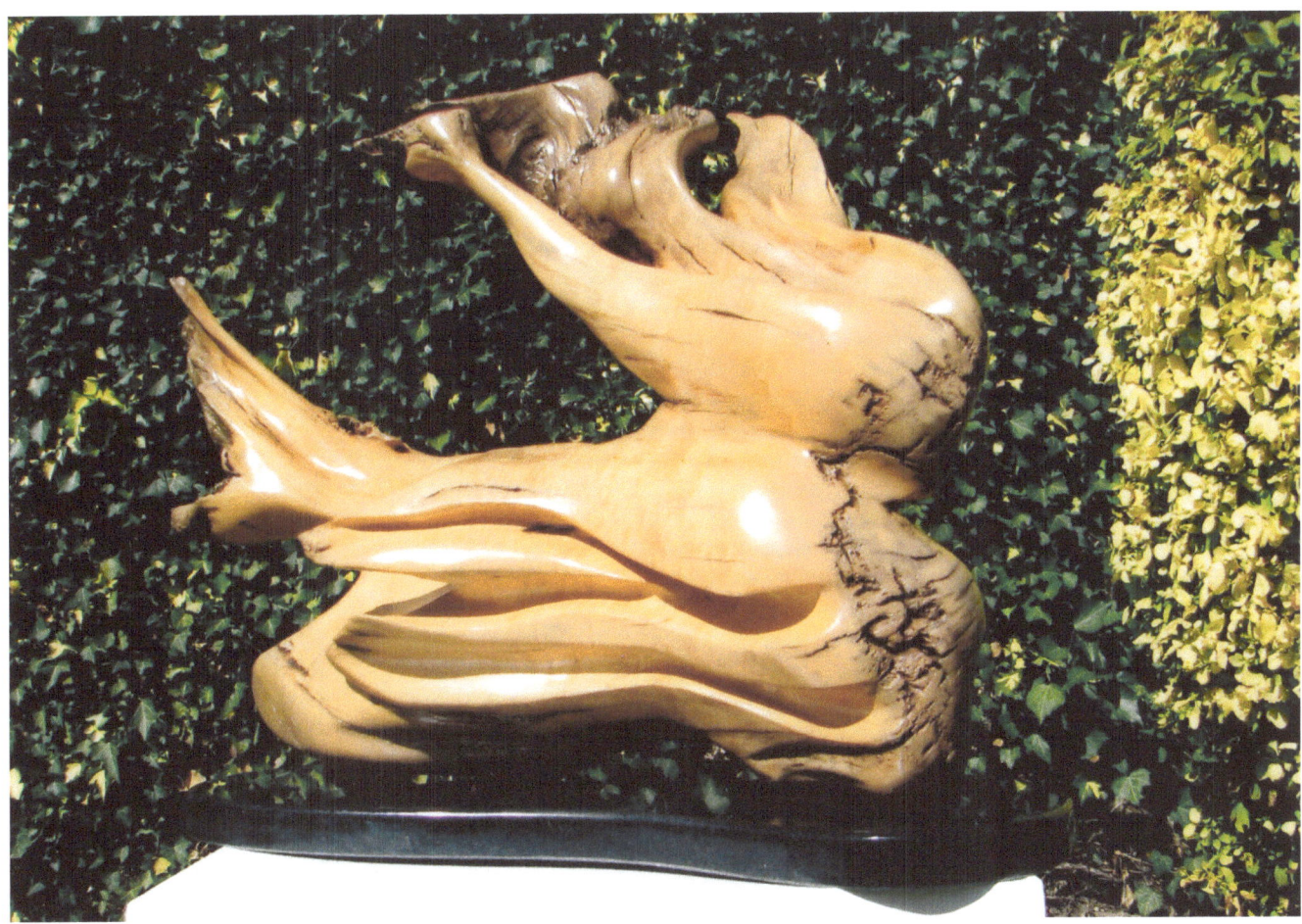

Technique | Illustration - Sculpture
Price Range | USD 1000 - USD 4750
Sales Report | USD 2500 (2018) - USD 4000 (2019)
Active Years | 50 years

Transitional
Huon Pine on Granite, h55cm w71cm d45cm
USD 3500

Nora Komoroczki (MANO)
ハンガリー | Hungary

卒業後、ハンガリーブダペストでジャーナリストとしてのキャリアをスタートさせ、その後マレーヴ・ハンガリー航空の機内誌の編集長となる。仕事を通じて世界の様々な地域を訪れ、美しい場所や興味深い人々に出会い、大いに刺激を受ける。その後、ハンガリーとスウェーデンでいくつかの絵画コースを受講しながら絵を描き始める。主に風景画の油絵を制作するが、人物画も好む。スウェーデン、イスラエル、ハンガリーで個展を開催。オーストリア、ベルギー、ルーマニア、ハンガリーでのグループ展に出展。作品はオーストラリア、アメリカ、イギリス、スウェーデン、ハンガリーなどのコレクターによって購入されている。

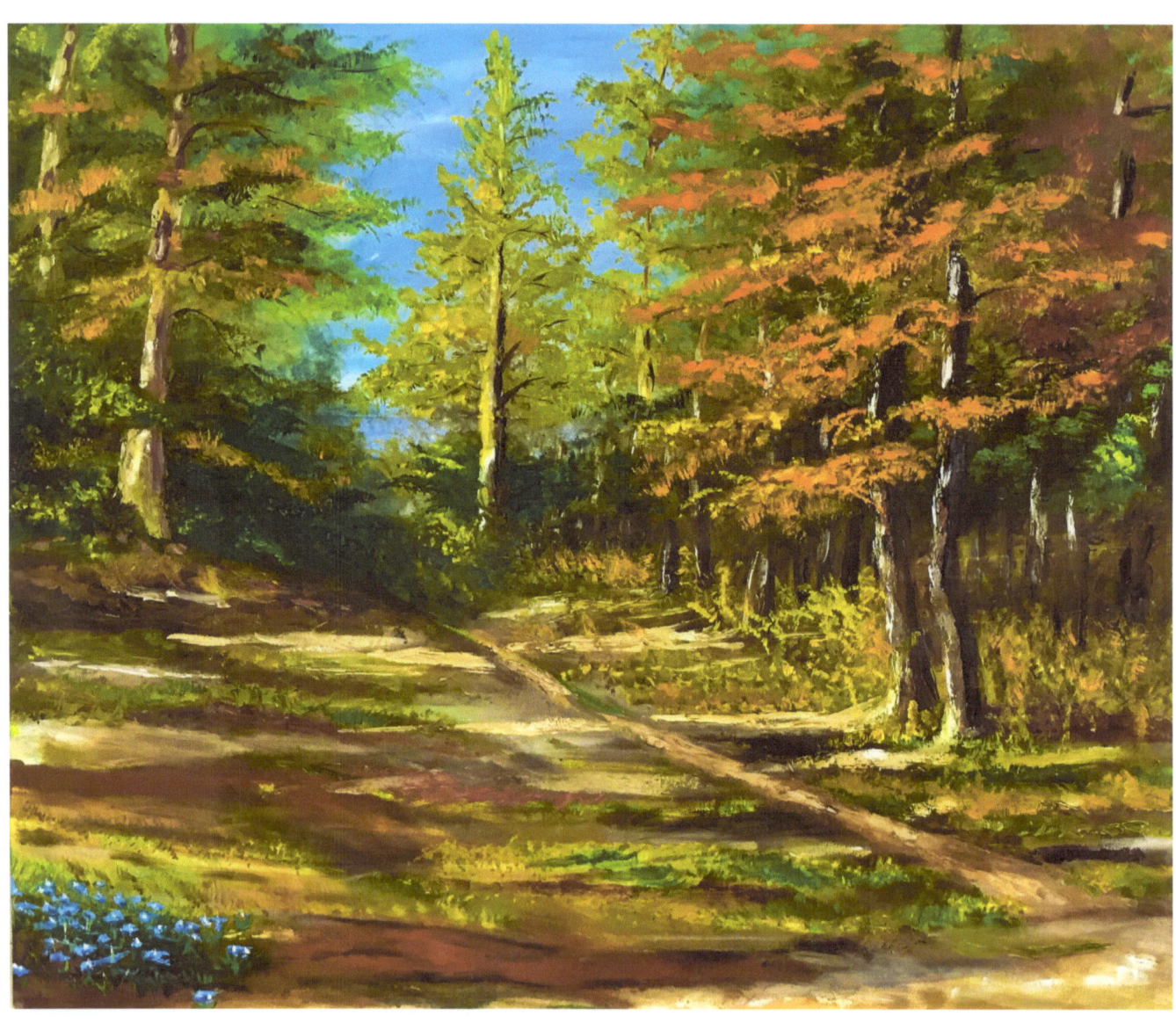

技術 | 絵画
価格帯 | USD 3000 - USD 11000
販売レポート | USD n/a [2018年] - USD n/a [2019年]
有効な年数 | 35年

Autumn Forest
Oil on canvas, 110 cm x 90 cm, 2014.
USD 11000

artnow0.webnode.com

After graduating from the University I started working as a journalist in Budapest. Later on becoming Editor in Chief of the inflight magazine of the Hungarian Airlines I could travel quite extensively, thus managed to visit wonderful places around the world and meet interesting people that inspired me to a great extent.I began painting, attended some painting courses both in Hungary and Sweden. I paint in oil on canvas, mainly landscapes, but I love to capture eyes and faces, as well. I had solo exhibitions in Sweden, Israel and Hungary and participated in group shows in Austria, Belgium, Romania and Hungary. My paintings were purchased by collectors in Australia, USA, UK, Sweden and Hungary.

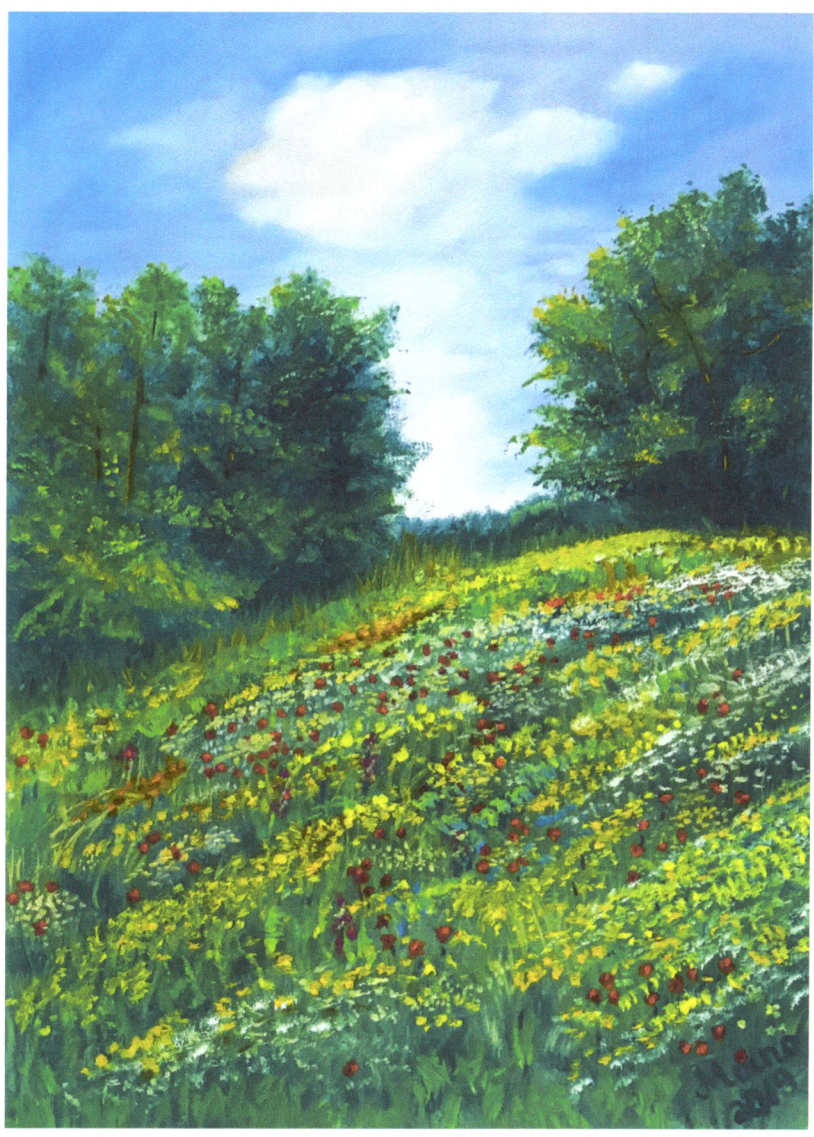

Technique | Painting
Price Range | USD 3000 - USD 11000
Sales Report | USD n/a (2018) - USD n/a (2019)
Active Years | 35 years

Floral scope
Oil on canvas, 80 cm x 60 cm, 2019.
USD 9600

Kaoru Kobayashi
日本 | Japan

芸術系の大学を卒業。作品を海外での個展開催や公的展覧会に出品。作品は植物、水、石、流れる雲などあらゆる自然からのインスピレーションを受けて制作する。日本の伝統的な模様や思想からも触発されている。アクリル絵具、墨汁、金粉、銀粉などを用いて優美な表現で紙に描く。

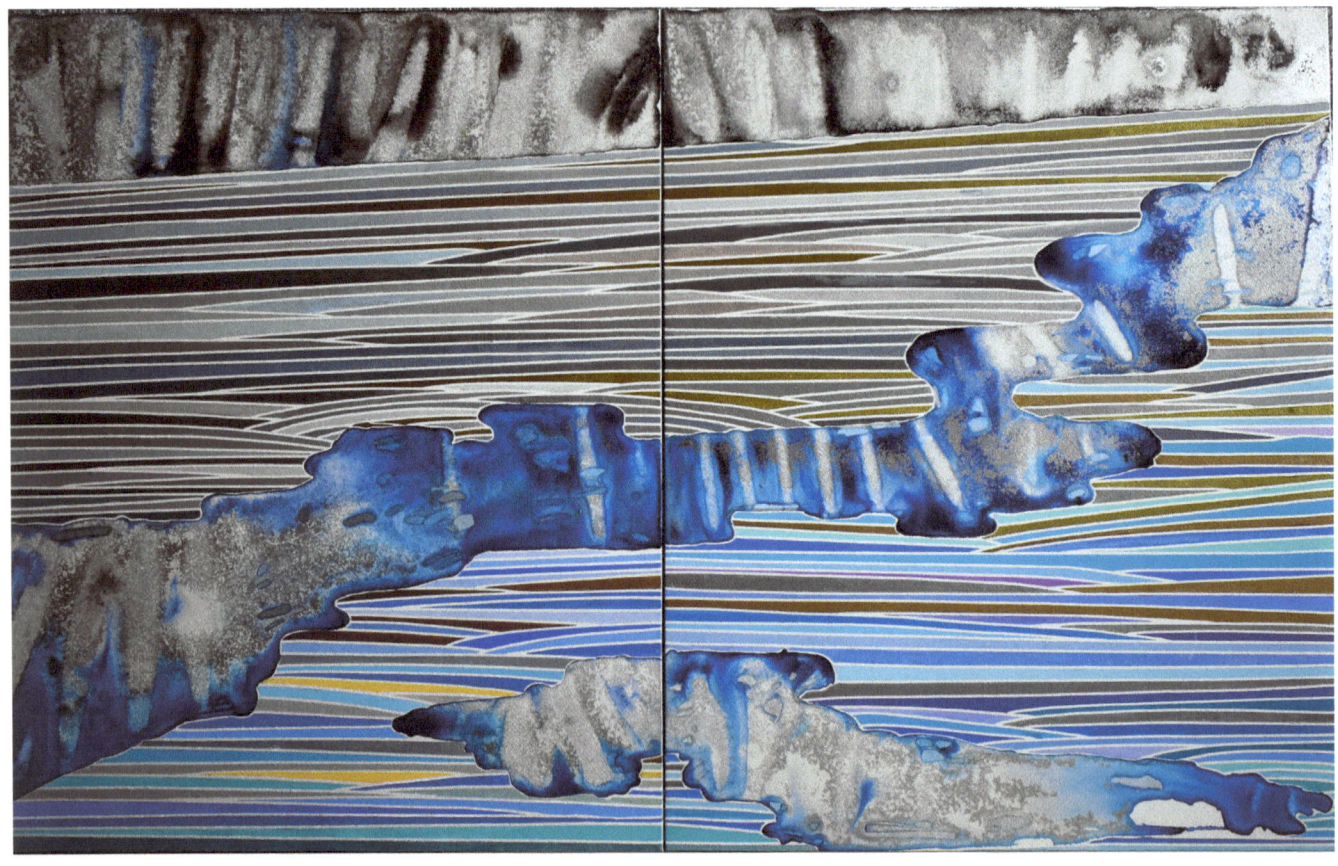

技術 | 絵画
価格帯 | USD 1000 - USD 5000
販売レポート | USD 10000 [2018年] - USD 25000 [2019年]
有効な年数 | 10年

From The Water
50x130 cm, 2020
USD 3000

aorukobayashi.wixsite.com/portfolio

Graduated from Art University. My work has been presented in solo and public exhibitions internationally. My work is inspired by plants, water, stones and claud flow...from all nature. And I get inspired by traditional Japanese patterns and motives. I use acrylic and Japanese ink, gold and silver powder and draw on paper for delicate expression.

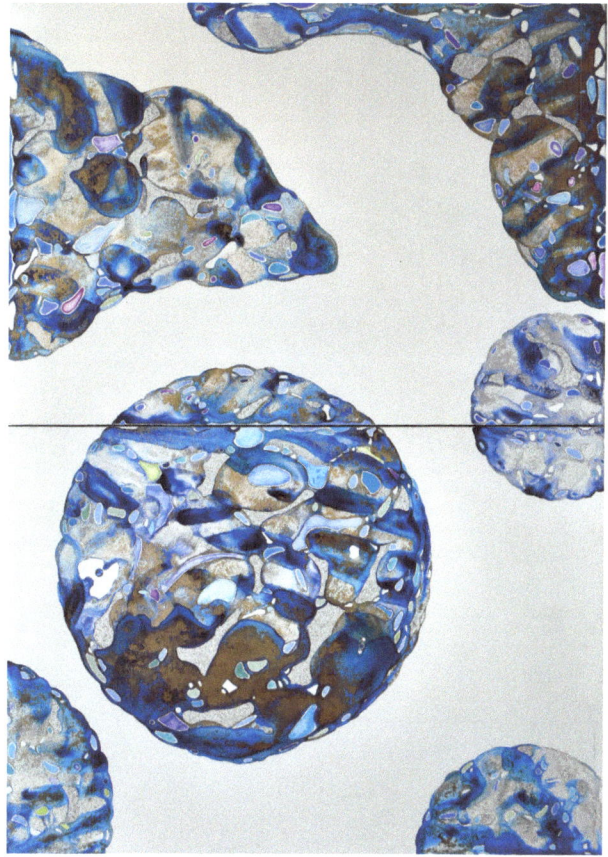

Technique | Painting
Price Range | USD 1000 - USD 5000
Sales Report | USD 10000 (2018) - USD 25000 (2019)
Active Years | 10 years

Far Away
100x73 cm, 2019
USD 3000

Gloria Keh
シンガポール | Singapore

Gloria Keh氏は幼少期から絵画を始め、油絵画家だった父、故Martin Fu氏は彼女の最初の師匠である。オーストラリアメルボルンで曼荼羅アートと象徴主義を学び、その後シンガポールのLa Salle art collegeにてアートセラピーの短期コースを受講。2008年に、非営利チャリティー奉仕プログラム「Circles of Love」を設立。自身のアートを人道支援に役立てている。活動拠点のシンガポールに加え、世界各地で70以上の展覧会に参加。最近の活動では、「Art Basel Week Red Dot Miami」で展示即売をおこなった。これまでに12の美術関連の賞を受賞している。

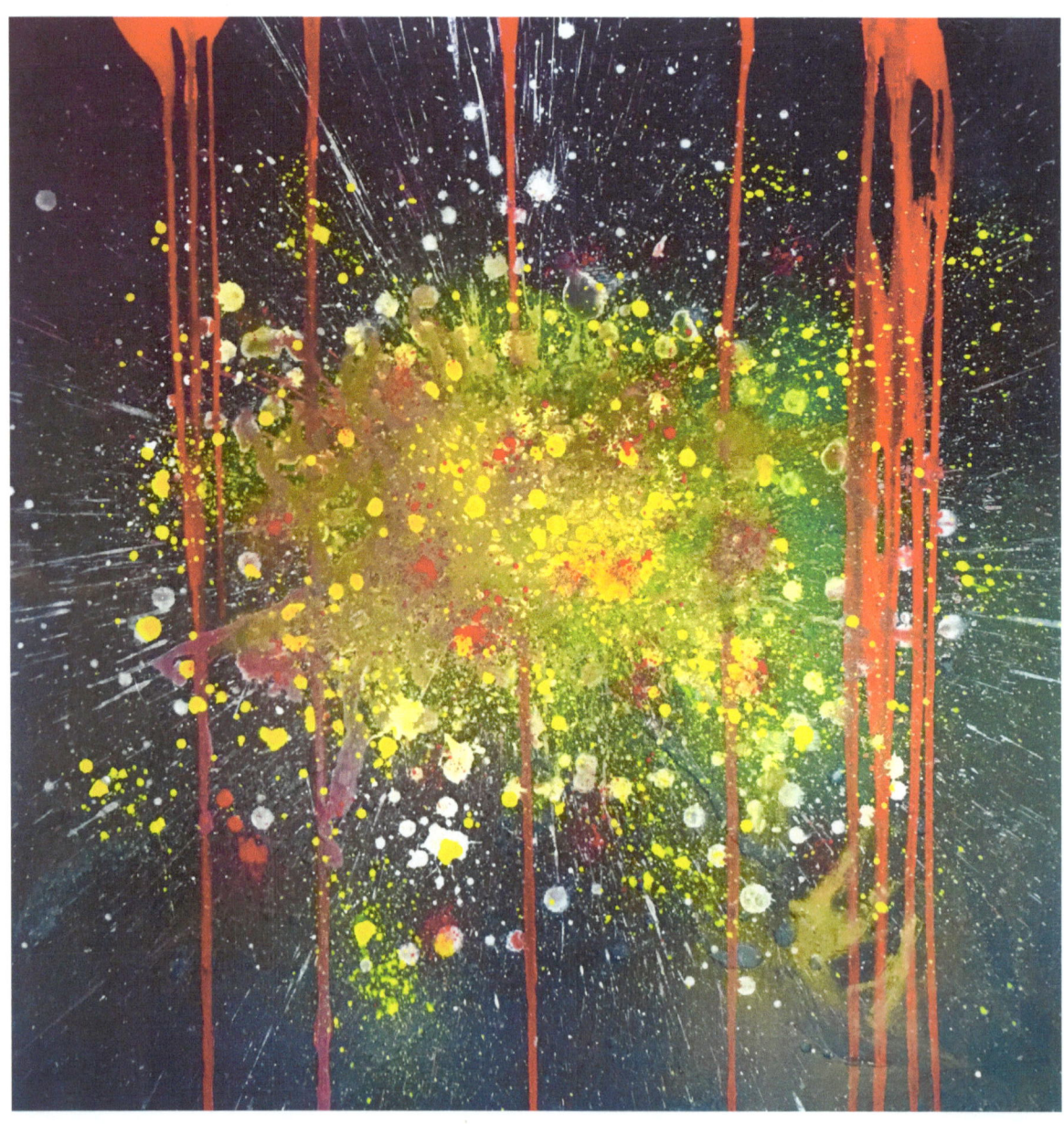

技術 | 絵画
価格帯 | USD 500 - USD 4000
販売レポート | USD n/a [2018年] - USD n/a [2019年]
有効な年数 | 11年

The Birth of A Star
Acrylic on canvas, 81 cm x 81cm, 2016
Price Upon Request

gloriakeh.com

Gloria Keh began painting since childhood, her late father the oil painter, Martin Fu was her first art teacher. She studied mandala art and symbolism in Melbourne, Australia and undertook a short course in art therapy at La Salle art college in Singapore. In 2008, Gloria founded Circles of Love, a non profit charity outreach programme using her art in the service to humanity. She has participated in over 70 art exhibitions, both in Singapore, where she lives, as well as internationally. Most recently she participated and sold at Art Basel Week Red Dot Miami. Gloria has won 12 international art awards.

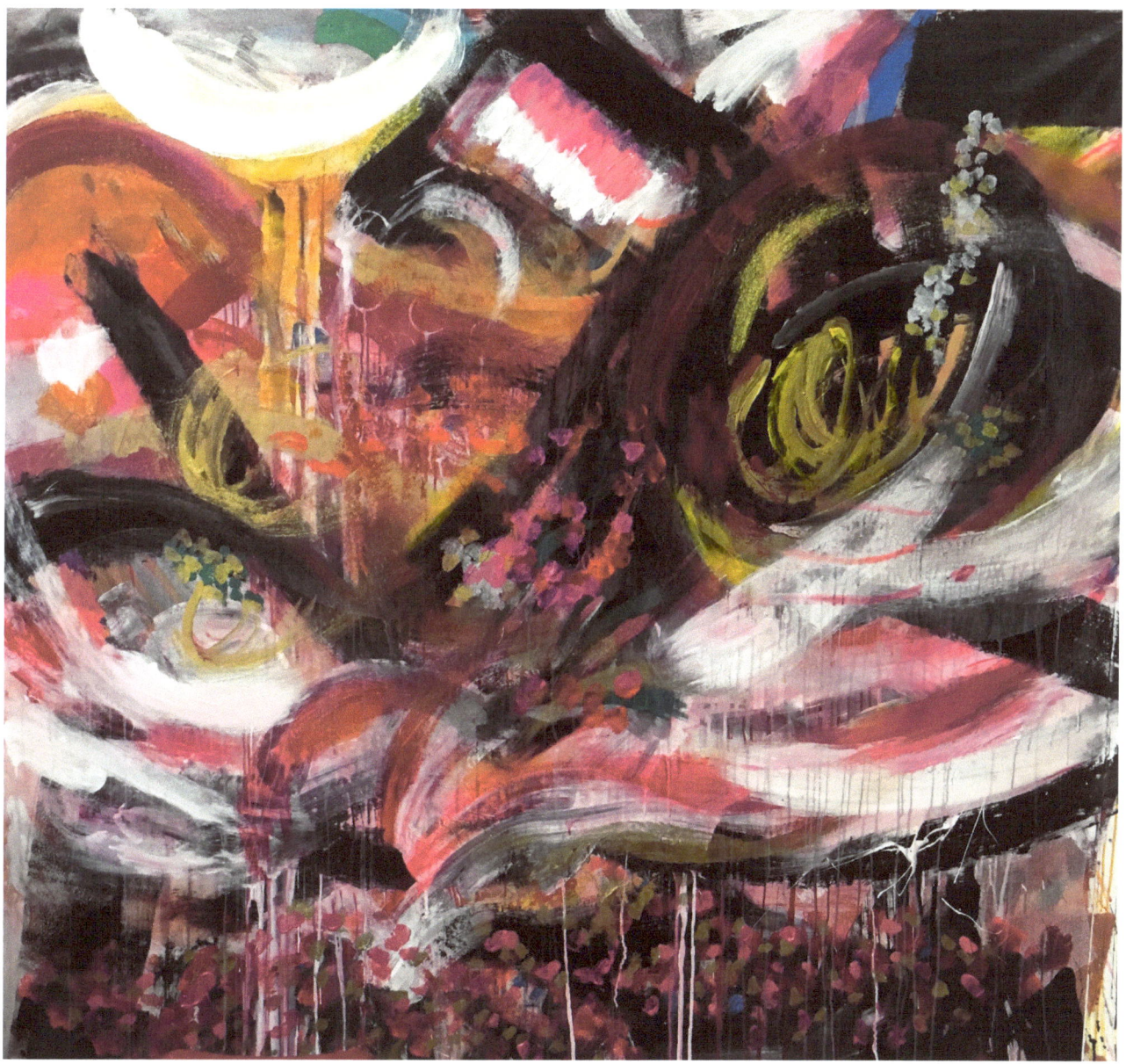

Technique | Painting
Price Range | USD 500 - USD 4000
Sales Report | USD n/a (2018) - USD n/a (2019)
Active Years | 11 years

Death of A Dragon (Yet The Dragon Never Dies)
Acrylic on canvas, 160 cm x 167 cm, 2018
Price Upon Request

Chace Gray
アメリカ | United States

写真家のChace Gray氏は西洋諸国の風景への畏怖を表現している。コンポラ写真の基準には従わず、作品に、より真実味と信憑性を持たせるためにフィルターをつけずに撮影している。画像のデジタル加工処理はおこなわず、自然の声に耳を傾けた作品を制作している。

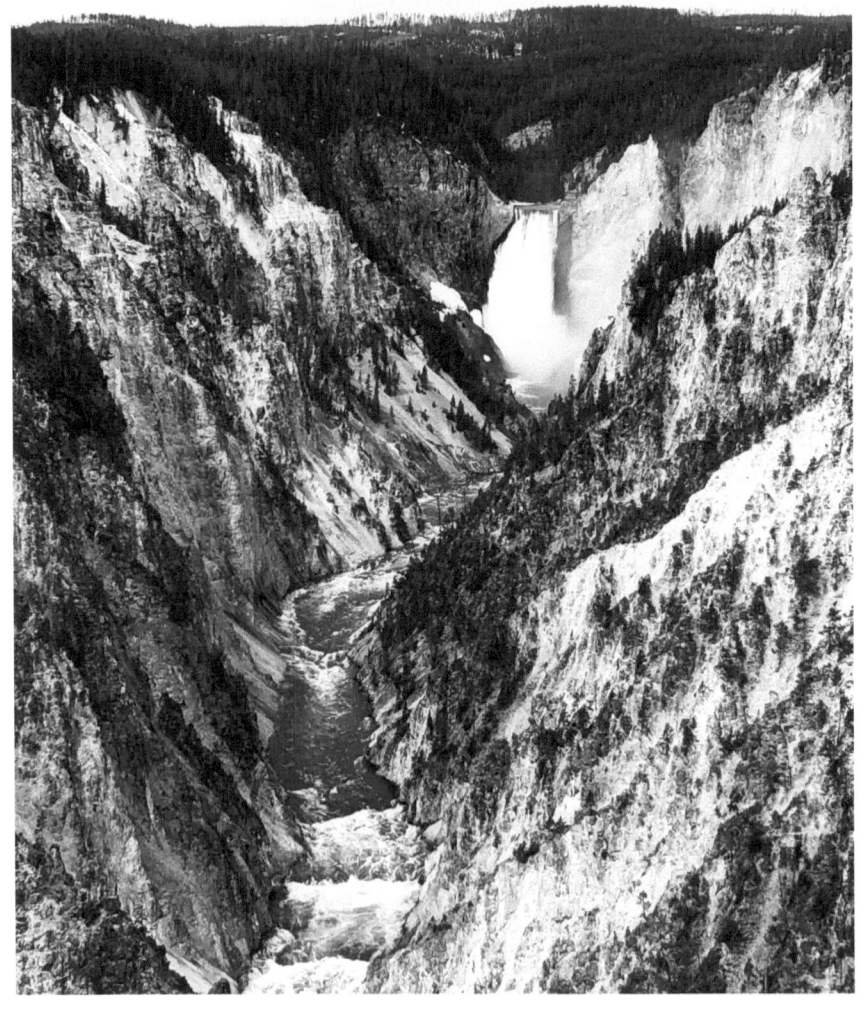

技術 | 写真
価格帯 | USD 750 - USD 1200
販売レポート | USD n/a [2018年] - USD n/a [2019年]
有効な年数 | 15年

Mother Earth
Price Upon Request

chacegray.com

Photographer Chace Gray captures the awe of the vistas of The West. Rejecting the norms of contemporary photography, Gray chooses an unfiltered approach that adds truth and authenticity to the work. By not digitally altering her photographs, the artist lets her surroundings speak for themselves.

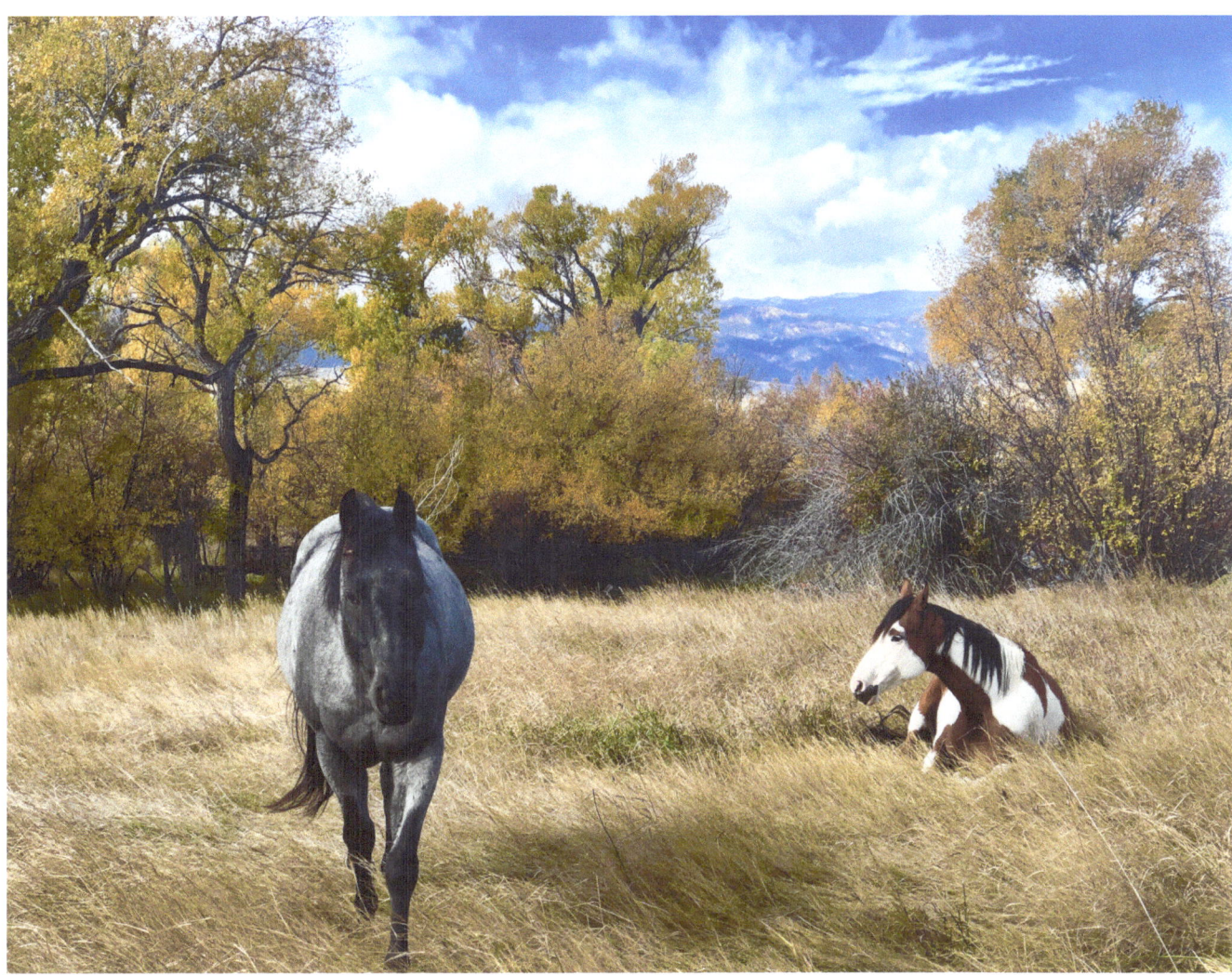

Technique | Photography
Price Range | USD 750 - USD 1200
Sales Report | USD n/a (2018) - USD n/a (2019)
Active Years | 15 years

Chief Horse
Price Upon Request

Jessica Alazraki
アメリカ | United States

メキシコシティで生まれ育つ。アナワク・メキシコ大学　コミュニケーション学学士取得パーソンズ美術大学（ニューヨーク市）　グラフィックデザインディプロマ取得2013年ニューヨーク芸術アカデミー　描絵、絵画コース修了2015-2016年　ニューヨーク芸術アカデミー　具象画修士課程修了マンハッタン、ブルックリン、ロングアイランド、ポキプシー、カリフォルニア、フィラデルフィア、ニューヨークのサザビーズオークションハウスなど、アメリカの40以上のギャラリーのグループ展に出展。様々な美術展に参加している。　2015-2016年　ニューヨーク芸術アカデミー　具象画修士課程修了マンハッタン、ブルックリン、ロングアイランド、ポキプシー、カリフォルニア、フィラデルフィア、ニューヨークのサザビーズオークションハウスなど、アメリカの40以上のギャラリーのグループ展に出展。様々な美術展に参加している。

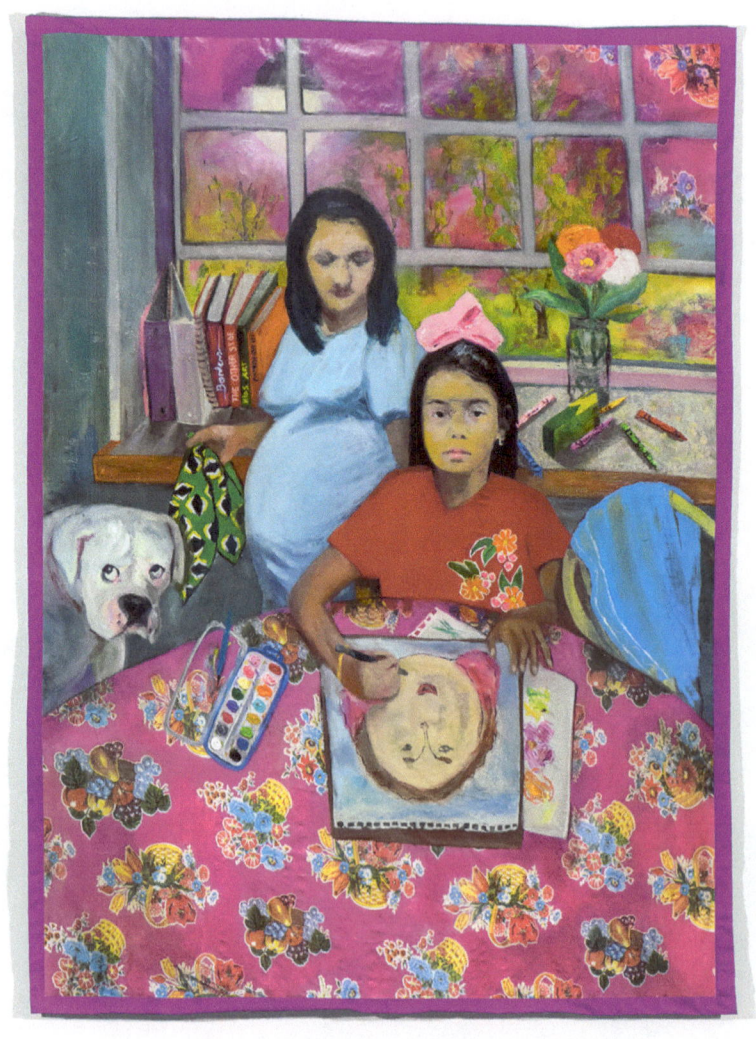

技術　|　絵画
価格帯　|　USD 3000
販売レポート　|　USD 10000 [2018年] - USD 12000 [2019年]
有効な年数　|　5年

Creating Figures

USD 3000

jessicaalazrakiart.com

I was born and raised in Mexico City and earned a bachelor's degree in Communications from Universidad Anáhuac, a Diploma in Graphic Design from Parsons School of Design in New York City, a Certificate in Drawing & Painting from The New York Academy of Art in 2013 and a year studies of the Master's Degree in Figurative Painting at the New York Academy of Art, New York City, 2015-2016. I have exhibited my paintings in the U.S.A. in over 40 group shows at galleries in Manhattan, Brooklyn, Long Island, Poughkeepsie, California, and Philadelphia as well as in Sotheby's Auction House in NY. I have participated in various museum exhibitions.

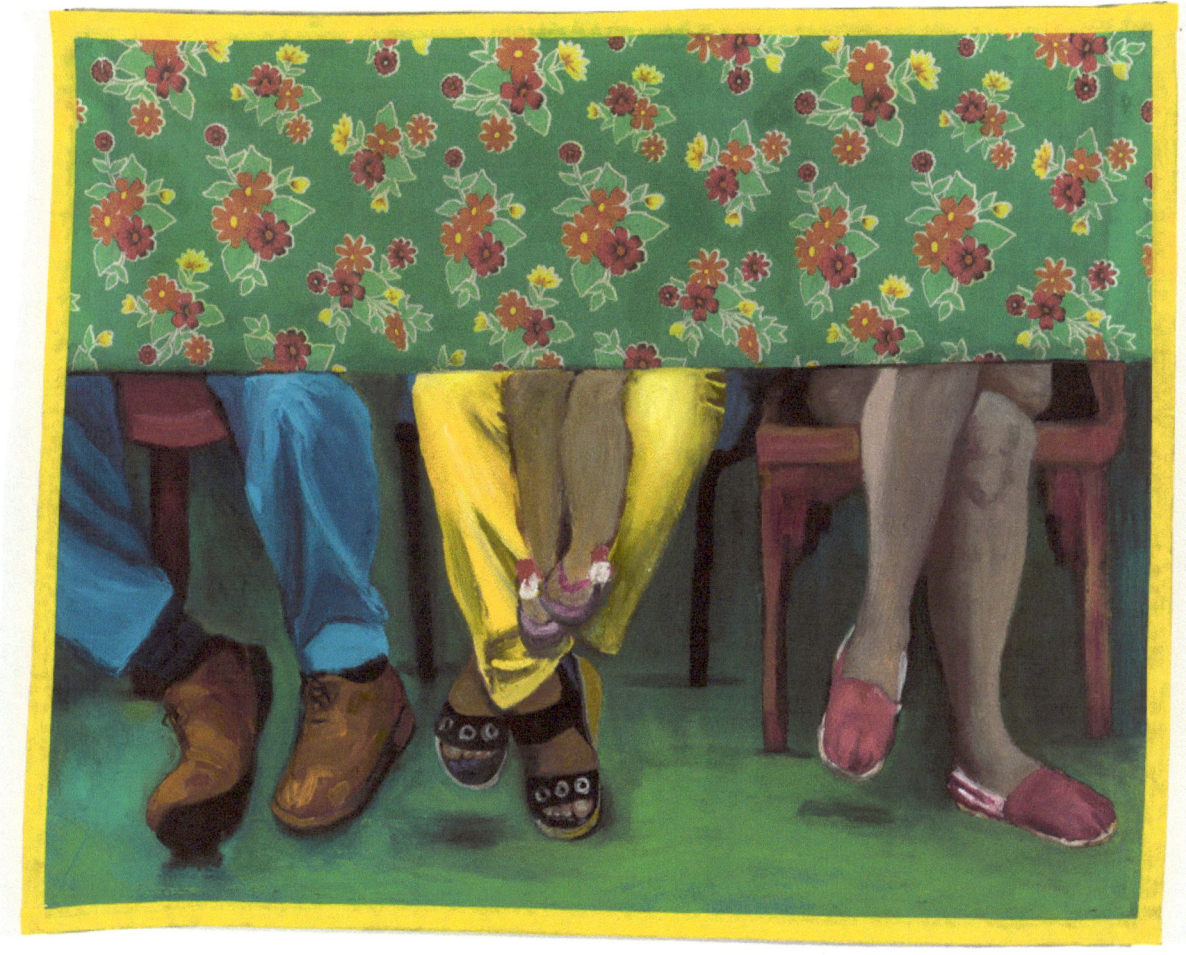

Technique | Painting
Price Range | USD 3000
Sales Report | USD 10000 (2018) - USD 12000 (2019)
Active Years | 5 years

Under the table

USD 3000

Michal Ashkenasi
イスラエル | Israel

キャリアのスタートは遅く、40歳の時に絵画教室に通い始め、1年後、講師にアートを本格的に学ぶよう勧められる。Haifa universityで3年間学んだ後、修士課程に進み7年間在籍した。作品は抽象画で、広々としたキャンバスに、小さく、詩的で明るい色合いで描く。これは壮大な宇宙の中での私たちの小ささを表現するためである。2大学より授与された、名誉教授と名誉文学修士の称号に加えて、計9つの賞を受賞。絵画の個展を30回、写真の個展を7回開催、グループ展には43回出展した。イスラエルを拠点に活動している。

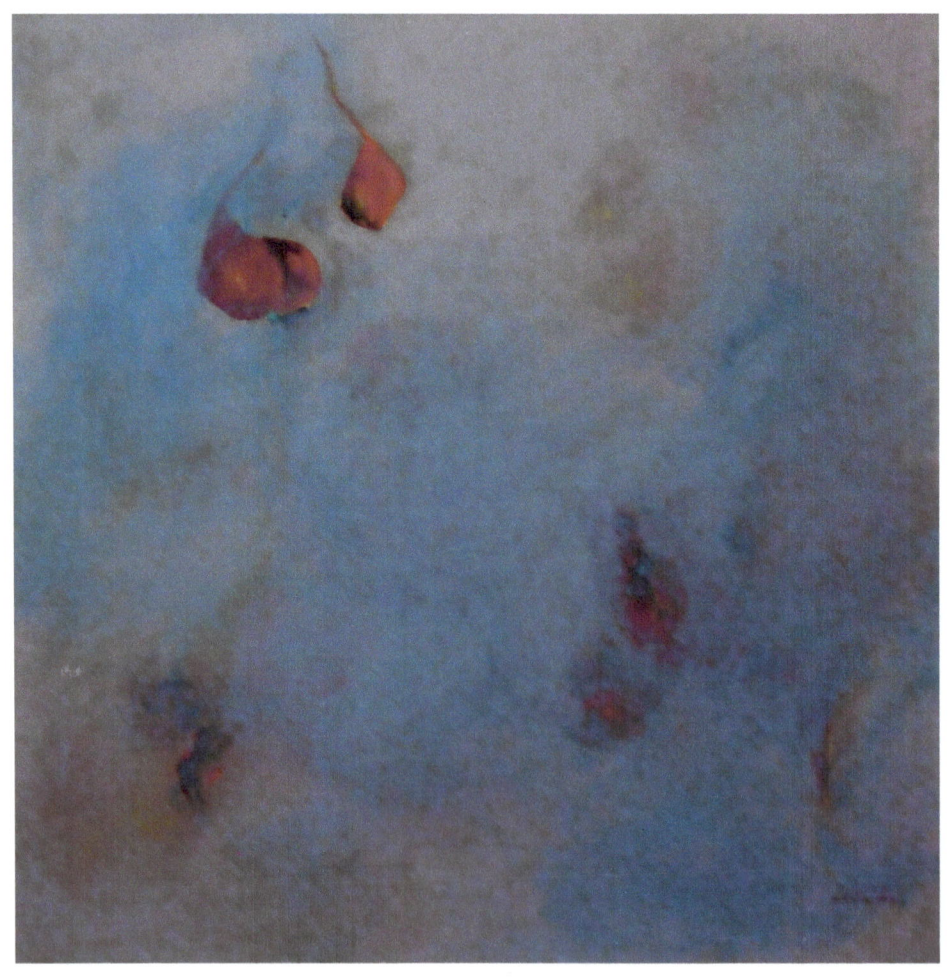

技術 | 絵画
価格帯 | USD 3000 - USD 8000
販売レポート | USD 4000 [2018年] - USD 3000 nis [2019年]
有効な年数 | 32年

Grey Sea
a/c 90/90cm. 2009
USD 4500

michalashkenasiart.com

I came to art late .when I was about 40 I went to a social class in painting and after a year the teacher told me to go and study art. I did 3 years in Haifa university and was accepted to Master Classes where I stayed 7 years . My work is abstract - minimal , lyrical and vivid colors with big expanses on the canvas and some small objects .The mean reason to show our smallness in the big Universe . received 9 awards aside of a Hon.Professor and a Hon. Magister Artium from 2 different Academia.Did 30 solo painting shows and 7 solo photography shows .43 groupshows. I live and work in Israel.

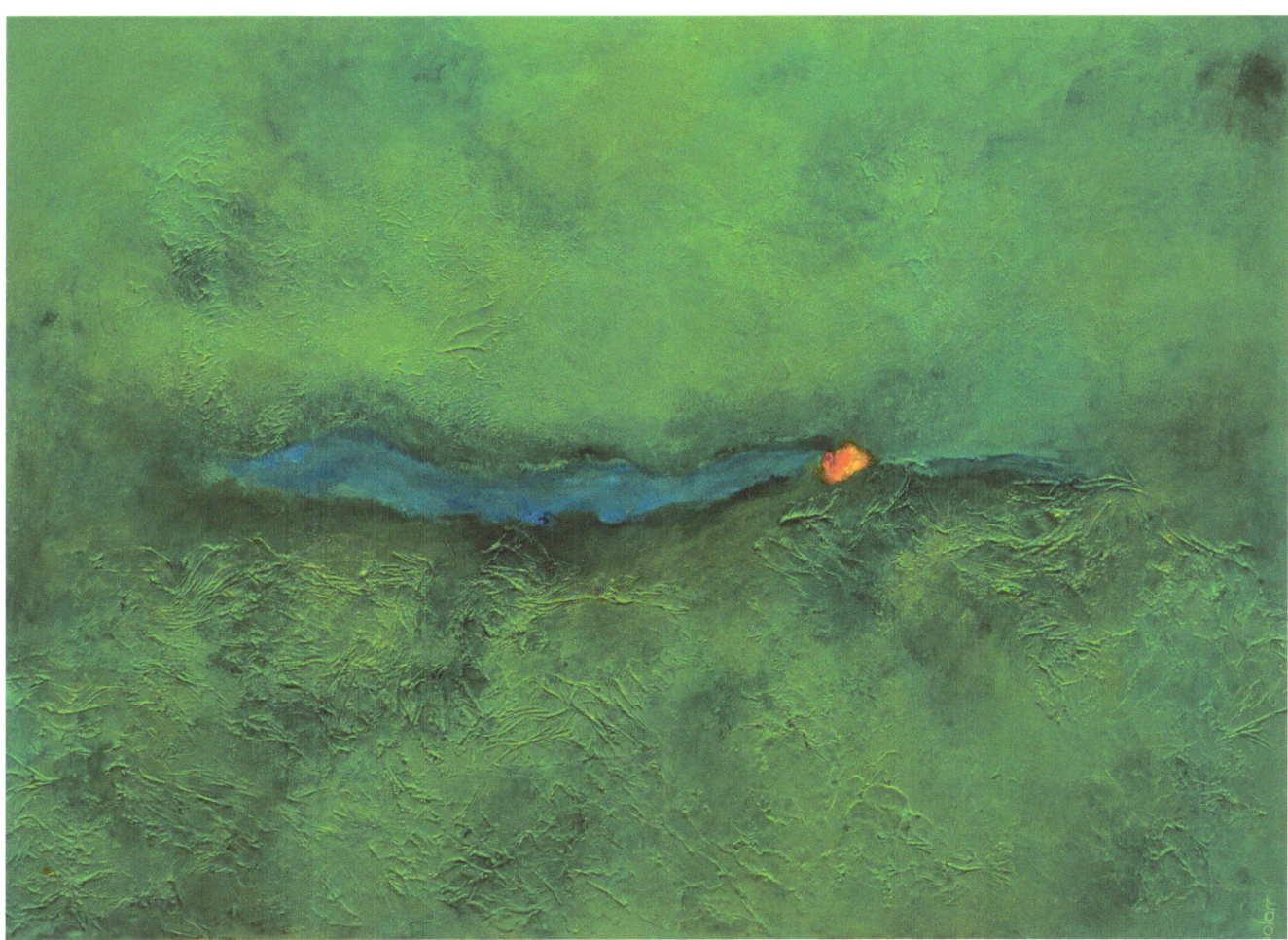

Technique | Painting
Price Range | USD 3000 - USD 8000
Sales Report | USD 4000 (2018) - USD 3000 nis (2019)
Active Years | 32 years

Two Lakes And One Point
a/c, 70/100cm. 2019
USD 5500

Alexander Saner
スイス | Switzerland

Alexander Saner氏は独学でアートを学んだスイス人アーティストである。スイス、バーセルの近くに位置するドイツのブライテンバッハ在住。若い頃は新聞向けの漫画家として活躍した。1993年より、立体彫刻作品を制作。彼の言葉によると、「対象物は題材による。静的作品の本当の動的な部分は、生きている観察者自身である。」独創的な彼による次の発言は、自身の作品にも影響を与えている。「アートとは余分なものを全て排除することである。」、「最も複雑なものは最もシンプルなものである。」、「シンプルさにより明確さを得る」、「もう取り除くものは何もなくなったら、作品は完成である。」

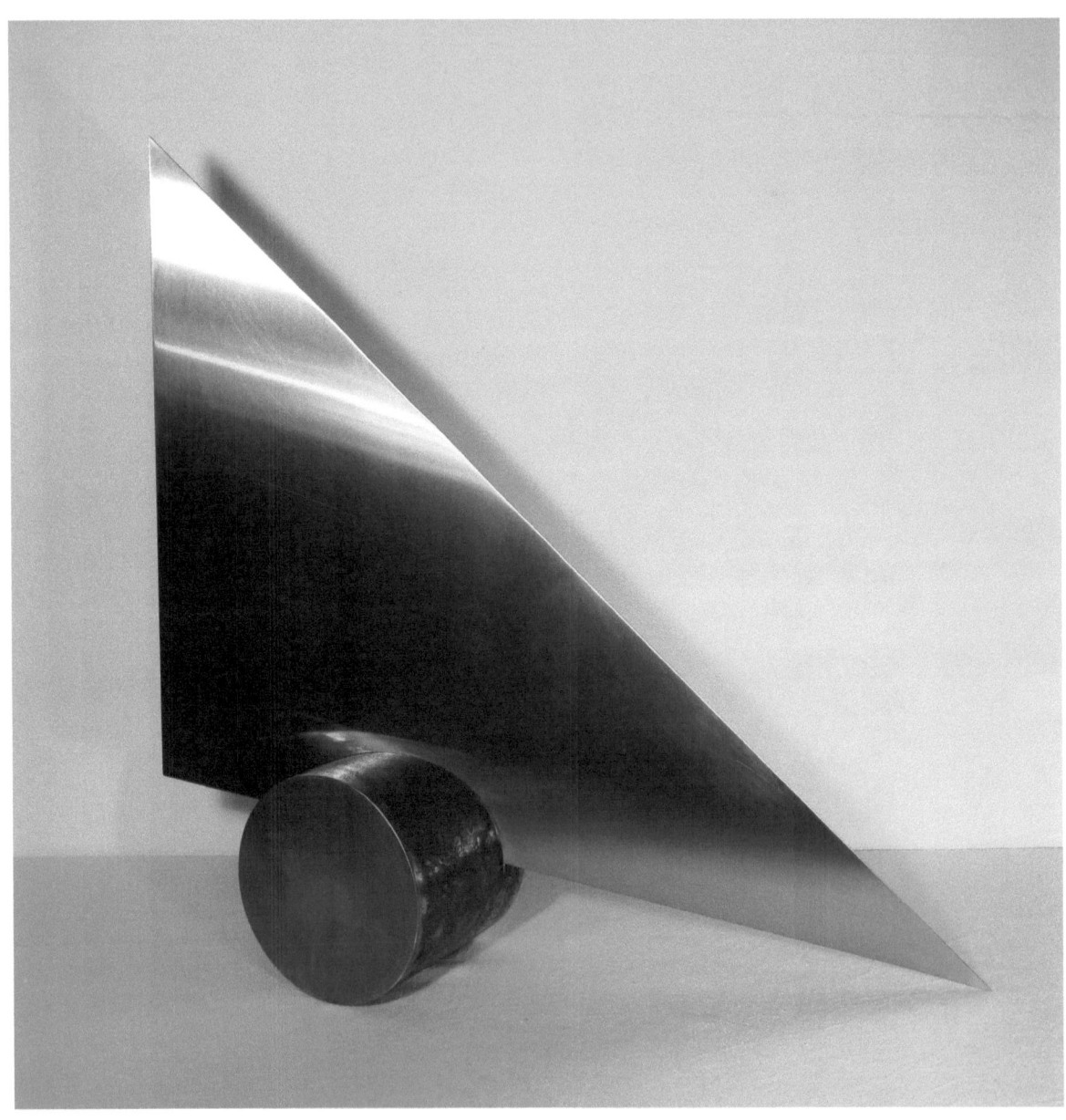

技術 | 彫刻
価格帯 | USD 3000 - USD 50000
販売レポート | USD n/a [2018年] - USD n/a [2019年]
有効な年数 | 27年

Cut 66
Steel, 90x80x33cm
USD 17000

swissart.ch/alexander-saner

Self-taught Swiss Artist, Alexander Saner lives in Breitenbach, near Basel. In his early years, he was actve as a cartoonist for newspapers. Since 1993 he has been creating three-dimensional art sculptures. In his own words:"the object depends on the subject. The real dynamic part of a static artwork is the living observer himself." The following Statements of creative personalities influence his work: -"Art is the Elimination everything superfluous." -"The greatest complexity is the greatest simplicity." -"Clarity through simplicity." -"I nothing can be taken away, the work is completed."

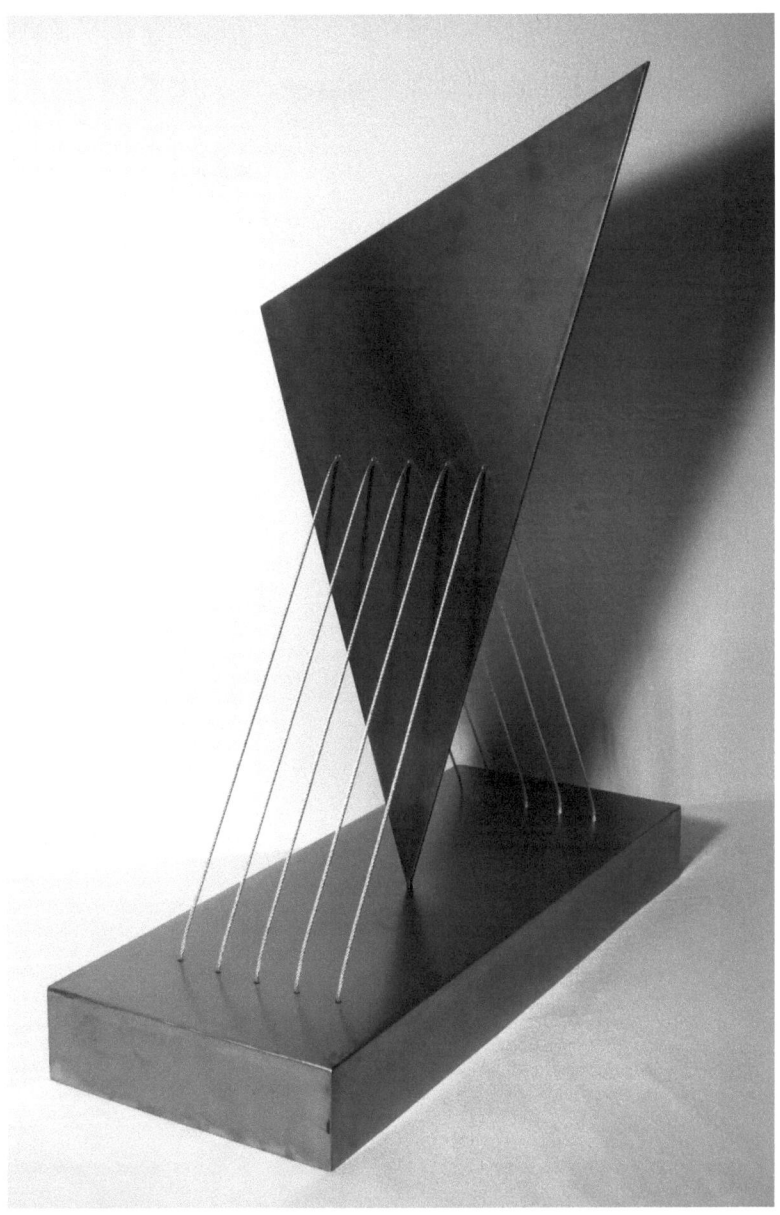

Technique | Sculpture
Price Range | USD 3000 - USD 50000
Sales Report | USD n/a (2018) - USD n/a (2019)
Active Years | 27 years

Tension 9

28x70x80cm

USD 19000

Makotu Nakagawa
日本 | Japan

死というテーマはアーティストにとってしばしば特別な興味の対象となり、Makotu Nakagawa氏にとってもそれは深い関りを持っている。彼の作品では、人生の様々な段階での亡き父の姿と肉体、その死、そして生と死の狭間を描写している。ほぼ10年間にわたり、自身より半世紀前に生まれた父との関係を記録し、父は制作活動の中心であった。年長者が死んでいく定めであるということはわかっていたが、当初は父が死ぬことへの不安から逃れるために始めたことだった。しかし、結果的にそれは目の前の現実を受け入れ、記録するという意味あいに変化していった。彼の作品は過去、現在、未来を映した優美な肖像画である。

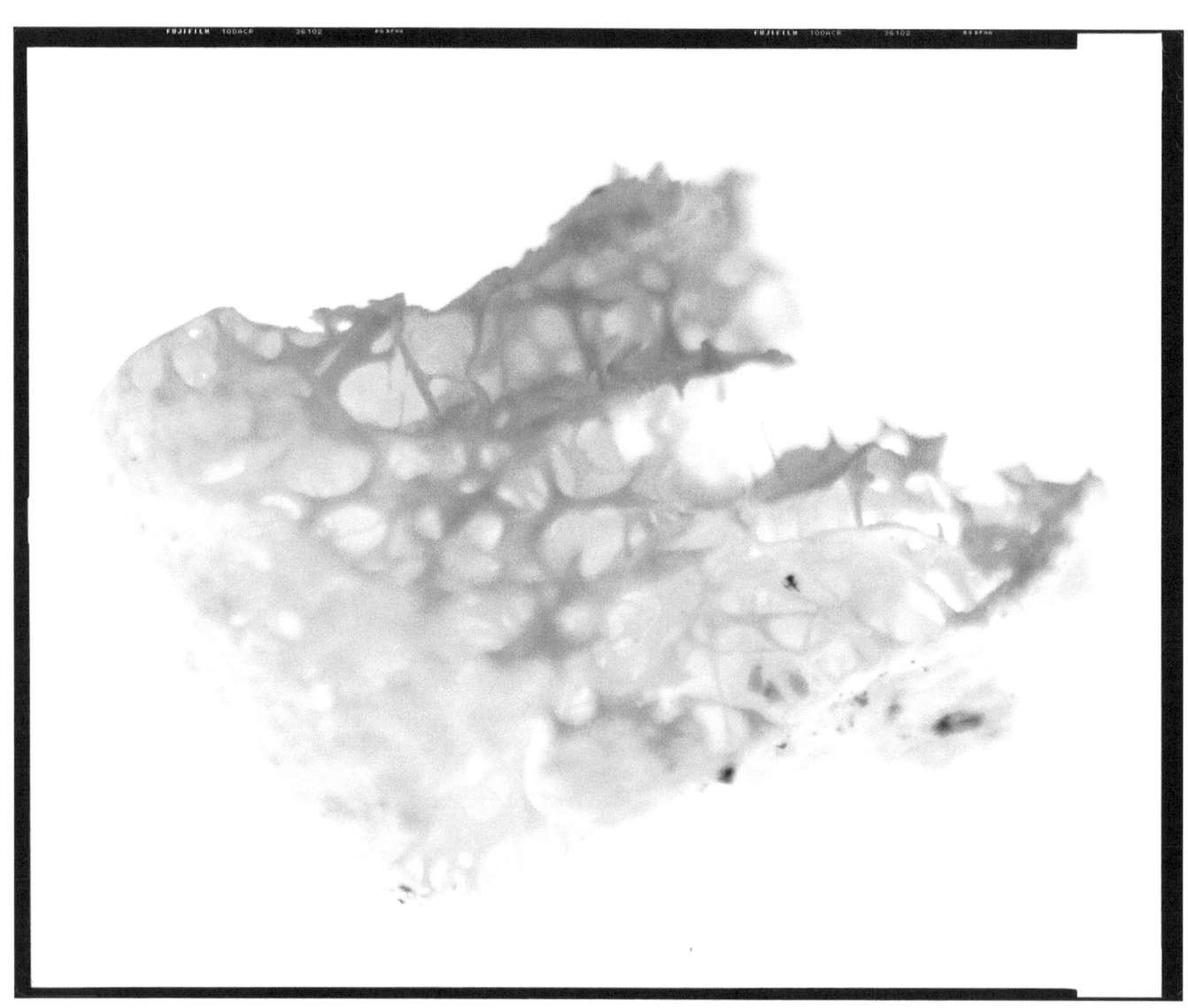

技術 | 写真
価格帯 | USD 500 - USD 3000
販売レポート | USD n/a [2018年] - USD n/a [2019年]
有効な年数 | 1年

Uro no ena - the remains of my father
Silver gelatin print, 19 x 23 x0 inch
USD 2606

makotu.net

The subject of death is often of particular interest and intrigue for artists, and for Makotu Nakagawa it is something he approaches with particular intimacy and clarity; depicting his late father and his body through numerous stages of life, death and the spaces in-between. For almost a decade, Makotu's father has been at the forefront of the work as he documented the relationship with the man born half a century before him. While it began as an escape from the anxiety of death – always being aware of his predecessor's mortality - unexpectedly it turned into a means to accept and record the reality that was in front of him. His work is a delicate portrait of what is, what was and what will be.

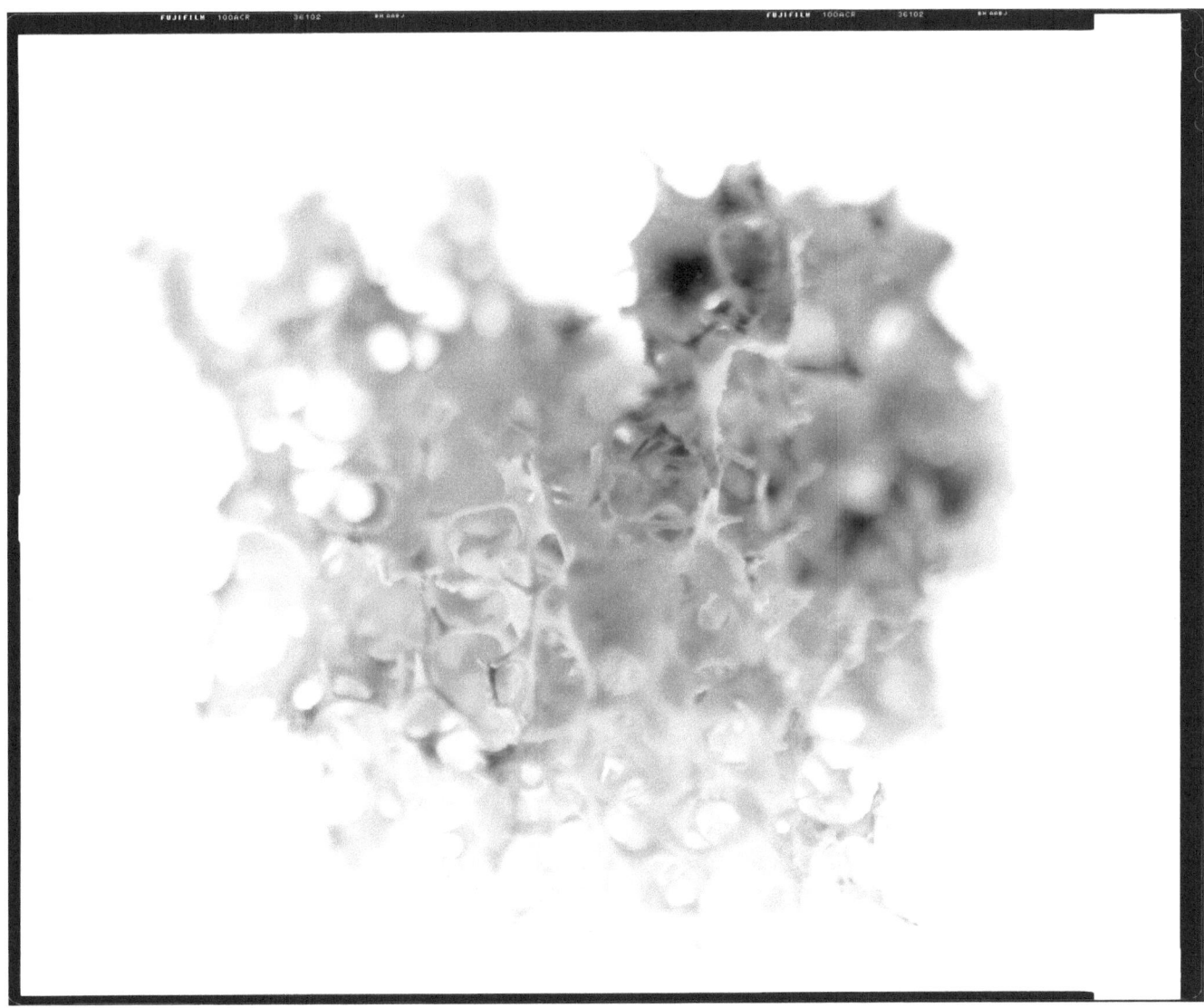

Technique | Photography
Price Range | USD 500 - USD 3000
Sales Report | USD n/a (2018) - USD n/a (2019)
Active Years | 1 year

Uro no ena - the remains of my father
Silver gelatin print, 19 x 23 x0 inch
USD 2606

WoonHyoung Choi

韓国 | South Korea

「Trust me（私を信じて）」というテーマで作品を制作している。アートの分野で自身が取り組んでいる事柄は「私は信じない」である。作品は、真実、嘘、「盗まれたもの」、「影響を受けたもの」などの間でさまよい、ユーモアの要素を加えている。「Trust me（私を信じて）」には様々なシリーズがあり、「Liar Liar（ライアー・ライアー）」は嘘と苦悩についてのテキスト作品、「Vaginoplasty（造膣術）」、「Horny Snowmen（欲情した雪だるま）」はメインテーマを性的にユーモラスに解釈したもの、その他に「Brainless（愚か者）」「Stolen（盗まれたもの）」「Pseudo（にせもの）」等、様々なスタイルと内容でテーマを解釈した作品を制作している。

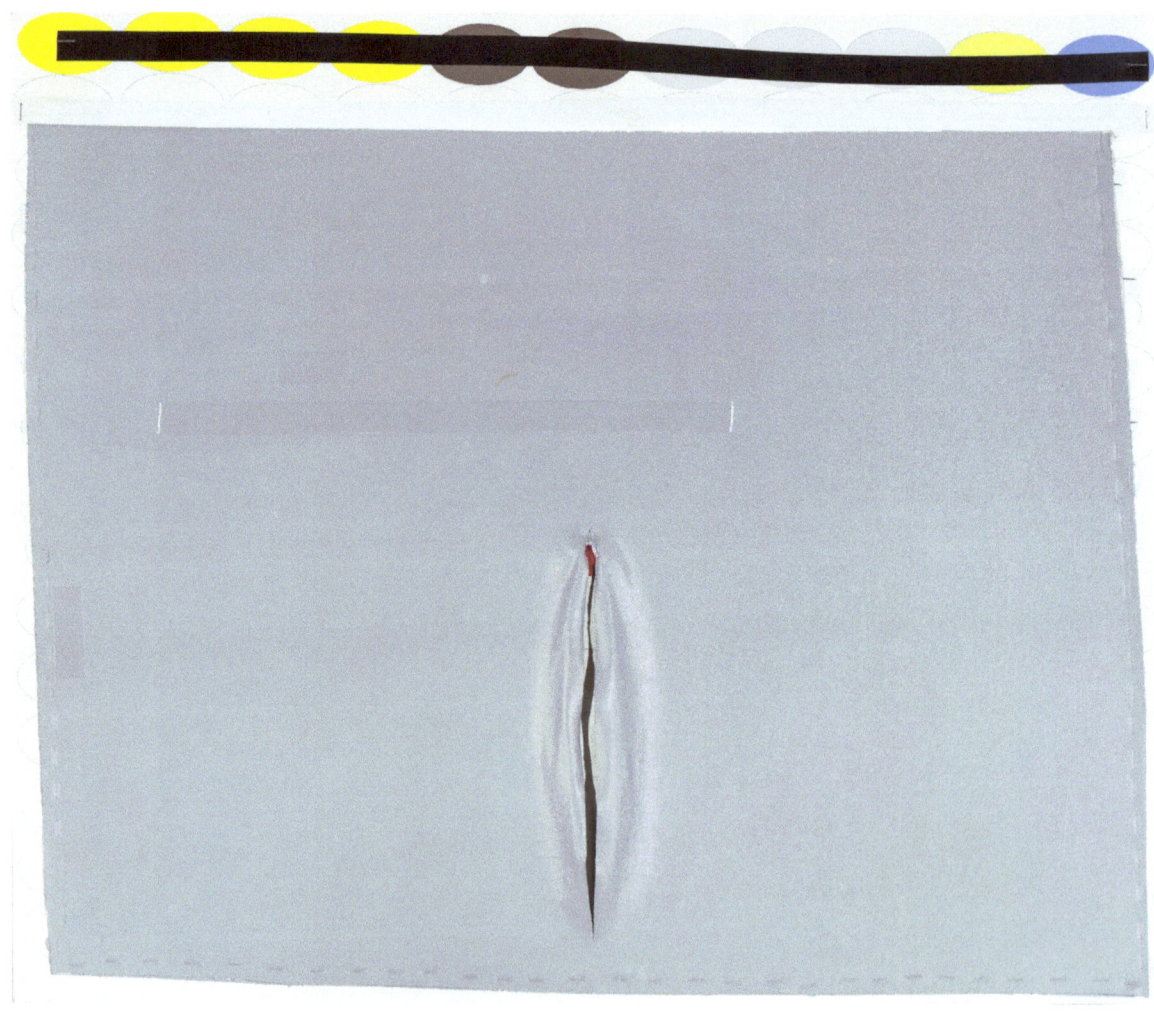

技術 | 絵画
価格帯 | USD 1000 - USD 20000
販売レポート | USD 54000 [2018年] - USD 42000 [2019年]
有効な年数 | 20年

Trust me
Mixed Media on Canvas, 80x100cm, 2019
USD 6000

woonhyoung.com

I create my works under the theme of "Trust me." The main issue I deal with in the field of art is "I don't believe." My works wander around truth, lies, the 'Stolen' and the 'Influenced' producing a sense of humor. There are a number of series under the theme "Trust me": 'Liar Liar' is a series of textual works on lying and cross, 'Vaginoplasty' and 'Horny Snowmen' is a sexually humorous interpretation of the main theme. There are also 'Brainless','Stolen' and 'Pseudo' series with which I work to create my theme in varying styles and contents.

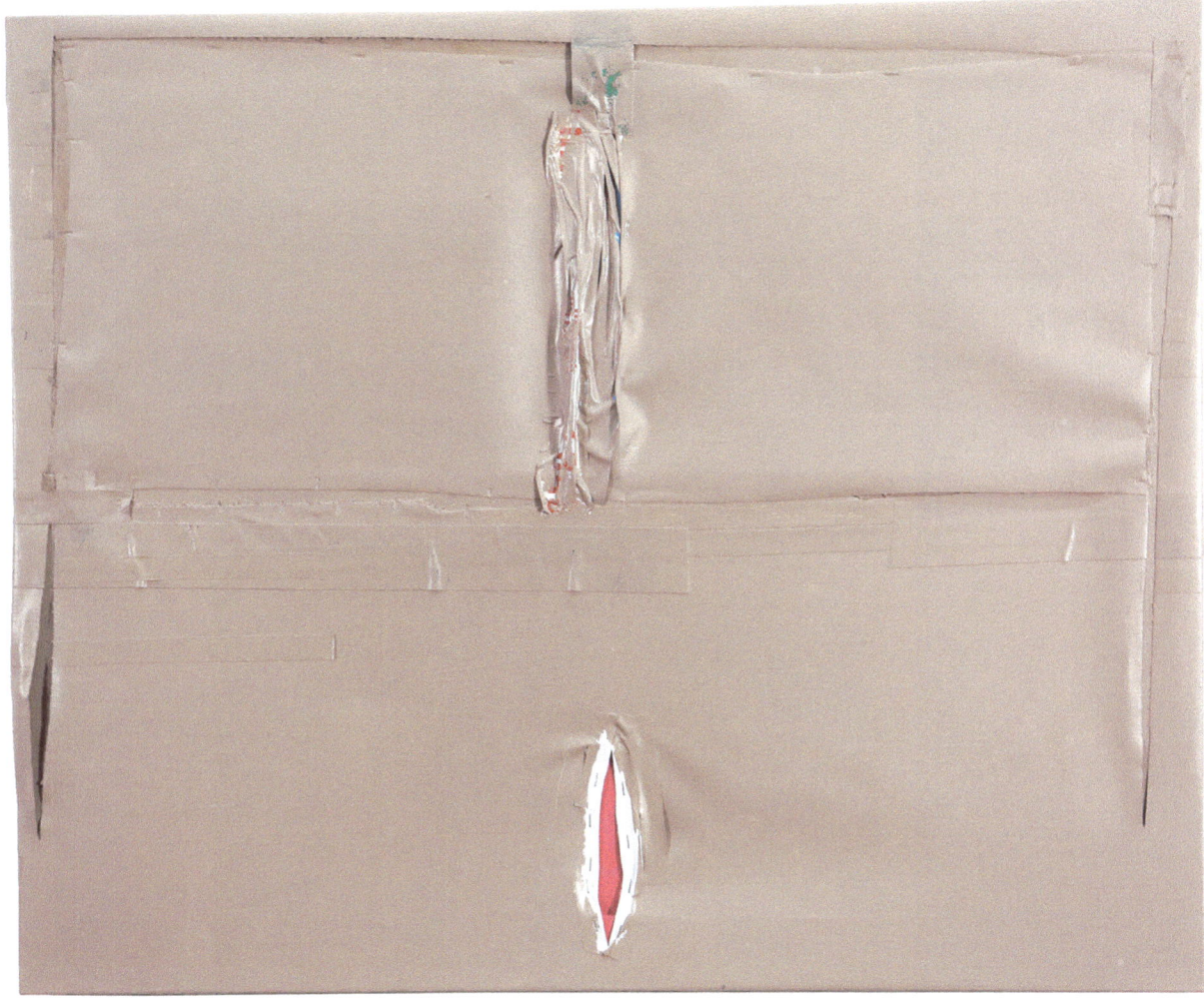

Technique | Painting
Price Range | USD 1000 - USD 20000
Sales Report | USD 54000 (2018) - USD 42000 (2019)
Active Years | 20 years

Trust me-Vaginoplasty
Mixed media on canvas, 72.7 x 90.9cm, 2019
USD 5500

Irena Orlov
アメリカ | United States

世界の美しさに常に刺激を受けており、それを何時間でも追及できる。全てが瞬く間に変わっていく流れが速い世界の中で、全く同じ世界に住み続けることはないと気づく。人生は一瞬のうちに展開していく。感性あふれる瞬間をとらえることが自身の作品の鍵となると考えている。

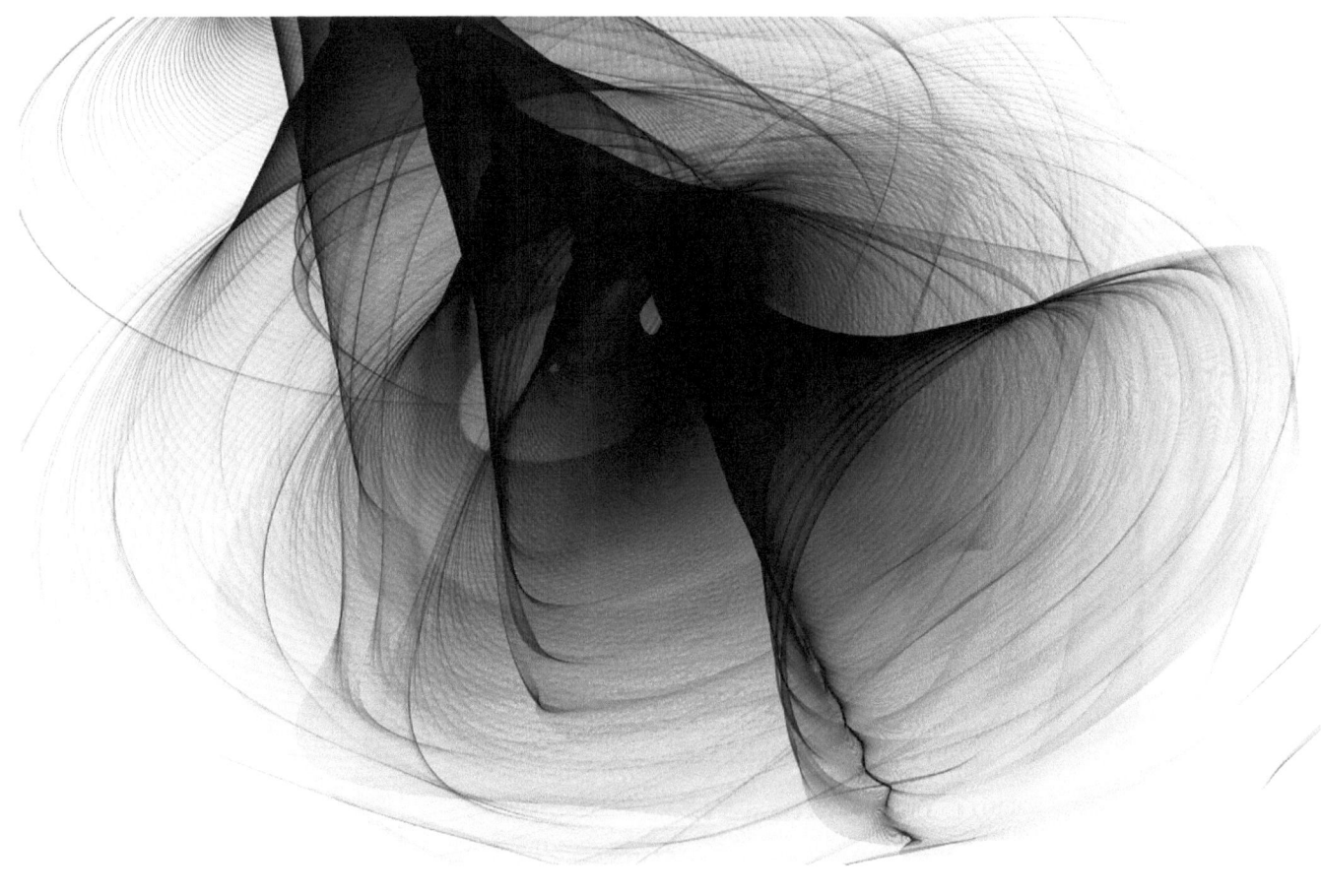

技術 | 絵画 - 混合メディア
価格帯 | USD 3500 - USD 50000
販売レポート | USD 175000 [2018年] - USD 250000 [2019年]
有効な年数 | 12年

Constant Energy
USD 6000

irenaorlov.com

I was and continue to be inspired by the beauty of the world around me and can spent hours to explore it. The rapid world at which is everything changed so fast, I discovered that I will never live in quite the same world. Life unfolds only in moments. Capturing moments that are full of emotion is the key to my art.

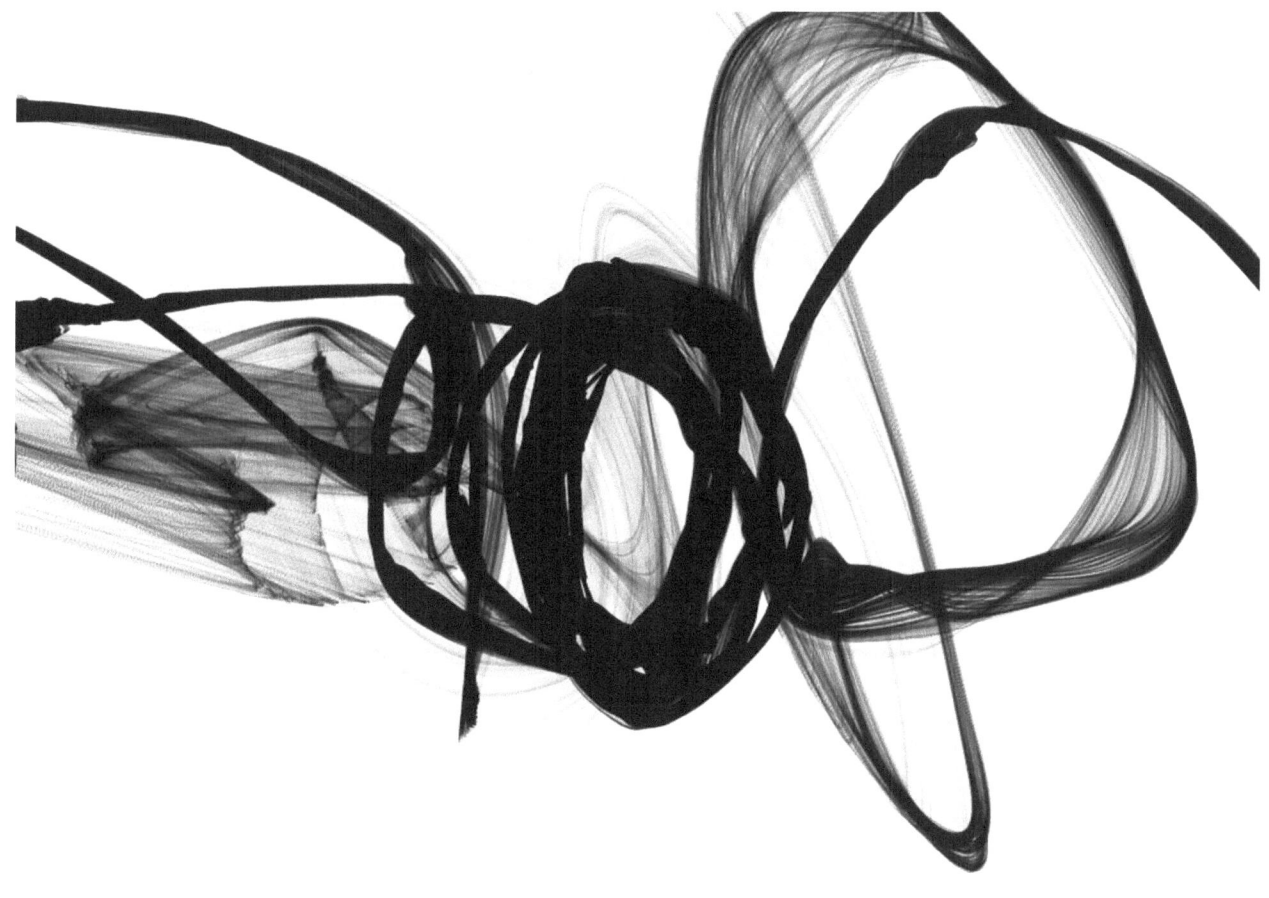

Technique | Painting - Mixed Media
Price Range | USD 3500 - USD 50000
Sales Report | USD 175000 (2018) - USD 250000 (2019)
Active Years | 12 years

The Energy

USD 8400

Antwan Thompson
アメリカ | United States

アメリカ合衆国メリーランド州出身。生まれつき耳が聞こえないが、聞くこと以外は全てできると考えている。

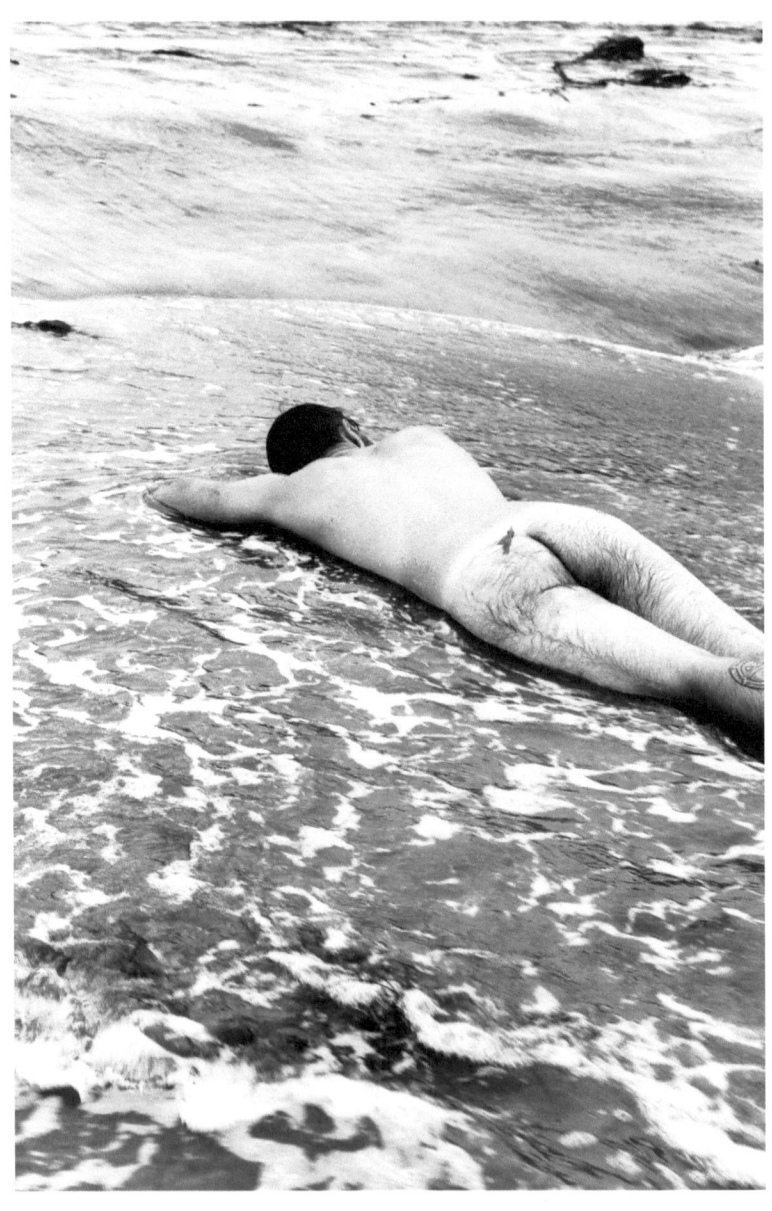

技術 | 写真
価格帯 | USD 100 - USD 300
販売レポート | USD n/a [2018年] - USD n/a [2019年]
有効な年数 | n/a 年

Mermaid
USD 100

antwanjthompson.com

Born and Raised deaf in Maryland ... this is my truth. Deaf can do anything except hear.

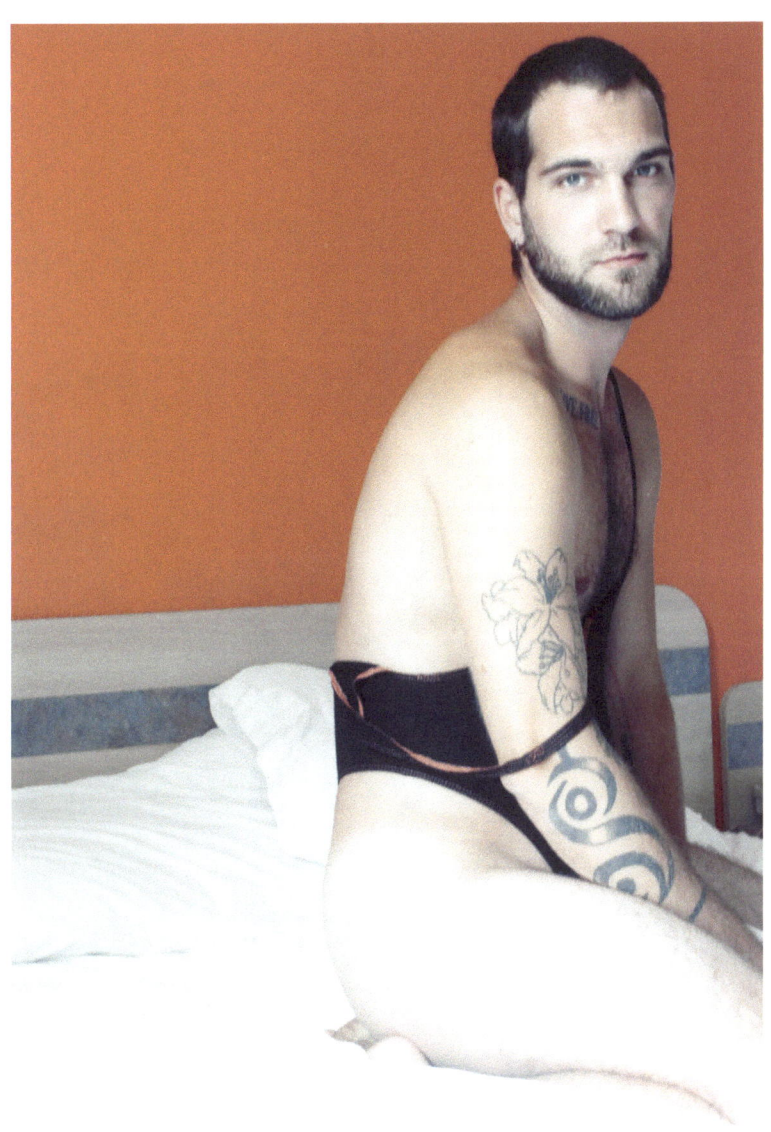

Technique | Photography
Price Range | USD 100 - USD 300
Sales Report | USD n/a (2018) - USD n/a (2019)
Active Years | n/a years

Awakening Moment

USD 150

Josephine Salvatrice Pititto
オーストラリア　|　Australia

1954年生まれ。1968年にオーストラリアへ移住。独学でアートを学び、1996年よりアーティスト活動を開始。水彩／油／アクリル絵具、インクなどの様々な画材を使用する。2005年にはイタリアのアーティスト・イン・レジデンスに招待された。作品は、ジェスチュラル・ペインティングと形象とのバランスを融合させたもので、彼は、ペン画を描くことにより、自分の思考と感情が自由に交差し、絵画は自分も含め、多くの人々が愛するアート作品を生み出すことの大きな喜びを与えてくれると述べている。

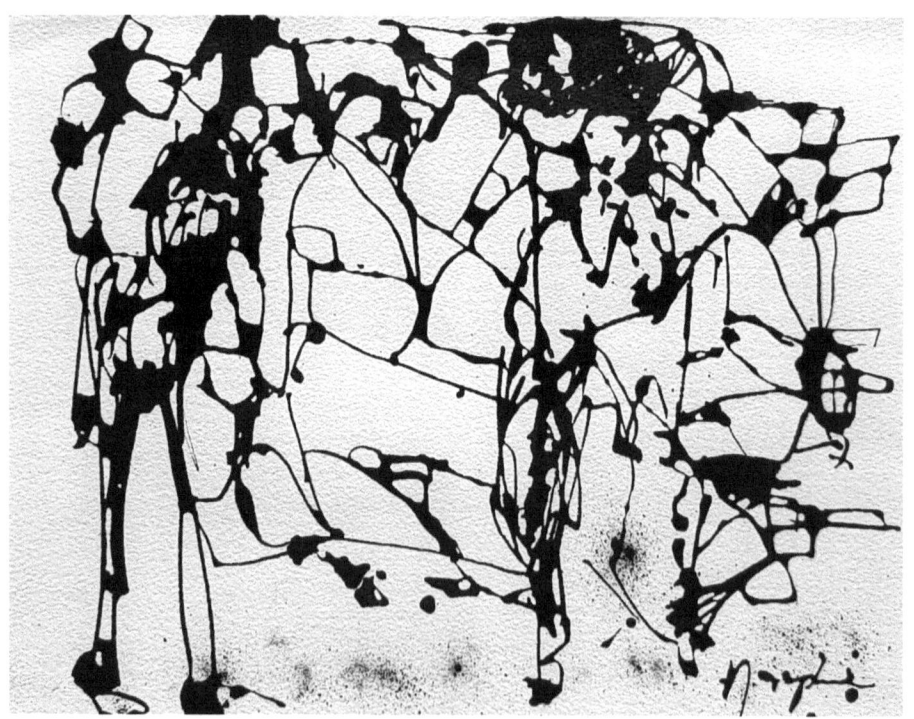

技術	絵画 - 図
価格帯	USD 1200 - USD 2800
販売レポート	USD n/a [2018年] - USD n/a [2019年]
有効な年数	23年

Tuscan Harmony
Oil on canvas. 96cmx54cm
USD 2800

josephinepitittoart.com

Born in 1954 .migrated to Australia 1968. Josephine is a self taught artist who has been practicing since 1996. The artist works across a range of mediums-including including watercolour,oils, acrylic,inks. The inks on paper and canvas were inspired by an invitation as an Artist in Residence in Italy in 2005. The drawings combine a balance between gestural abstraction and figuration. "Ink drawing allows my thoughts and emotions to flow freely". Painting has truly given me the greatest pleasure in producing art the people love as well as I do.

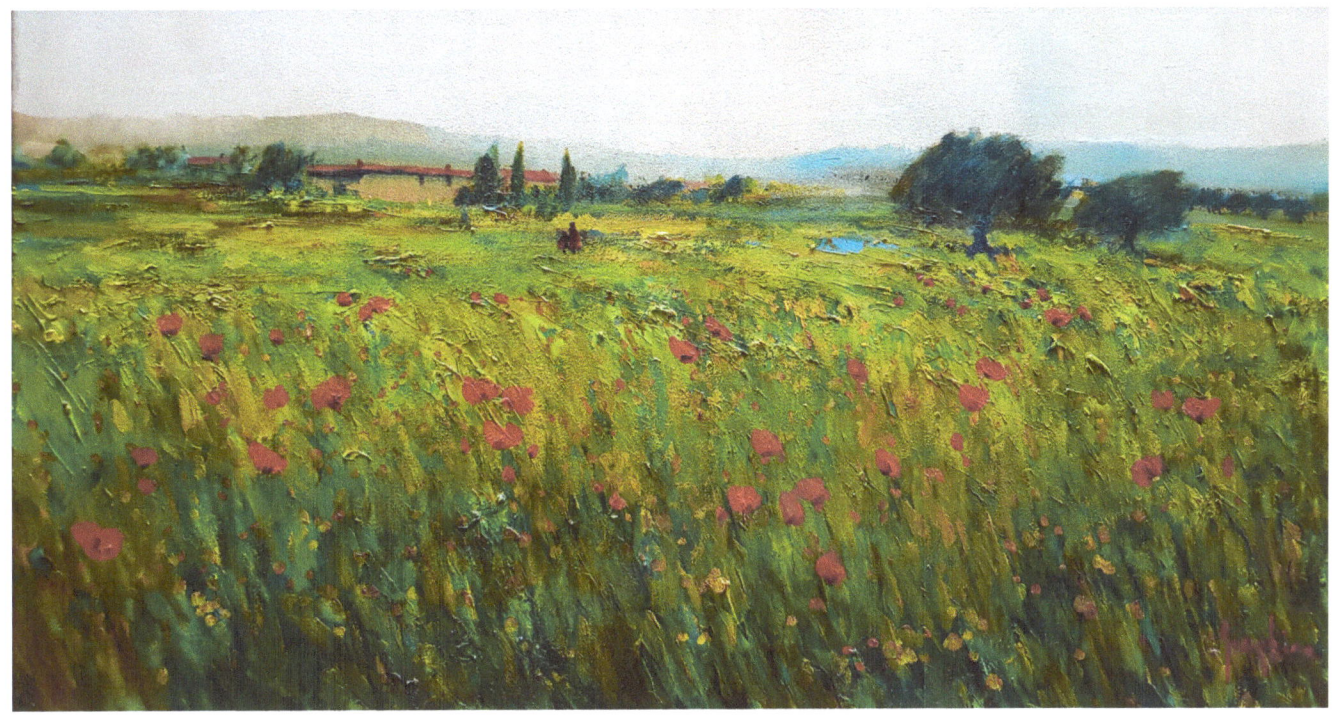

Technique | Painting - Illustration
Price Range | USD 1200 - USD 2800
Sales Report | USD n/a (2018) - USD n/a (2019)
Active Years | 23 years

Gathering
Ink on watercolour paper. 36cmx28cm
USD 2000

David Whitfield
フランス | France

絵画は、絵画自体、アーティスト、そして鑑賞者の3つの要素で成り立っており、アーティストと絵画の関係は、アーティストの制作中の作品に対する情熱的、個人的かつ感情的な探検の道のりとコミットメントである。しかし、ひとたび作品が完成すると、鑑賞者たちに見てもらうべく世に出て、それによって作品の潜在能力を発揮させることができる。作品の評価は見る者の解釈によるものであり、作品を分類することは、そのタイトルに対するオープンで偏りのない観点からの解釈を制限してしまうとして考えている。

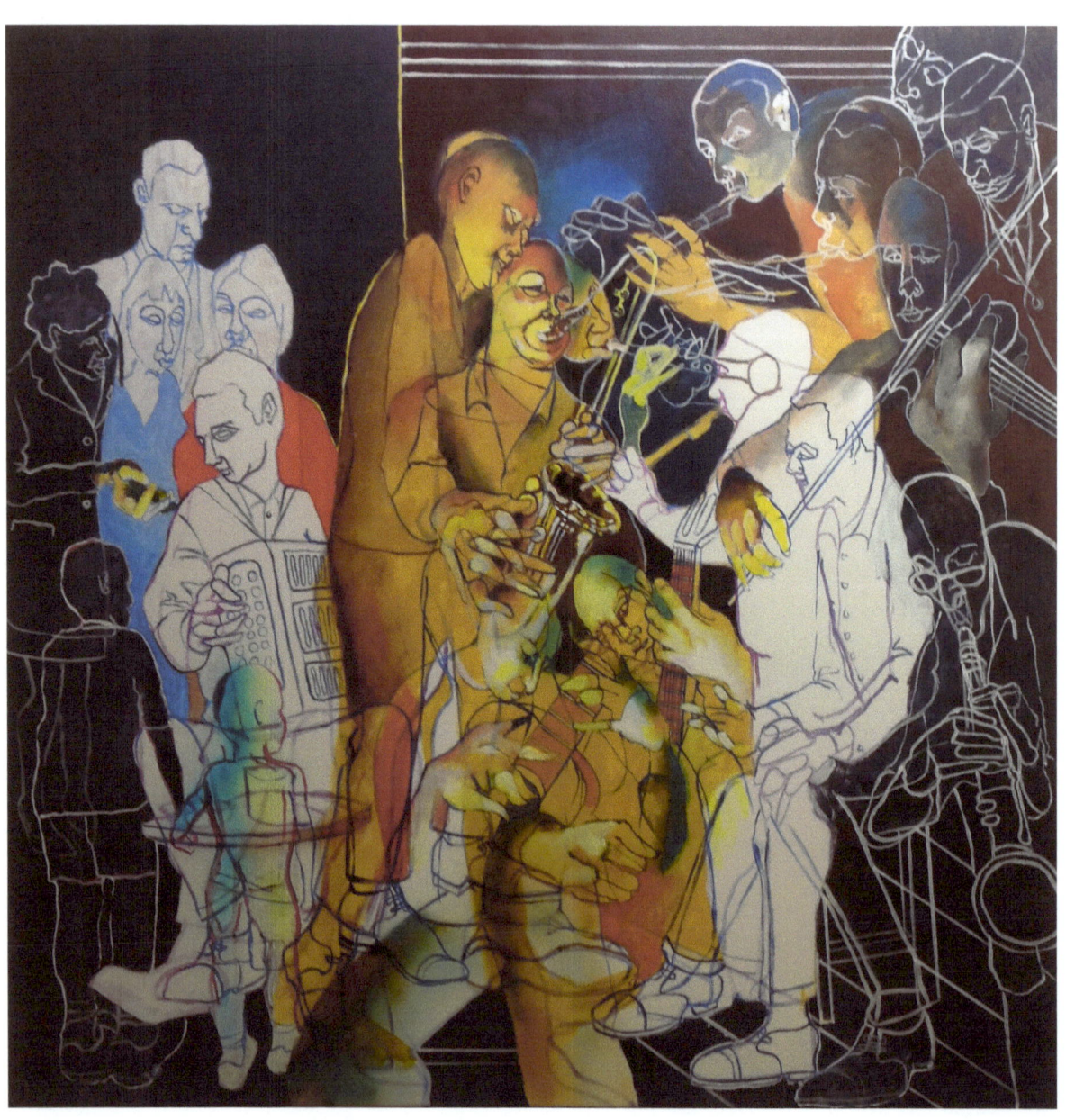

技術 | 絵画
価格帯 | USD n/a - USD n/a
販売レポート | USD n/a [2018年] - USD n/a [2019年]
有効な年数 | n/a 年

Untitled
Acrylic on canvas
USD 2500

davidwwhitfield.com

A painting requires three components to bring it to life, the work itself, the artist and the viewer. The relationship between the artist and the painting is of an intense private emotional journey of exploration and commitment from the artist to the ongoing work. However once finished it lies waiting to be brought into the world to be presented to the viewer only then can it assume an identity that will fulfill its potential. The judgement rests upon those who interpret the image set before them, by labeling the work would surely restrict any interpretation from an open unbiased point of view toward that of the title itself.

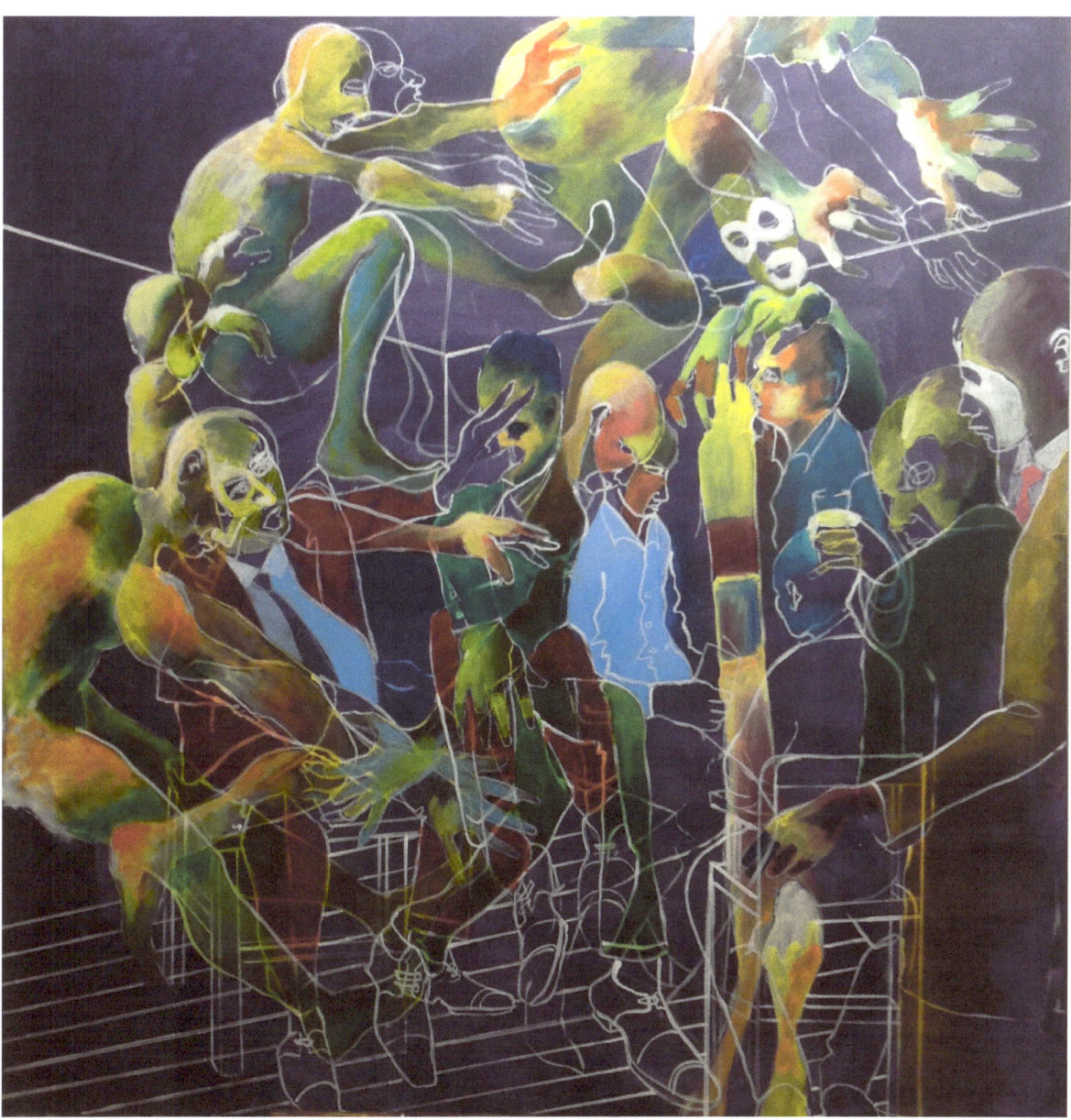

Technique | Painting
Price Range | USD n/a - USD n/a
Sales Report | USD n/a (2018) - USD n/a (2019)
Active Years | n/a years

Untitled
Acrylic on canvas
USD 2500

Linda Lasson
スウェーデン | Sweden

Linda Lasson氏はスウェーデン北部在住のテキスタイルアーティストである。防水帆布をはじめ、異なる素材の生地に刺繍糸や黒糸を縫い付ける手法の作品を制作。周りの自然からや、時には先住民への接し方や気候変動などの政治的なトピックにより作品へのインスピレーションを得ている。

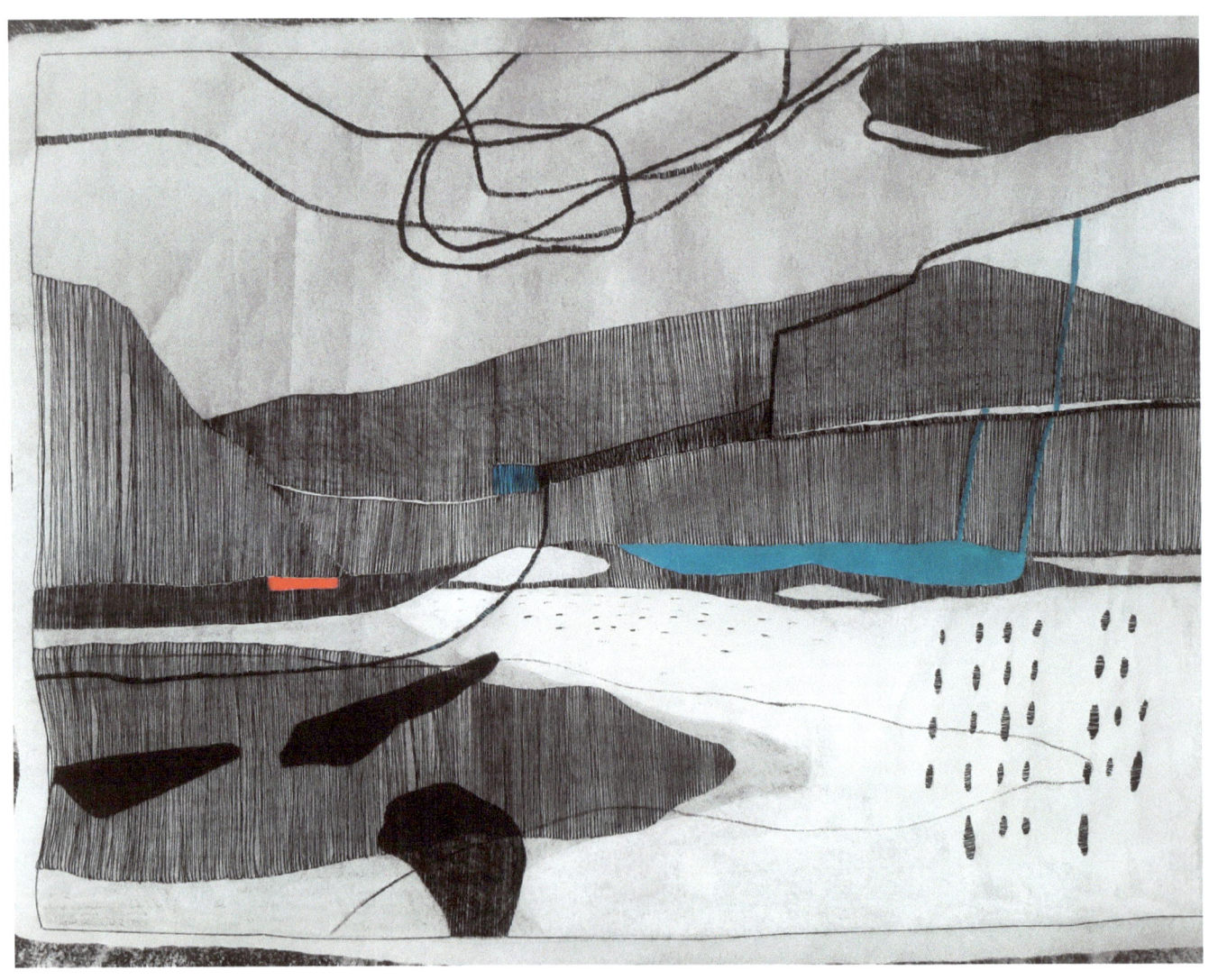

技術 | 刺繍
価格帯 | USD 200 - USD n/a
販売レポート | USD n/a [2018年] - USD n/a [2019年]
有効な年数 | 5年

Orange Stripe
USD 1500

lindalassonhemsida24.sr

My name is Linda Lasson and I work as a textile artist in the north of Sweden. I work with embroidery ,black thread, on different materials such as tarp. I get my inspiration from the surrounding nature. And also political topics about how we treat our indigenous people and climatchanges.

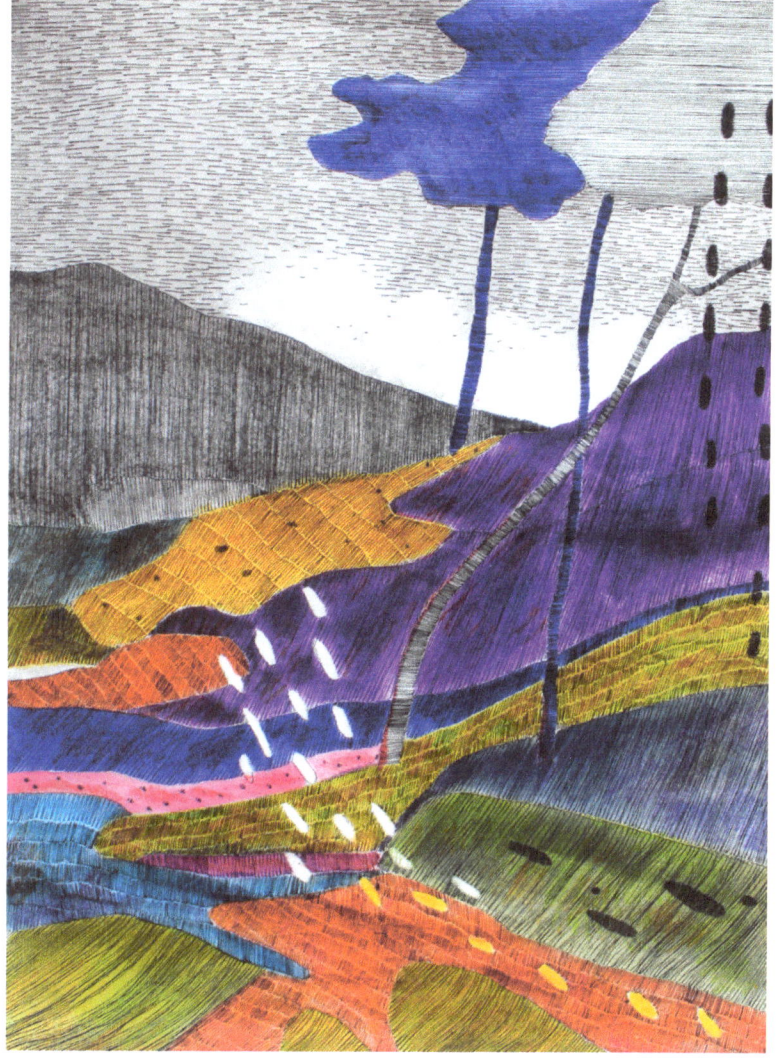

Technique | Embroidery
Price Range | USD 200 - USD n/a
Sales Report | USD n/a (2018) - USD n/a (2019)
Active Years | 5 years

Mountain
USD 1500

Paula
スペイン | Spain

Paula Menchen氏の作品は、描画、版画、絵画を交差させたもので、この3つの技法の共通点を探究している。Otis Art Institute of Parsons School of Design芸術学部で絵画とイラストレーションを重点的に学ぶ。それより以前には、Parsons school of Design、The New Schoolでも学んだ。ロンドン、アムステルダム、スペイン、イタリア、アメリカ（主にカリフォルニア）などの展示会で作品を出展。2015年にスタジオのあるロンドンからスペインに戻ってからは、マルベーリャのthe Kasser Rassu Galleryで個展を初開催した。翌年、Kunst Heute Volume 2016に招待され、作品が特集された。

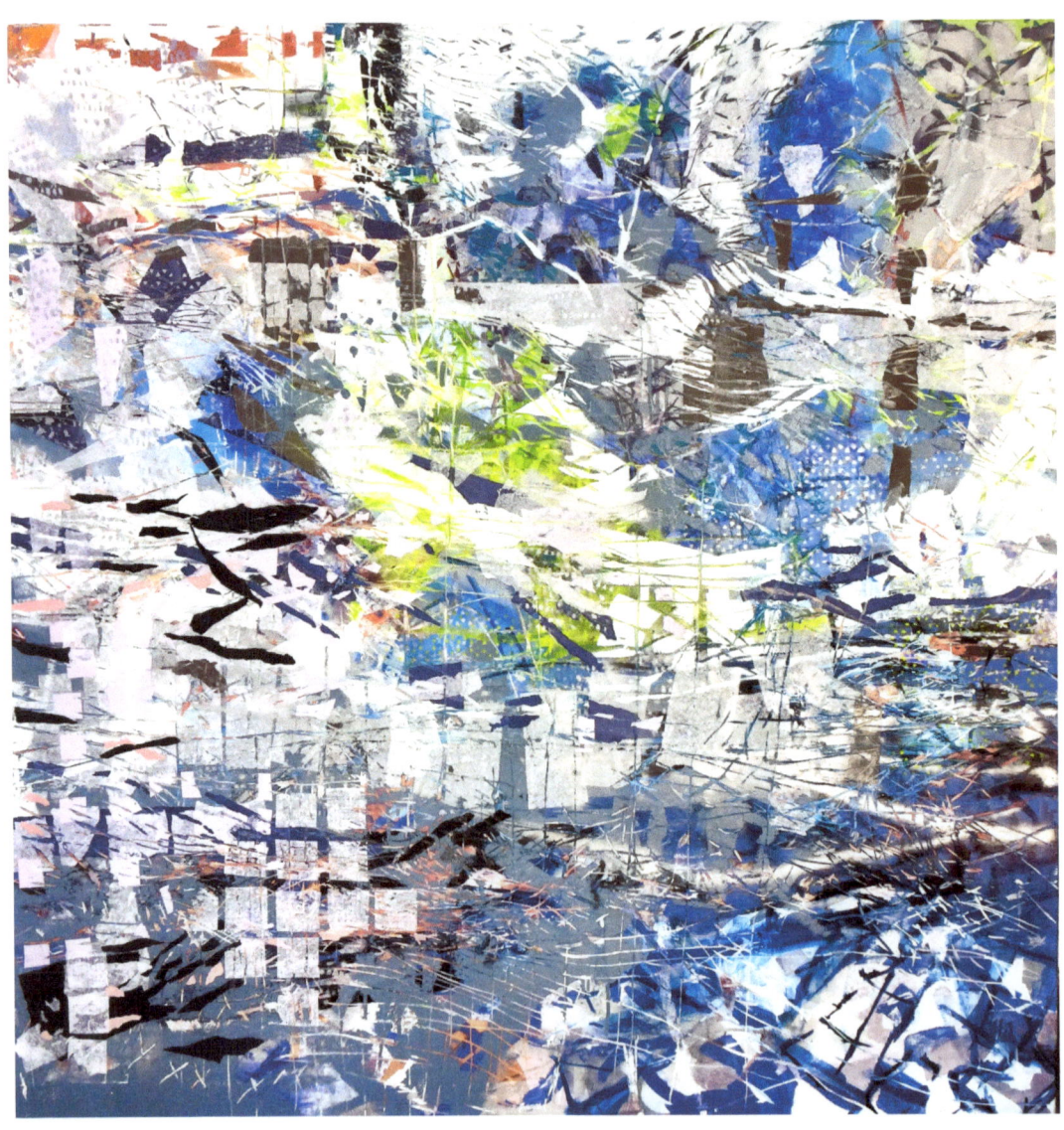

技術	混合メディア
価格帯	USD 1500 - USD 5000
販売レポート	USD 20000 [2018年] - USD 3500 [2019年]
有効な年数	20年

Electric Fences

USD 3200

paulamenchen.com

Paula's work poetically investigates the intersection between art, drawing, painting and printmaking. Combining the tactility and texture of Washi Rice Papers and the techniques of Mixografia Printmaking creating lush and intricate patterns and layers. Paula graduated from Otis Art Institute of Parsons School of Design where she majored in Fine Arts with an emphasis on painting and installation Art. She has exhibited her works in London, Amsterdam, Spain, Italy and America. Sanding, cutting, burning, smoothing and grinding surfaces that become impressions, footprints and traces. Paula looks for a constant dialogue between opposites and the complimentary. Analyzing a material front and back, perforated surfaces that become impressions of the past, present and future.

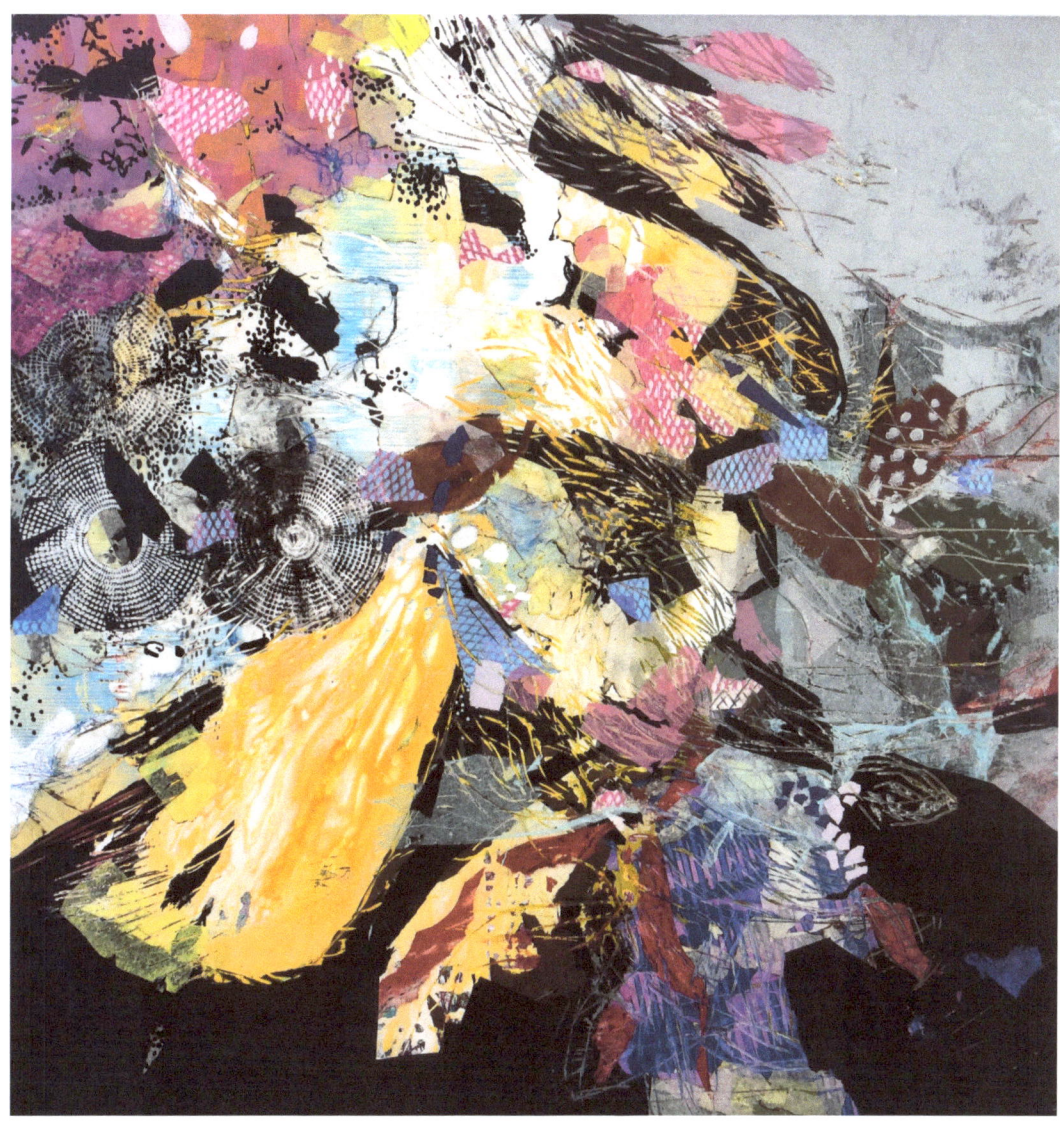

Technique | Mixed Media
Price Range | USD 1500 - USD 5000
Sales Report | USD 20000 (2018) - USD 3500 (2019)
Active Years | 20 years

Pressed Magnolia Flower
USD 2700

Bob Vanderbob
ベルギー | Belgium

ブリュッセルを拠点に活動しているアーティスト兼作曲家のBob Vanderbob氏は、テクノ人間の状態の詩的ビジョンを表現する現代の神話である人工神話を素早く作り出すために、アート、科学、SFの相互作用を探究している。彼のインスタレーションは意義の切望や、生態系の退化、政変、技術的進歩の中での美を追求している。

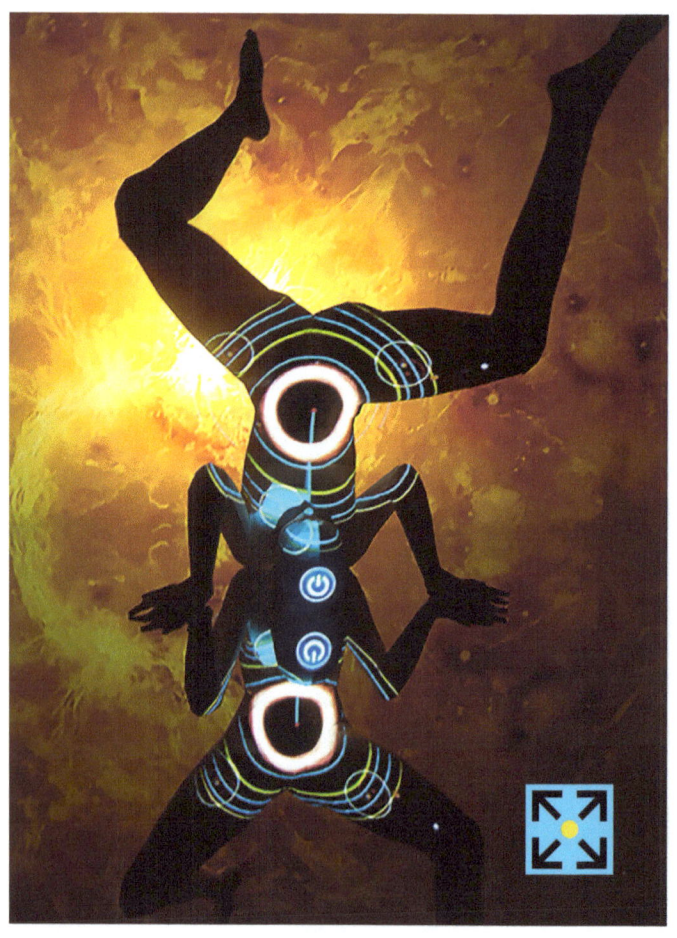

技術 | マルチメディアデザイン
価格帯 | USD 20000 - USD 50000
販売レポート | USD n/a [2018年] - USD n/a [2019年]
有効な年数 | 10年

Fecundity
Multimedia Installation
USD 50000

bobvanderbob.com

Brussels-based artist and composer Bob Vanderbob explores the interaction of art, science and science fiction to conjure up *artificial mythology*, a modern mythscape conveying a poetic vision of the techno-human condition. His installations probe our longing for meaning and beauty in the context of ecological degradation, political turmoil and technological acceleration.

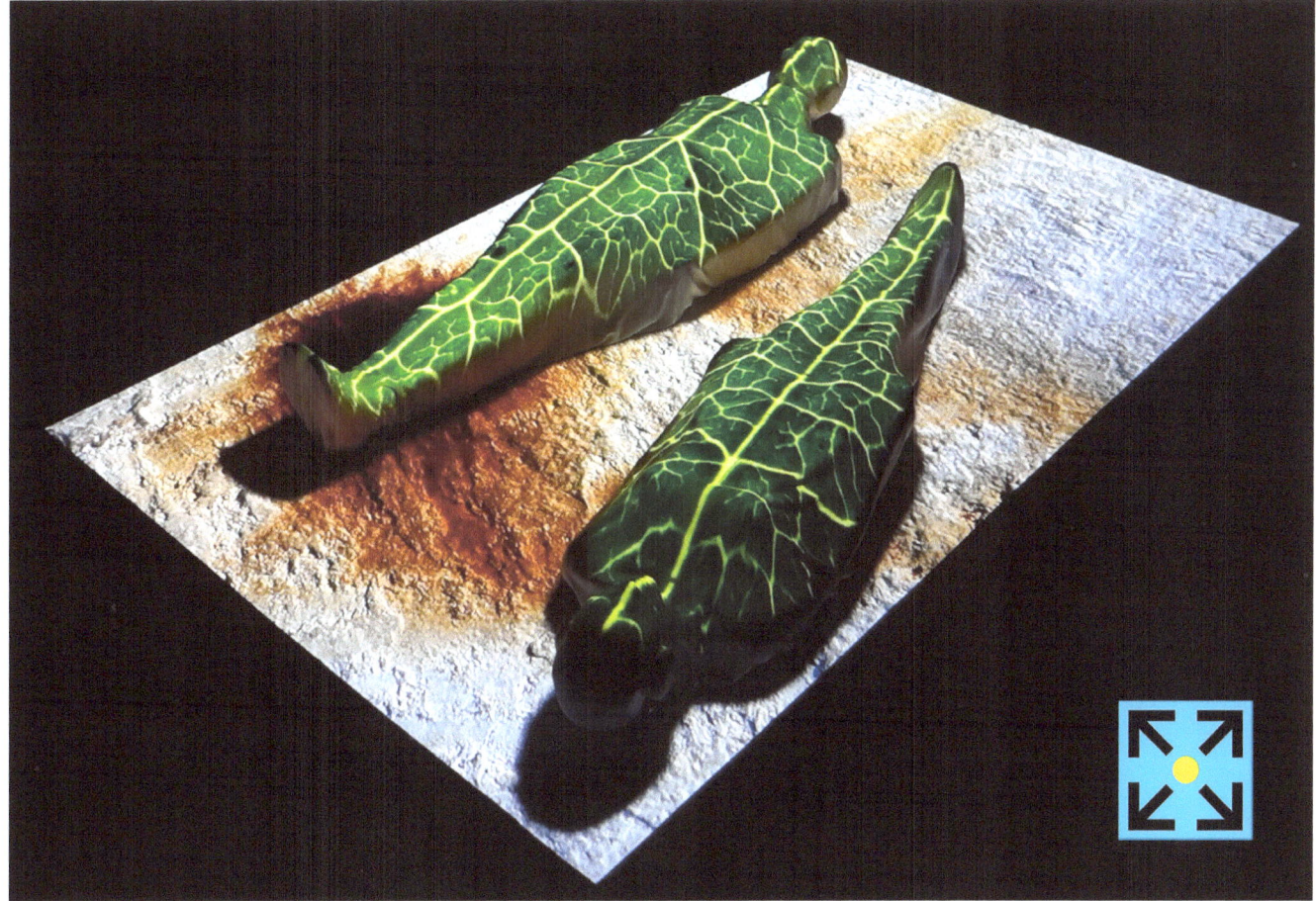

Technique | Multimedia Installation
Price Range | USD 20000 - USD 50000
Sales Report | USD n/a (2018) - USD n/a (2019)
Active Years | 10 years

Excavation
Multimedia Installation
USD 45000

Laurent Pheulpin
スイス | Switzerland

自身の写真への情熱は、15年前のデジタル画像の到来がきっかけとなった。撮影場所を少し訪れてすぐに撮影の楽しさと無限の可能性を発見した。化学者でもある彼は、光が波でできているのか、粒子でできているのかはまだわからないが、好きなようにモノブロックを設置し、それを調節できることをありがたく思っている。光の不在は混乱を招き、光はその付属品によってのみ定義される主題を溶かしてしまう。また、様々な年齢層の人形に焦点を当てた写真によって老化とエロチシズムを私たちの関係についても探究している。2006年の初出展以降世界各地の様々な展示会で自身のビジョンを共有している。

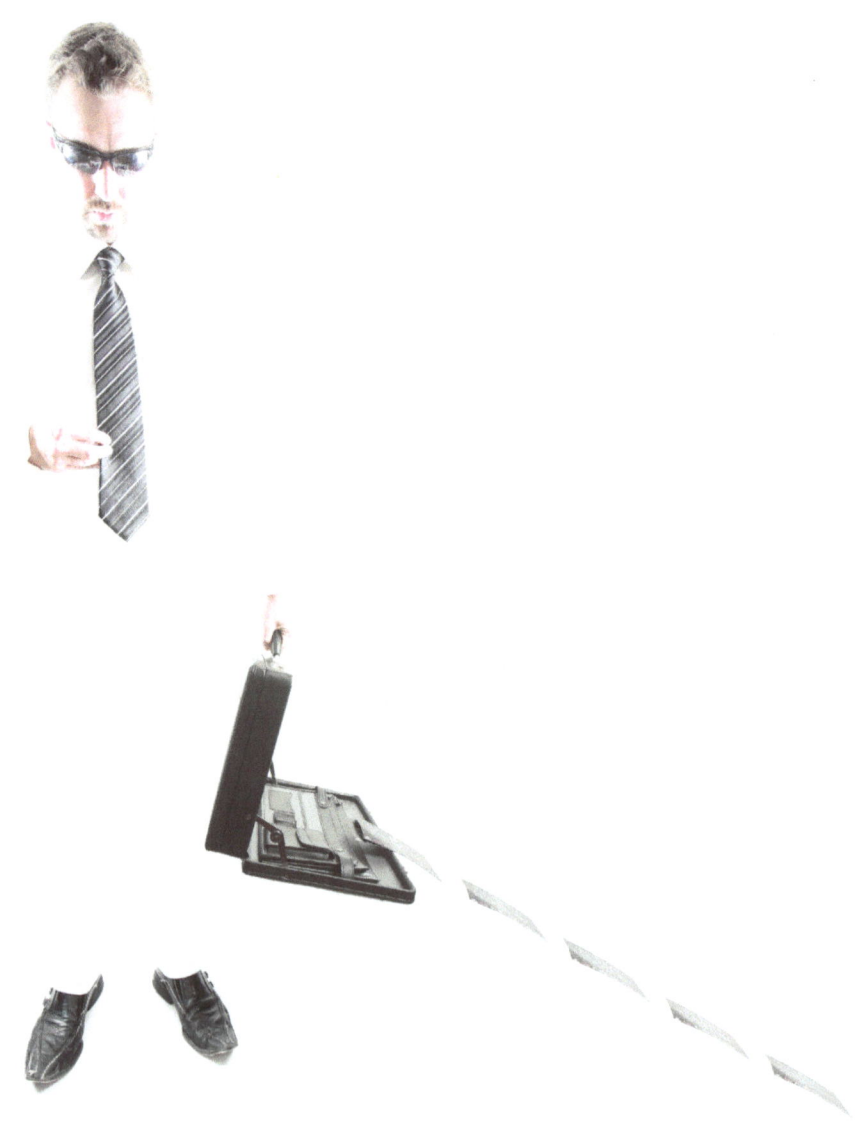

技術 | 写真
価格帯 | USD 500 - USD 1000
販売レポート | USD 50000 [2018年] - USD 70000 [2019年]
有効な年数 | 14年

MGH x Sin (Alpha)
USD 500

laurentphotographie.wordpress.com

My passion for photography emerged 15 years ago with the advent of digital imaging. After a brief visit to the photo-landscape, I discovered the joys of the studio and its infinite possibilities. As a chemist I still do not know if the light is made of waves or particles, but I appreciate the fact of modulating it by orienting my monoblocks according to my desires. Light can express disarray by its absence or dissolve the subject that will be defined only by its accessories. I also sought to explore our relationship with aging and eroticism through a series of photos featuring dolls of all ages. My first exhibition took place in 2006 and since then, I share my vision in different exhibitions around the world.

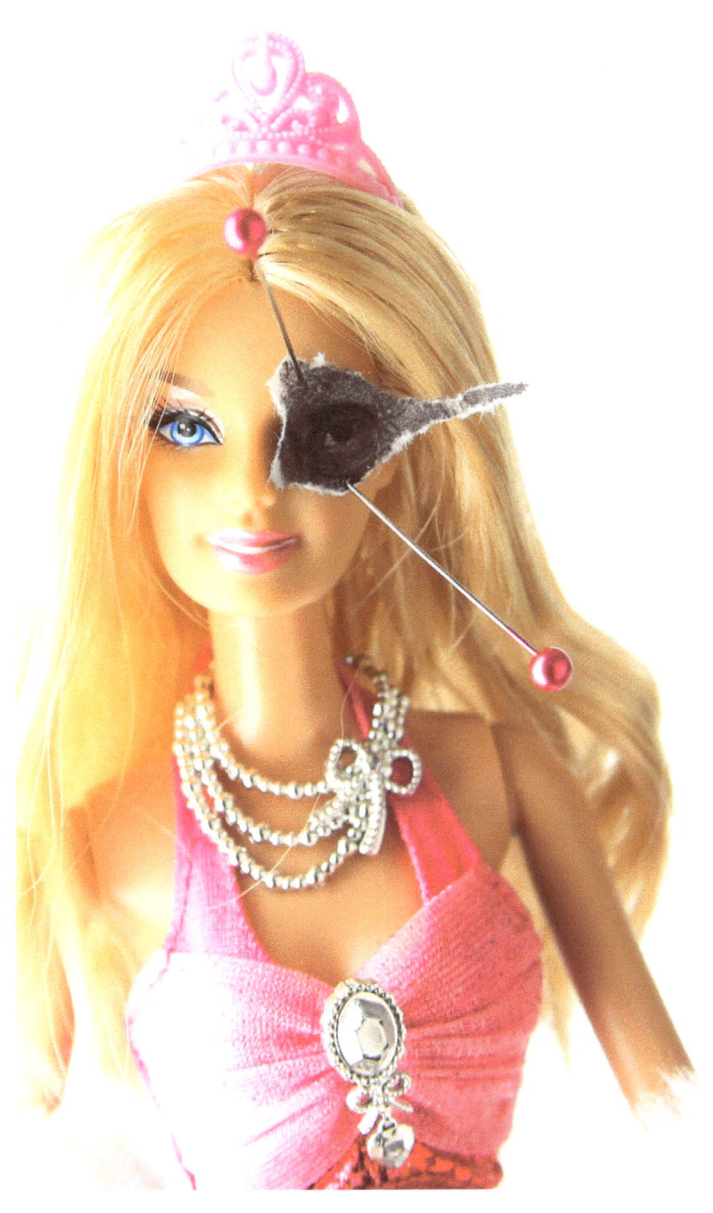

Technique | Photography
Price Range | USD 500 - USD 1000
Sales Report | USD 50000 (2018) - USD 70000 (2019)
Active Years | 14 years

Ojo 5
USD 800

Jasmine Seo
アメリカ | United States

Jasmine Seo氏はシアトル在住の啓蒙思想を持ち、人生を前向きにとらえる超現実主義者である。主に様々なパステルを用いた作品を制作するが、イラストレーションと版画の技法を組み合わせ、自分たちだけではなく、社会全体がよりよい調和と平和を生み出すために人々の理解と知識を高めるための力強いコミュニケーション手段としての作品作りを楽しんでいる。彼女は、アートは意識と意識を繋ぐためのツールとしてだけではなく、心の内を探り、繋ぎなおすための鍵であると信じている。

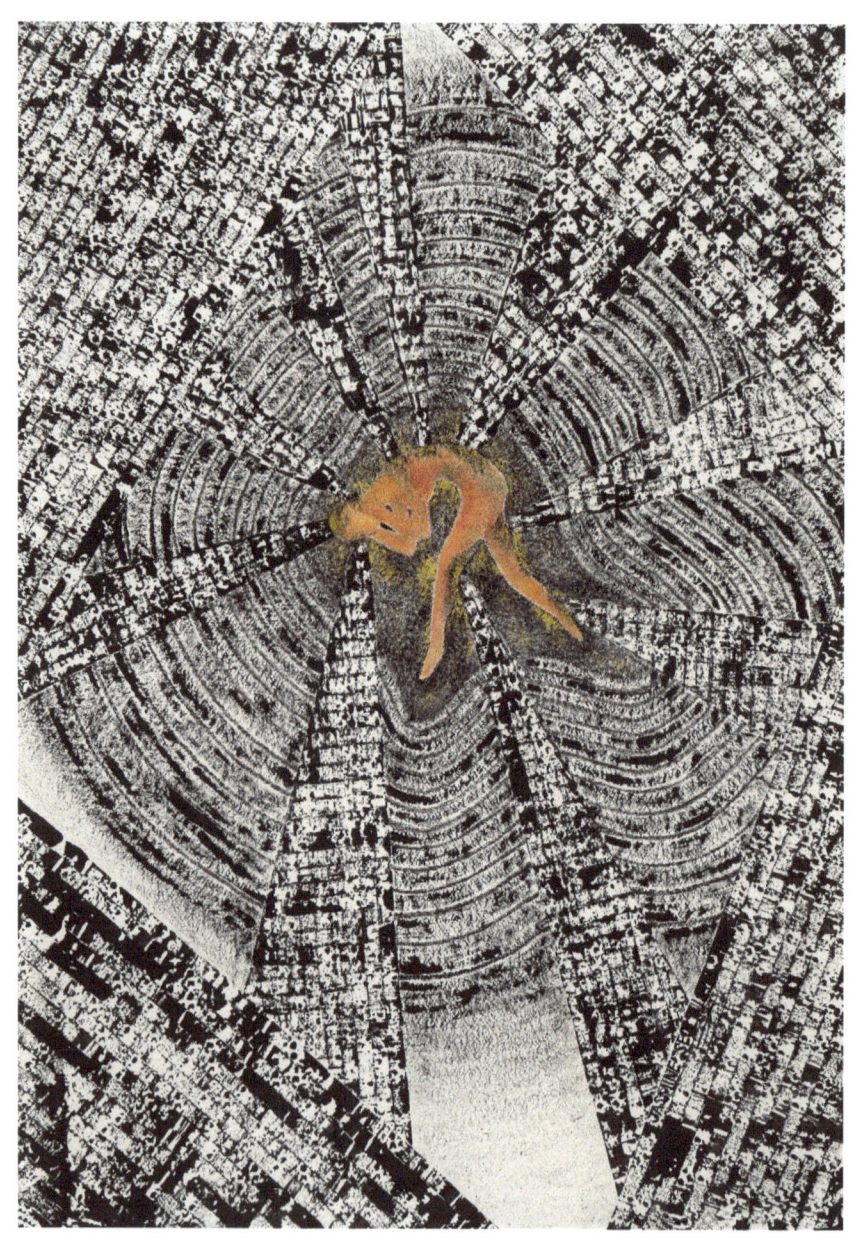

技術 | 絵画 - 図 - 混合メディア - 版画

価格帯 | USD 300 - USD 3200

販売レポート | USD 4600 [2018年] - USD 7200 [2019年]

有効な年数 | 4年

Le Penseur
Ink and Pastels, 30x22 in, 2019
USD 1050

jasmineseo.com

Jasmine Seo is a Seattle based surrealist with a propensity for enlightenment and an optimistic approach to life. Although she mostly works with different pastels, she has been particularly enjoying incorporating illustration and printmaking techniques in her artwork as a powerful communication tool to help our society broaden their sense of understanding and wisdom for better harmony and peace, not only within ourselves but also in our life. Jasmine firmly believes that art isn't just as a communication tool that can connect mind to mind but a key to trace back to our inner world and re-connect.

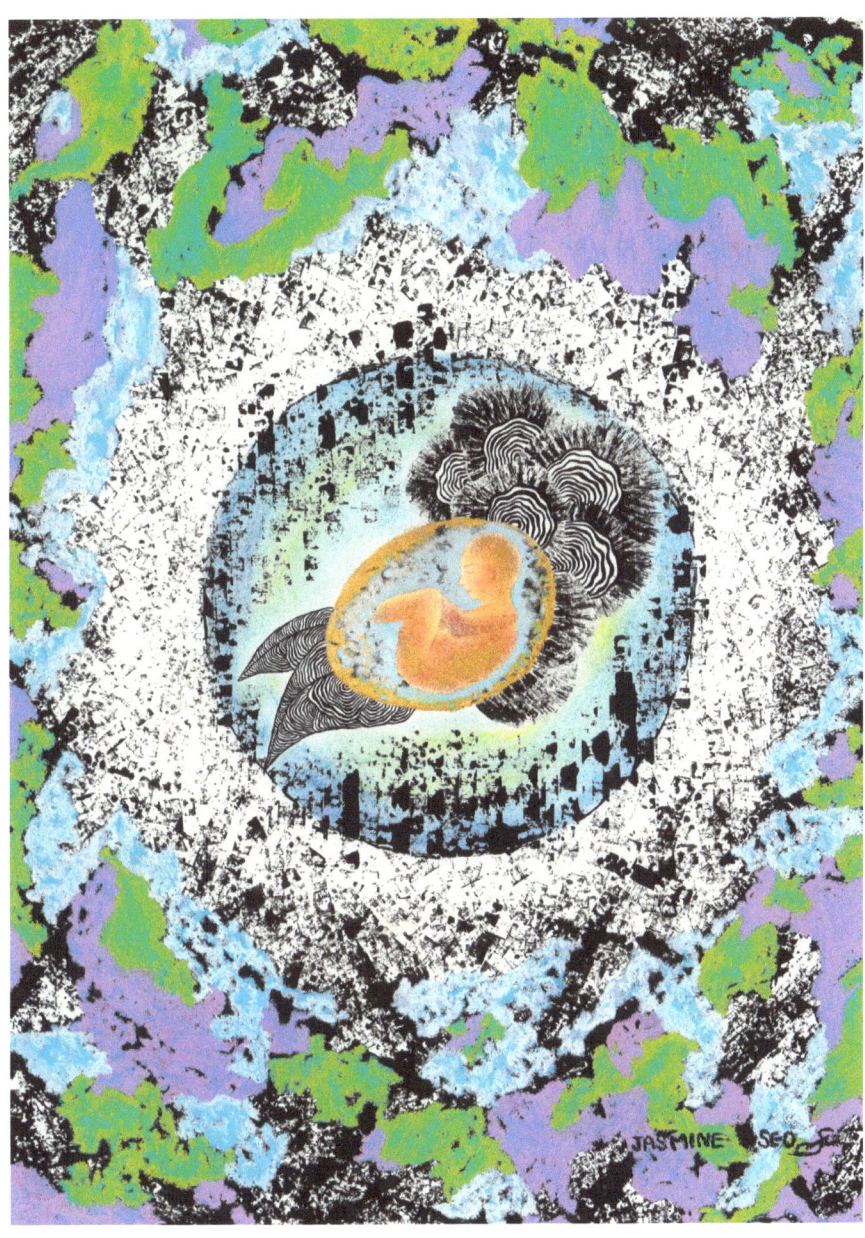

Technique | Painting - Illustration - Mixed Media - Printmaking
Price Range | USD 300 - USD 3200
Sales Report | USD 4600 (2018) - USD 7200 (2019)
Active Years | 4 years

Howling Moon
Ink and Pastels, 30x22 in, 2019
USD 1200

Jaana Heikkinen
フィンランド | Finland

フィンランド出身のアーティスト。Finnish Academy of Fine Arts卒業。アーティストとして、新たな素材や技法を見つけるといつも胸が弾む。しばしば同じ題材に対して描画、絵画、彫刻などからのアプローチをおこなう場合がある。自身にとって作品制作は内なる自分に出会う旅である。象徴主義、自然の神秘、神話など、様々な側面を持つ人間の意識に惹かれる。人と自然についての具象美術を制作し、また、作品では動物も多く取り入れている。動物は人間の本能と潜在意識、内なるパワーと私たちが自然の一部であるということの象徴であるとしている。自身にとってアートとは、自分が存在し、人として成長するための手段であると考えている。

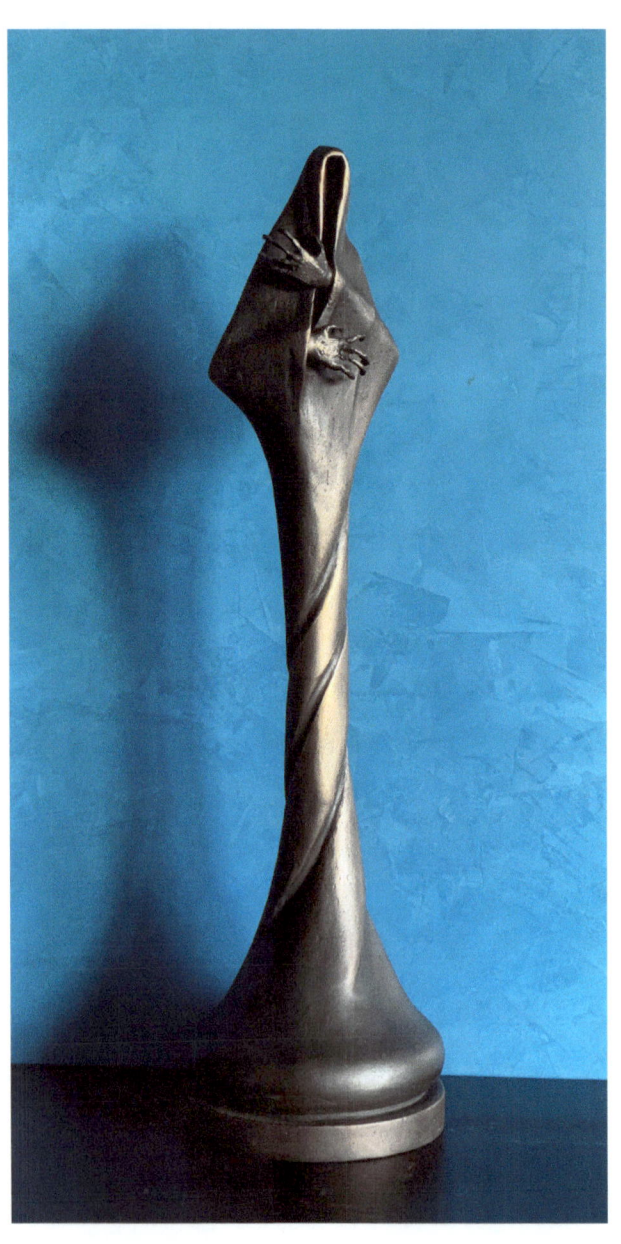

技術 | 絵画 - 図 - 彫刻
価格帯 | USD 300 - USD 10000
販売レポート | USD 9000 [2018年] - USD 10000 [2019年]
有効な年数 | 30年

Shadow 1/8
USD 5000

jaanaheikkinen.com

I'm an artist from Finland, graduated from the Finnish Academy of Fine Arts. As an artist, I get easily excited about new materials and techniques. I often work on the same subject by drawing, painting and sculpting. For me, making art is a journey to my inner world. I'm interested in symbolism, the mysticism of nature, mythology – the human mind with its various dimensions. I make representational arts about people and nature. I use a lot of animal subjects in my work. They symbolize to me the instinctive and subconscious side of human, our inner powers and the nature we are part of. Art is a way for me to exist, to be developed as a human.

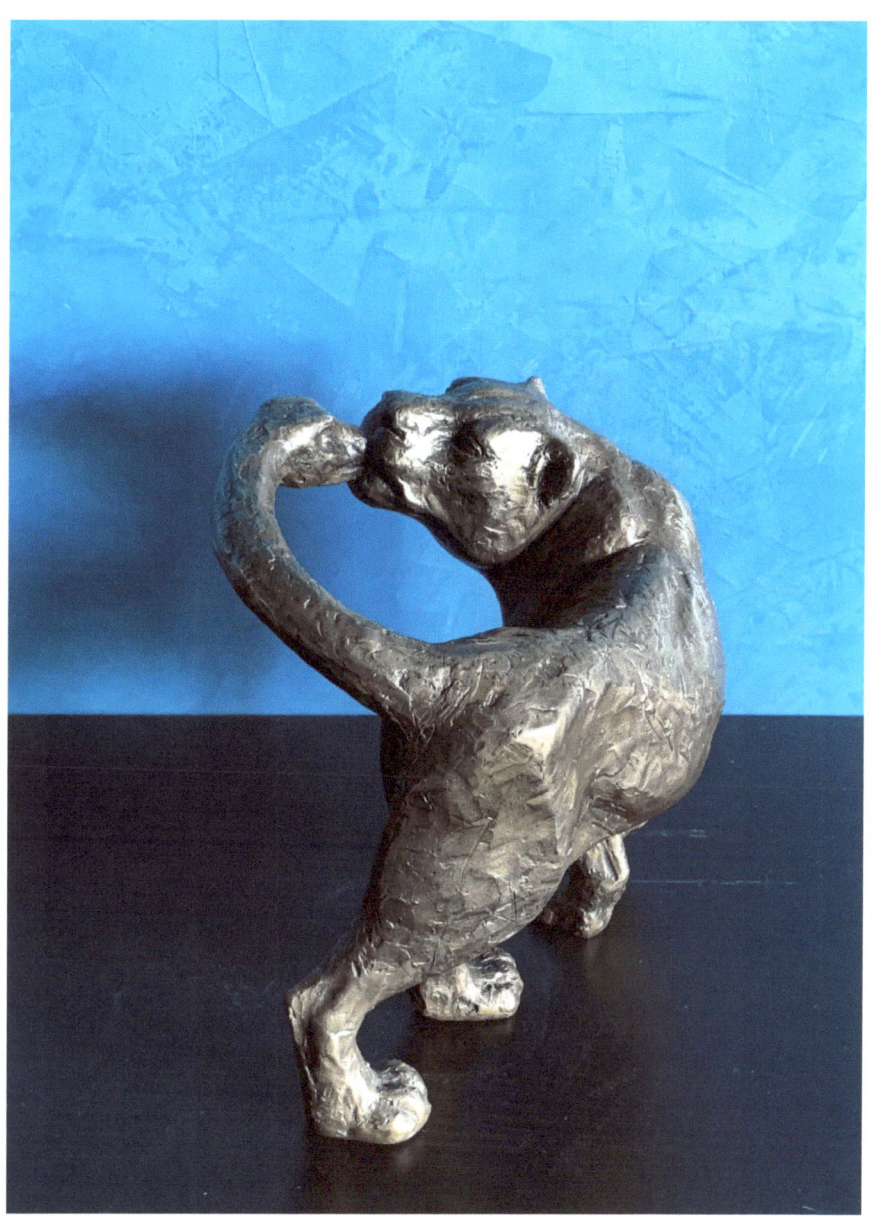

Technique | Painting - Illustration - Sculpture
Price Range | USD 300 - USD 10000
Sales Report | USD 9000 (2018) - USD 10000 (2019)
Active Years | 30 years

The Strenght 3/8
USD 4000

Mika Yajima
日本 | Japan

ヤジマミカ氏は、フリーランスを始めた頃から、繊維素材を使用したオリジナル技法で主に建築スペース向けの注文作品を制作している。極細糸と金属を用いて、軽さと重さ、固さと柔らかさなど反対の性質を用いた組み合わせが作品の特徴である。学生時代から続けている古代の伝統的技法と材料を現代アートに転換させる方法で、機械やデジタルツールではできない表現をおこなっている。現在は、一貫したテーマを基に、様々なスタイルの表現方法に重点を置いている。Lorenzo il Magnificoで国際賞、第12回フローランス・ビエンナーレ2019テキスタイル＆ファイバーアート部門で、素数を用いたスプラング・タペストリーで準グランプリを受賞。

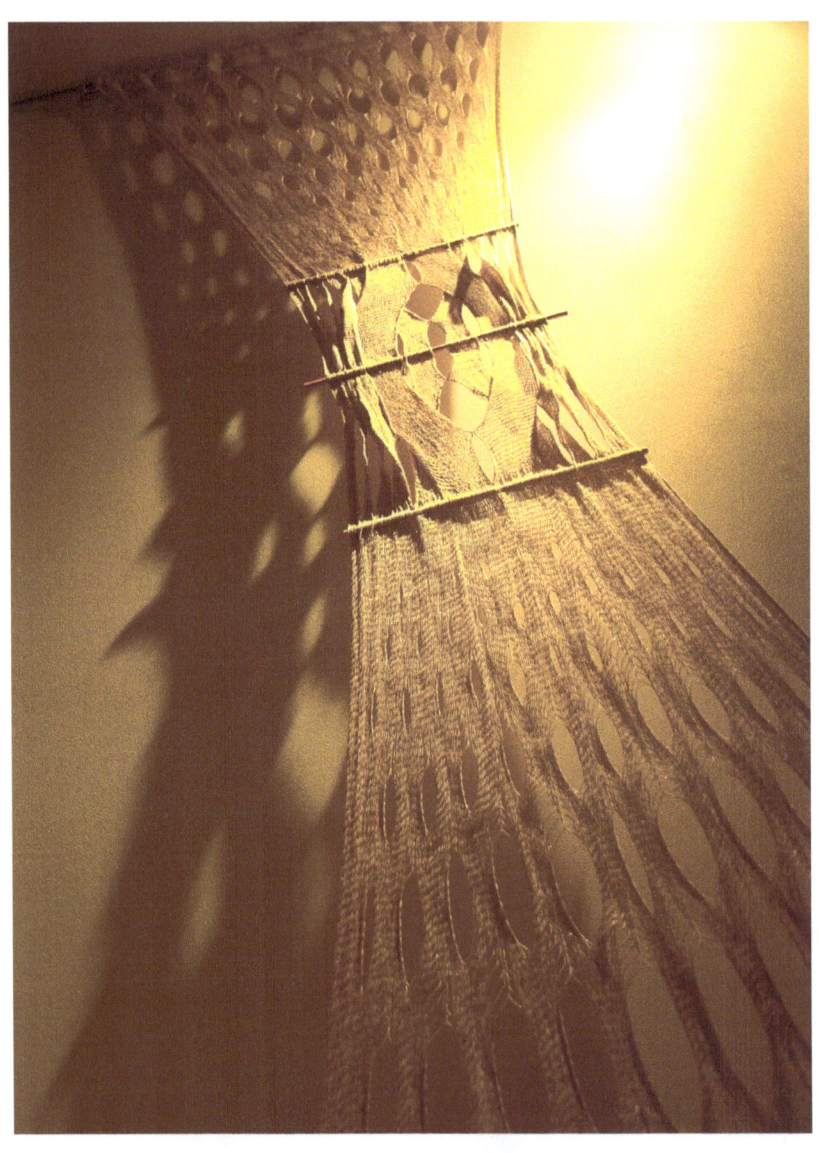

技術 | 繊維 作業
価格帯 | USD 300 - USD 33000
販売レポート | USD n/a [2018年] - USD n/a [2019年]
有効な年数 | 27年

Prime in Reverse | 2019 Prized work
Sprang works | Size: 2600(H) x 100(W) x 15(D) /mm | Materials: Ramie and gold rayon thread, Brass pipes and sticks. Price Upon Request

mikayajima.com

From the start of her freelance career, Mika Yajima produced mainly on order artwork for architectural spaces by using original techniques with fiber material. A paradoxical combination of thin thread & metal, light & heavy, soft & hard, and the like are her hallmarks. In recent years, she has made a transformation from and ancient traditional techniques and materials to the contemporary arts that continues from her art college days, something that cannot be done with machines or digital tools. And she is now focusing a variety style of expressions what based on a consistent theme. She has received the International Award 'Lorenzo il Magnifico' the 2nd Prize in Textile & Fiber Art category at Florence Biennale XII 2019 by Sprang-tapestry using Prime numbers.

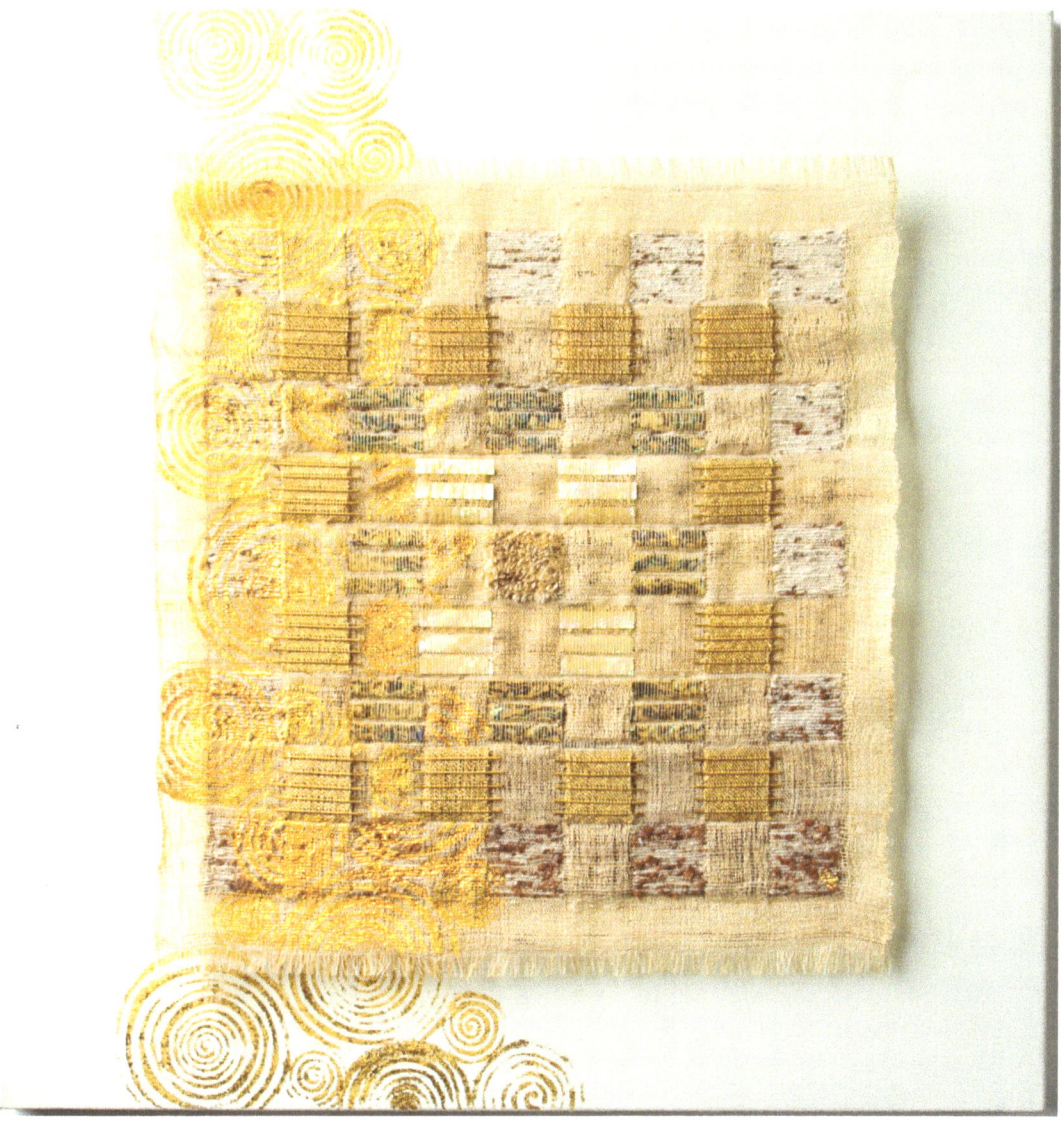

Technique | Textile & Fiber Work
Price Range | USD 300 - USD 33000
Sales Report | USD n/a (2018) - USD n/a (2019)
Active Years | 27 years

9x9 Composition 渦 Whirlpool | 2016 Prized work
Technique: Hand spun & double-weaved tapestry, Gold leaf work, Tapestry on canvas, Mixed-collage. | Size: 730(H)x730(W)x27(D)/mm | Price Upon Request

Jøran Juveli Marstrander
ノルウェー | Norway

写真撮影はカメラで捉えられるものだけでおこなう。(フォトショップは編集のためにだけ使用する)長時間露光を一度おこない、動きを加える独自のしかけで撮影をおこなう。変化の多いこの技法では、同じものは二度と撮れないため彼が本当にこだわる品質のものが撮影できる。また、比喩的ではない作品を制作することで、鑑賞者が自らの想像力で解釈できる余韻を残している。光に魅了され、40ミリにもなるアクリル板に現像するため、魅惑的な光の屈折を持つ作品となる。ノルウェー、Brick Lane Gallery London、ボローニャ、マドリッド、ヨーテボリ、ヴェネツィア・ビエンナーレ(Tiziano賞受賞)、Miami Art Week、Art Expo New Yorkなどで個展やグループ展を開催。

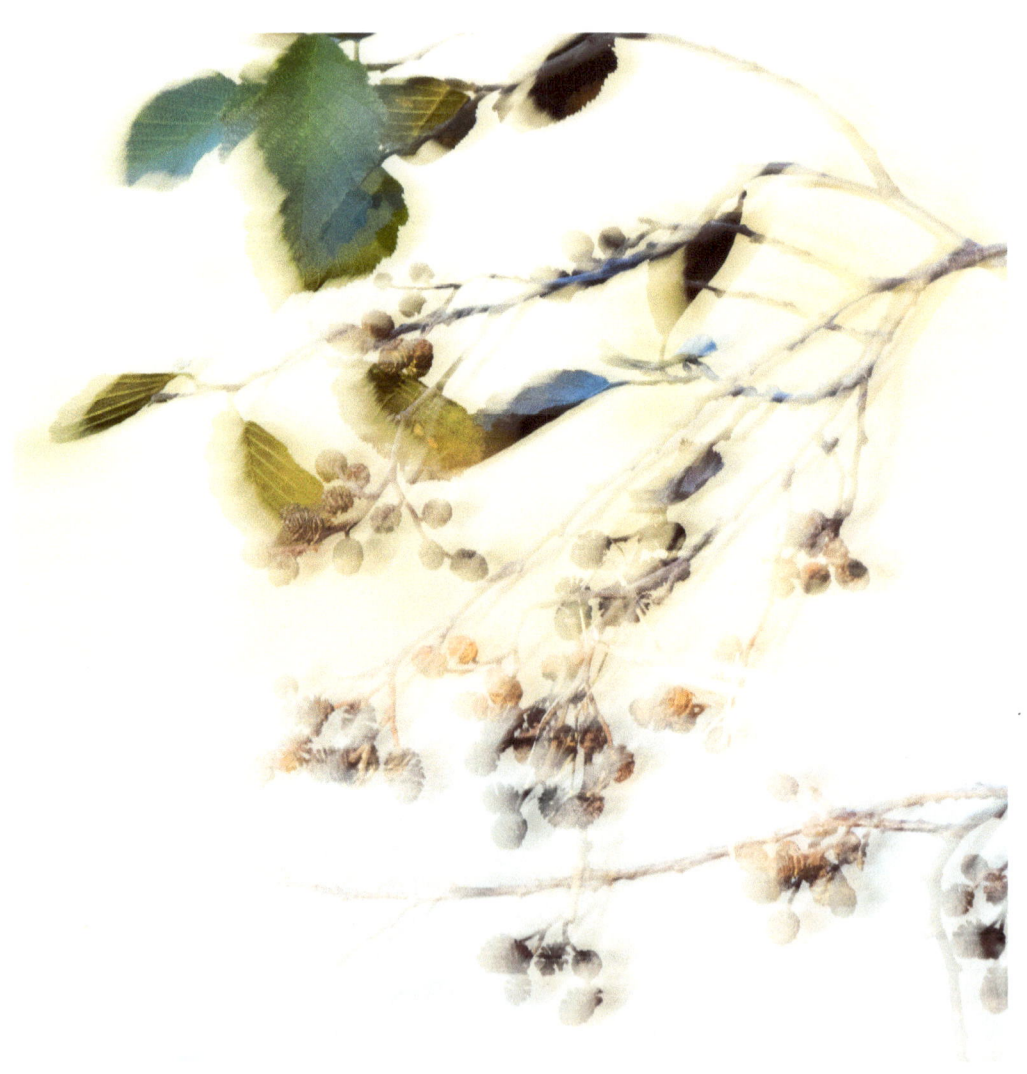

技術 | 写真
価格帯 | USD 1800 - USD n/a
販売レポート | USD n/a [2018年] - USD n/a [2019年]
有効な年数 | 12年

Whisperings 1
Art Photography 2019
Price Upon Request

juvelifoto.com

It is what I can achieve with only the camera that catches me the most about photography (Photoshop only used as a darkroom). I am using one exposure, long time and movement to create my own magic. This technique with many variables makes it impossible to repeat the same motive twice, a quality I greatly appreciate. By working non-figuratively I want to give more room for the viewer's own imaginations. My fascination with light is the reason why I love copying directly onto acrylic, up to 40 mm thick - then the refraction becomes magical!. Exhibitions: Solo/joint exhibitions in Norway, Brick Lane Gallery London, Bologna, Madrid, Gothenburg, Biennale of the Nations Venice (got the Tiziano Prize), Miami Art Week, Art Expo New York.

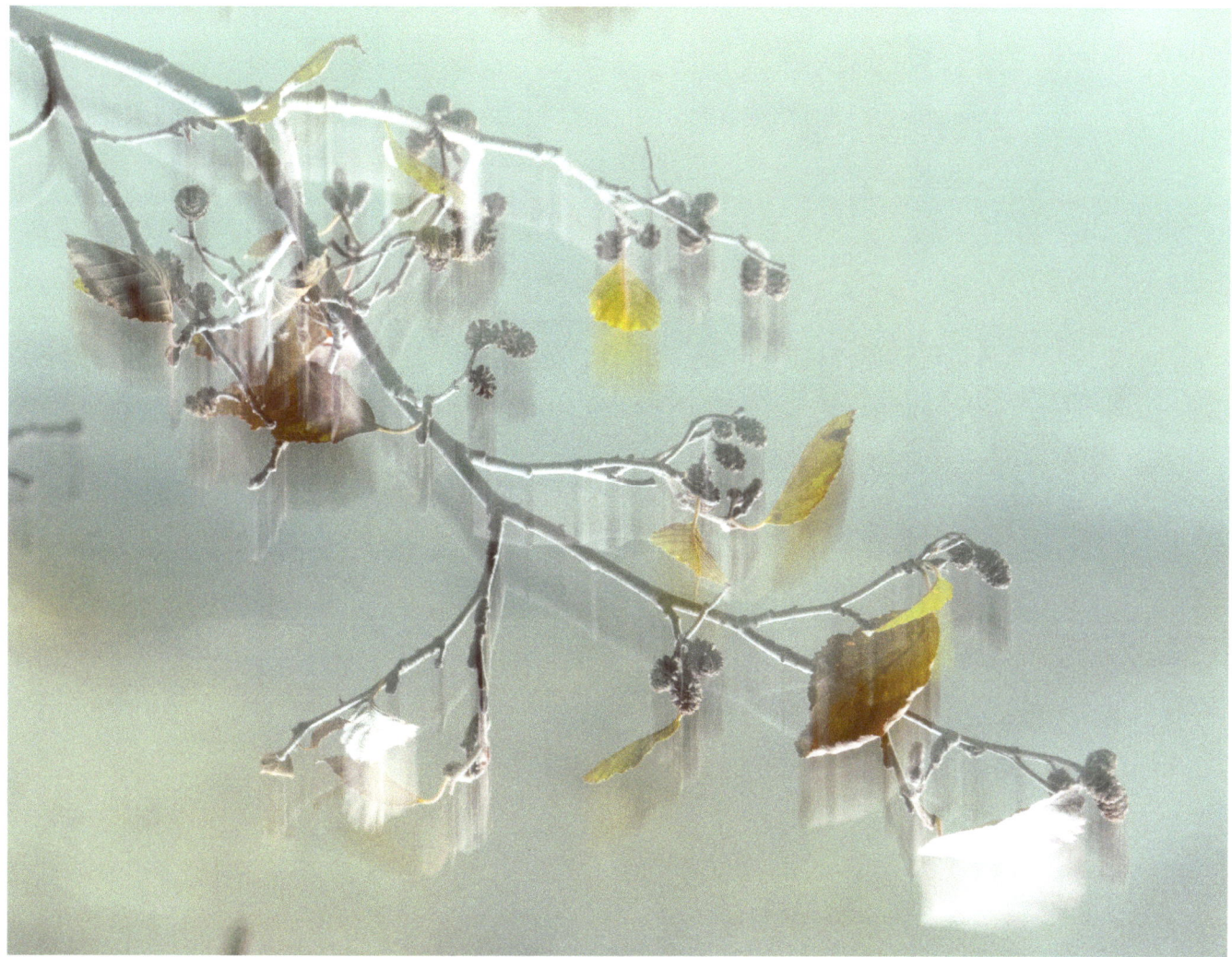

Technique | Photography
Price Range | USD 1800 - USD n/a
Sales Report | USD n/a (2018) - USD n/a (2019)
Active Years | 12 years

Whisperings 2
Art Photography 2019
Price Upon Request

Yaroslava Liseeva
ロシア | Russia

私たちは全てが移り変わりが激しく、せわしなく、互いに繋がりあった世界に生きている。YAROSLAVA氏は、感情や精神的な側面に訴えかける作品を制作している。現代は情報、ソーシャルネットワークやニュースが溢れすぎていて脳が情報過多になってしまっているため、それをいったん停止し、自分自身の目で世界を見て、耳で聞き、感じることが重要だと考えている。正しく軌道修正すれば、私たちはたくさんのものを見て、感じ、その意味をとらえることができる。作品では、風景のイメージに焦点を当て、木々、海、湖、風、火などの力強く、豊かで流れるような世界を描いている。もしこの現象を五感全てを使って観察してみると、自然は隠された本質を見せてくれ、その普遍的で神話的な特性に気づくことができるだろう。

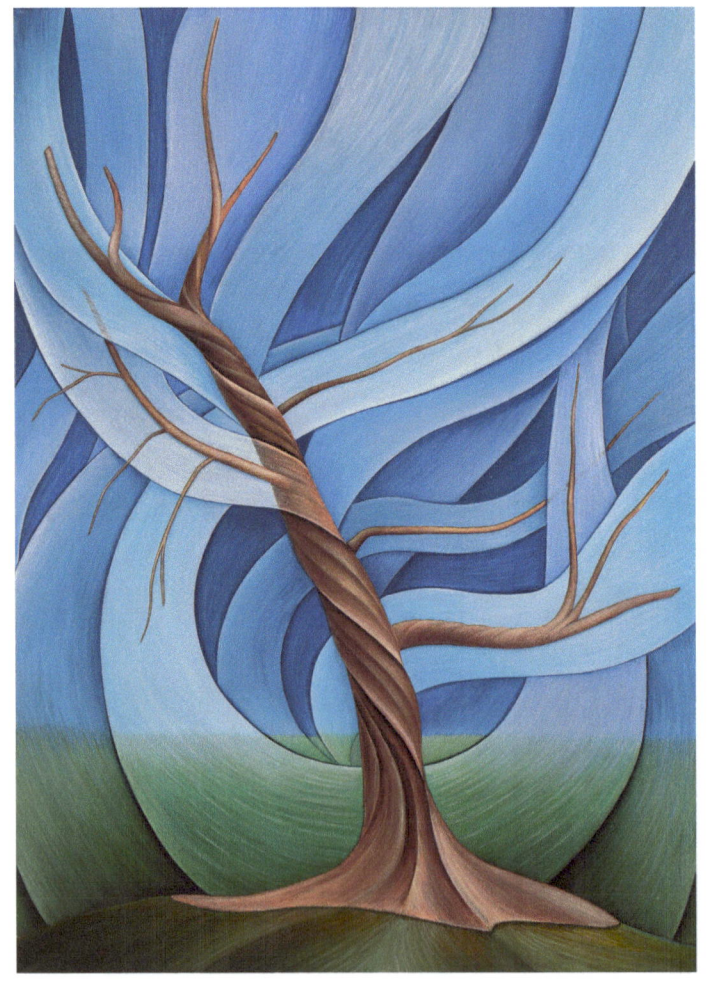

技術 | 絵画
価格帯 | USD 5000 - USD 10000
販売レポート | USD n/a [2018年] - USD n/a [2019年]
有効な年数 | 20年

Catching the Flow
Oil on canvas, 110x80 cm, 2019
USD 8000

yarlis.org

We live in the world where everything is inconstant and changing, moving and interconnecting. In my works I appeal to emotional and spiritual dimensions. Nowadays when our minds are overloaded with tons of information, social networks, news, it is very important just to make a stop and to open the eyes and see the world around, listen to it, feel it. We can see and feel so many things and meanings, when we tune ourselves for that. Focusing on landscape images I try to create dynamic, voluminous and flowing world. The trees, the oceans, the lakes, wind, fire... The real things. But if we observe these phenomena with all our senses, they open for us their metaphorical essence and acquire universal, mythological characteristics.

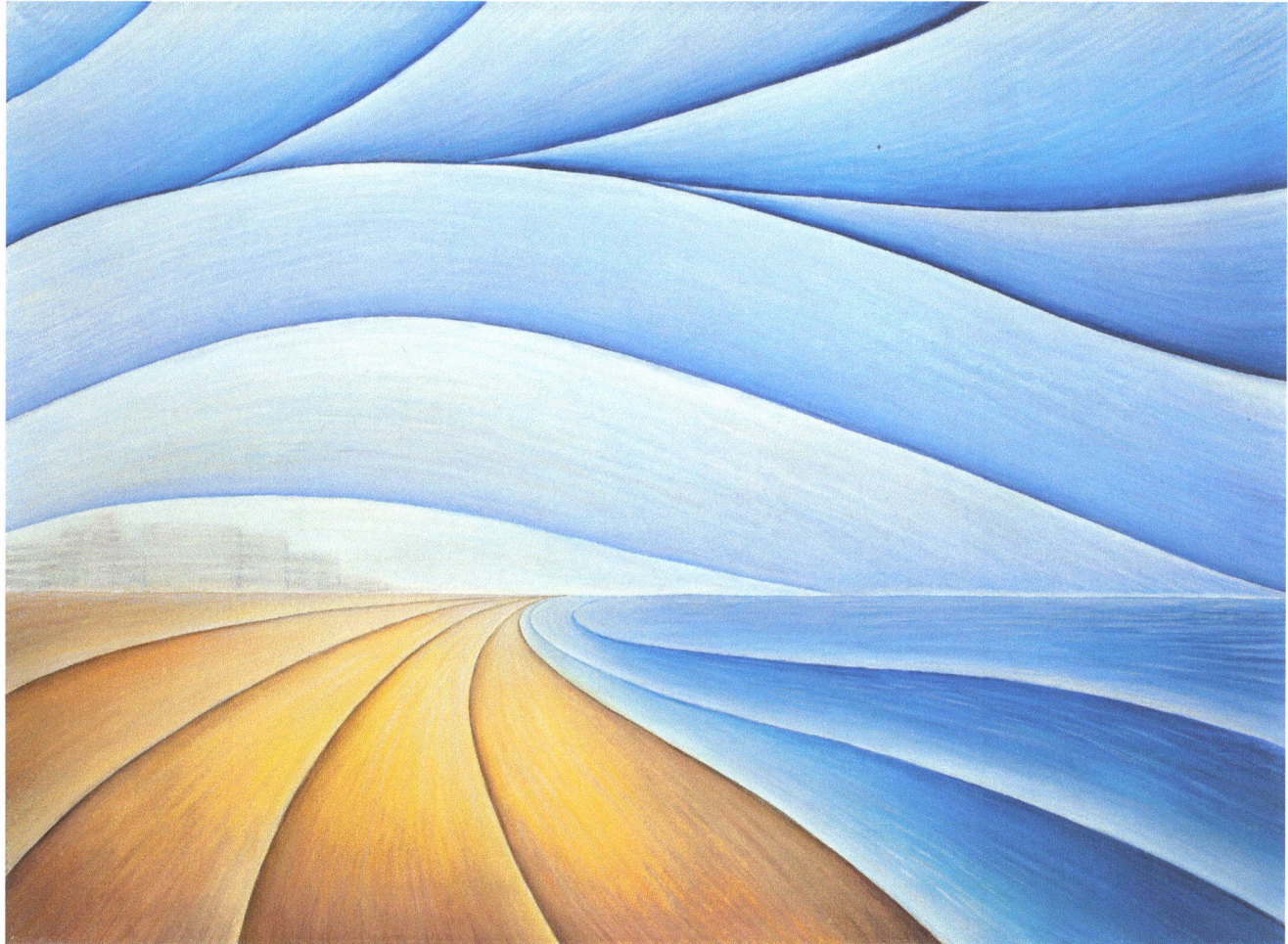

Technique | Painting
Price Range | USD 5000 - USD 10000
Sales Report | USD n/a (2018) - USD n/a (2019)
Active Years | 20 years

Emptiness. Solitude The Way.
Oil on canvas. 70x100x4 cm. 2019
USD 8000

Veronica Ibargüengoitia

メキシコ - アメリカ | Mexico - United States

メキシコシティ出身。2009年よりヒューストンとテキサスで暮らしている。密集した都市構造と巨大な建物に囲まれたこれらの都市から絵画の制作工程と芸術的センスを学んだ。Ibargüengoitia氏は、絵画作品に層状、急カーブ、隙間などで展開するための空間を残している。彼女は、鑑賞者が彼女の方法でその幾何学的形態世界に入っていくことを想像する。鑑賞者はその中にいるのか出てしまったかわからないまま、仕組まれた視点と静かな空間の中での謎解きを徐々に楽しみ始める。また、ヒューストン美術館によるフェローシッププログラムに参加しており、Houston Artadia Fellows of 2020を受賞した。

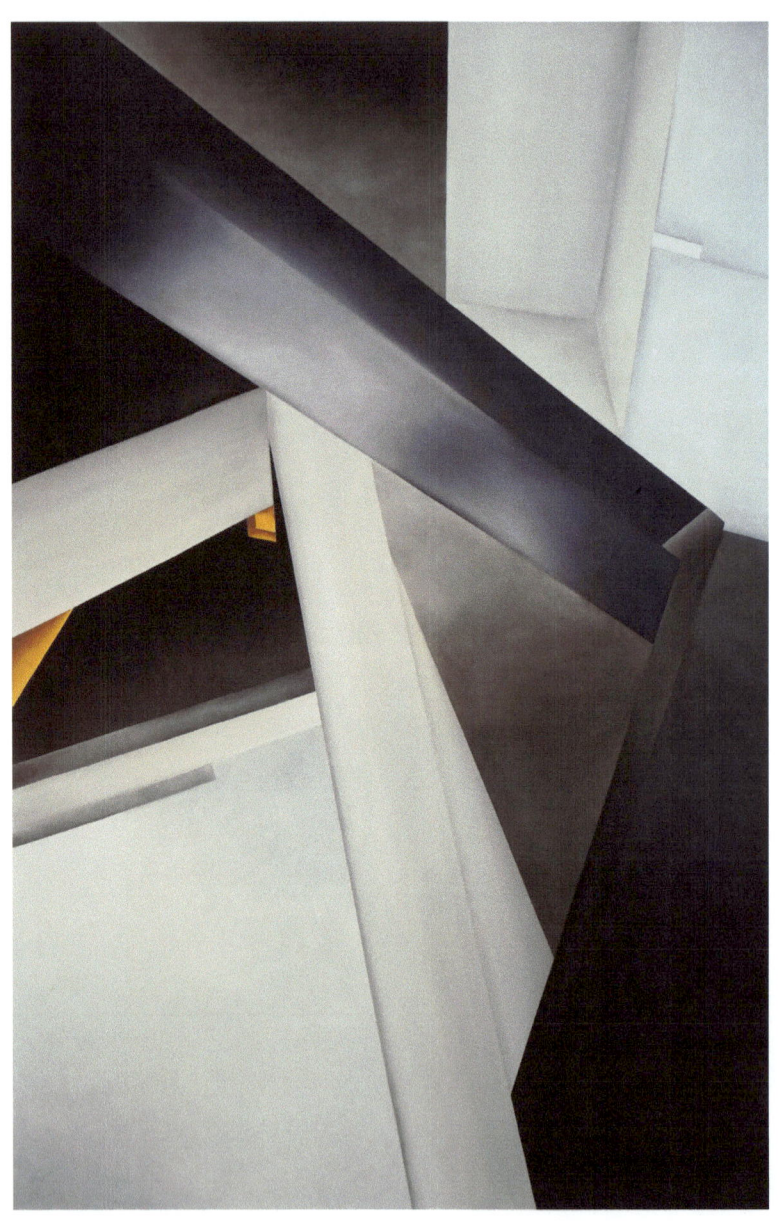

技術 | 絵画

価格帯 | USD 950 - USD 12000

販売レポート | USD n/a [2018年] - USD n/a [2019年]

有効な年数 | 15年

Montrose 5100

USD 4100

veronicaibarguengoitia.com

Veronica is originally from Mexico City, and since 2009, she has lived in Houston, Texas. Both these cities, with their dense urban fabric and large-scale architectural forms, have informed her painting process and artistic questions. Ibargüengoitia creates spaces within her paintings which will unfold in layers, sharp turns and empty places. She imagines the viewer thinking her way to enter inside her geometric forms. Step by step, the viewer will find pleasure in the conundrum behind the forced perspectives and quiet areas, not knowing if she is already in or out. Ibargüengoitia is part of the fellowship program Block XX from the Museum of Fine Arts Houston and awarded the Houston Artadia Fellows of 2020.

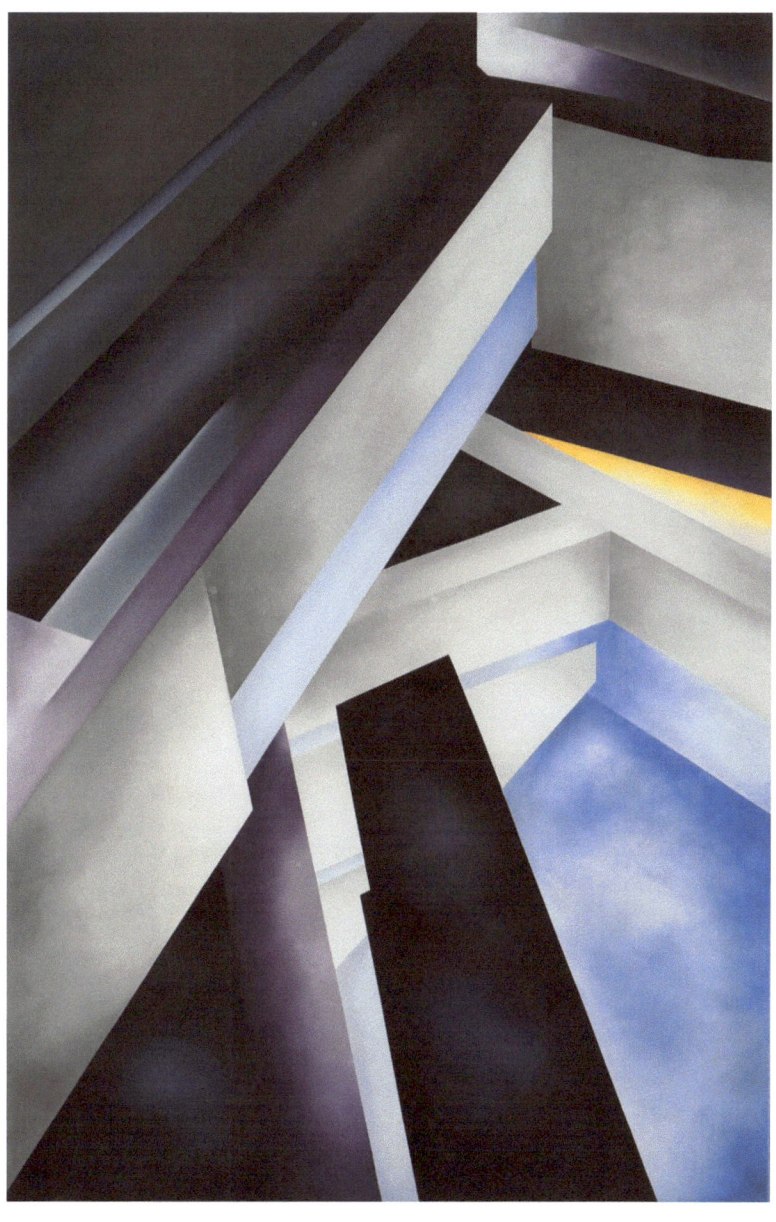

Technique | Painting
Price Range | USD 950 - USD 12000
Sales Report | USD n/a (2018) - USD n/a (2019)
Active Years | 15 years

Montrose 5101
USD 4100

Max Werner
アメリカ | United States

ベルギーゲント出身。ロンドンのByam Shaw School of ArtとThe Slade School UCLで美術を学ぶ。1997年までロンドンでエッチング(銅版画)の指導をおこない、その後アルゼンチンへ移住し、2003年まで過ごす。現在はアメリカを拠点に活動している。

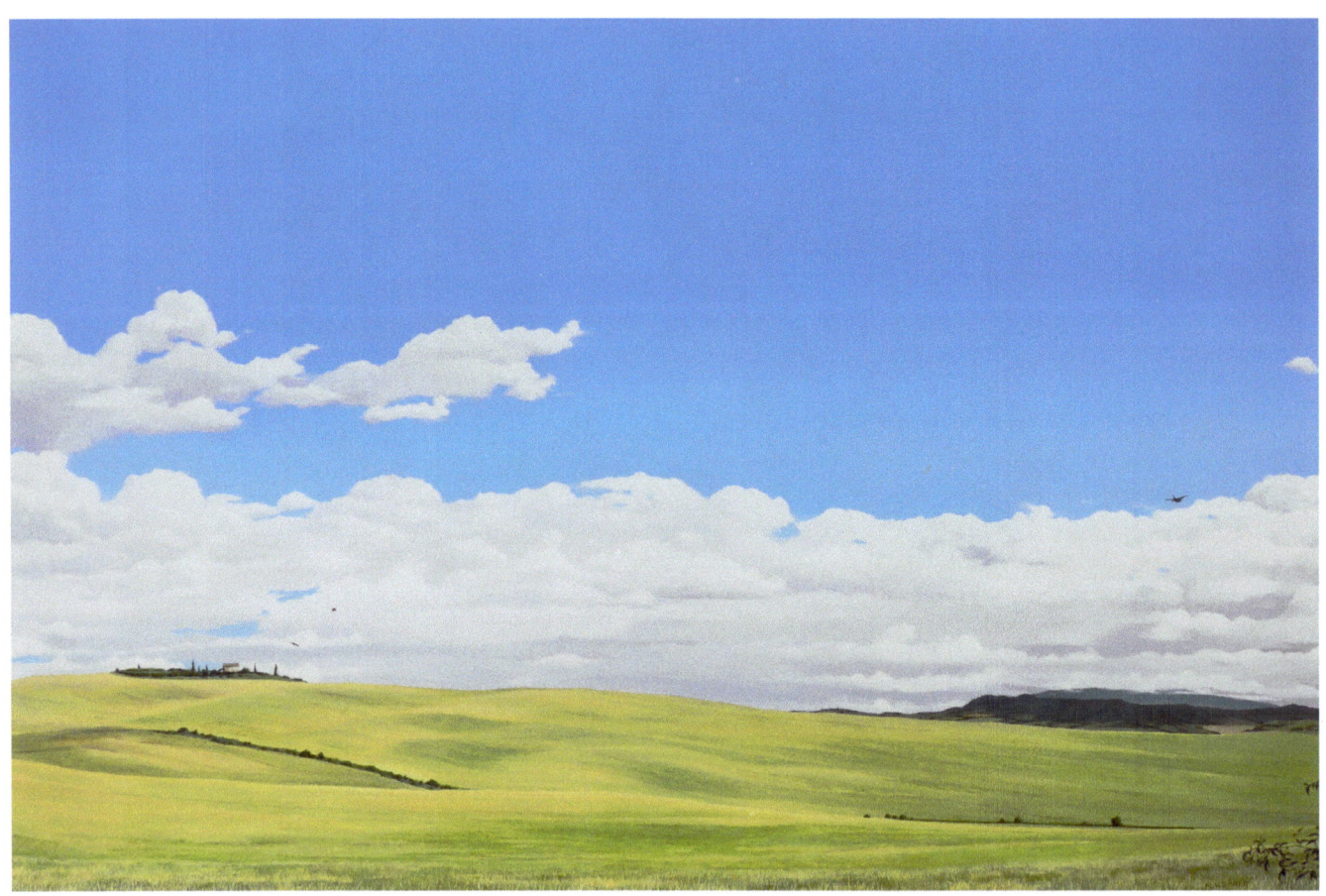

技術 | 絵画
価格帯 | USD 500 - USD 30000
販売レポート | USD n/a [2018年] - USD n/a [2019年]
有効な年数 | 35年

Birds In the Tuscan Sky

USD 12000

maxwernerart.com

Born in Ghent, Belgium. Studied Fine Art in London at the Byam Shaw School of Art and The Slade School UCL. Taught etching in London until 1997, then moved to Argentina until 2003. Currently lives and works in the USA.

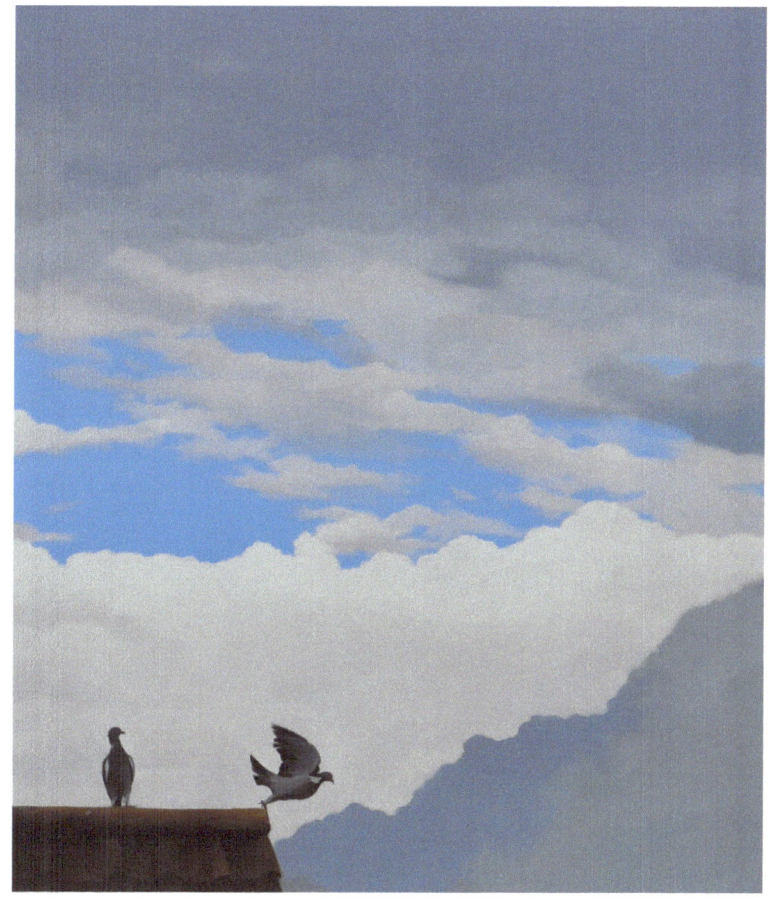

Technique | Painting
Price Range | USD 500 - USD 30000
Sales Report | USD n/a (2018) - USD n/a (2019)
Active Years | 35 years

Where Are You Going?
USD 3700

Gustavs Filipsons
ラトビア | Latvia

Gustavs氏にとって作品を作る唯一の目的と理由は、私たち自身の中にある未知のものと交流するためである。それは、本当の自分自身との繋がりを探すことであり、人が皆共通して持つものだとしている。また、新たな形やオリジナルな作品を生み出すことも目標にしている。

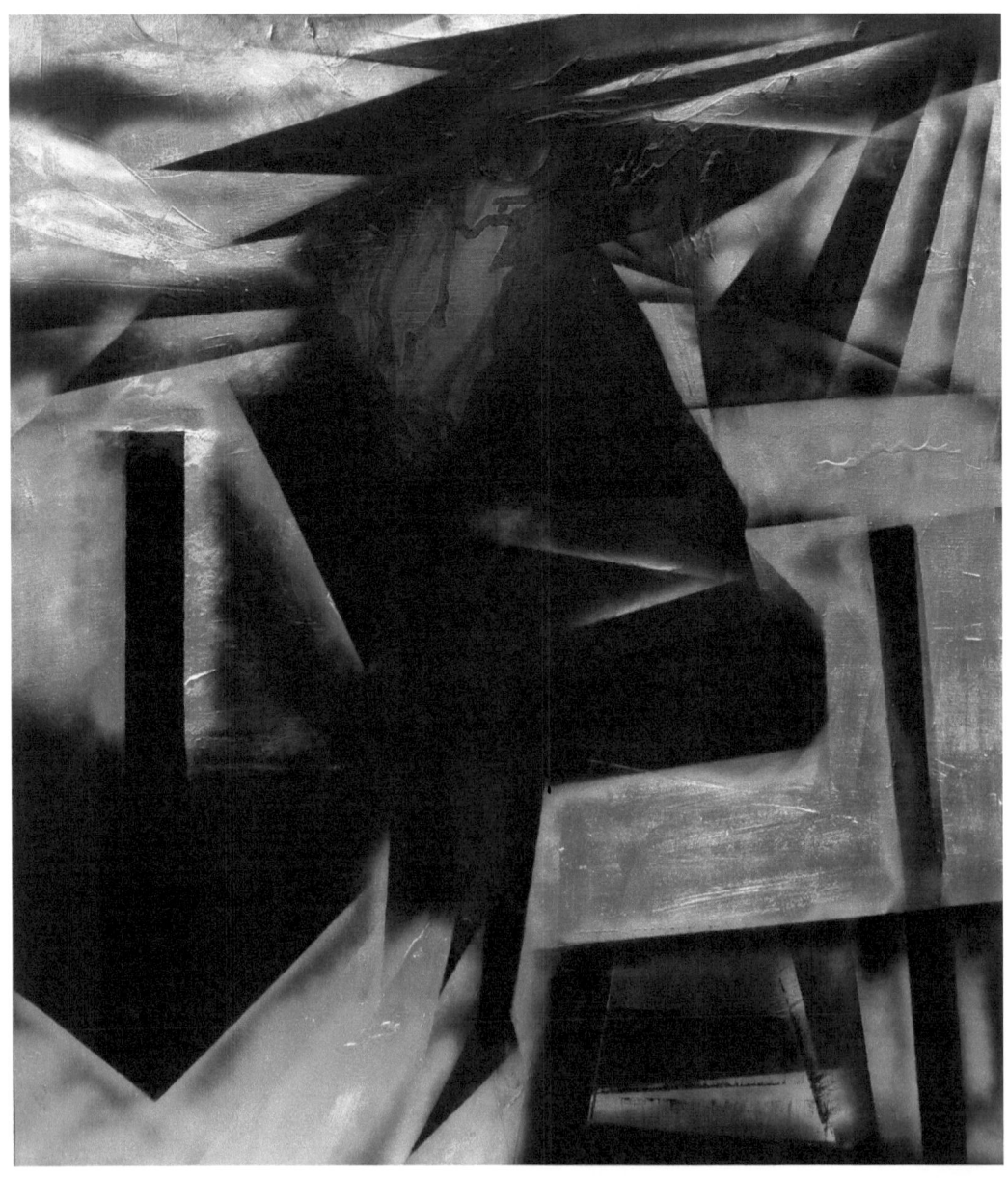

技術 | 絵画
価格帯 | USD 2500 - USD 8000
販売レポート | USD 4400 [2018年] - USD 3000 [2019年]
有効な年数 | 25年

At The Sea
Oil, acrylic, spray paint on canvas, 160x140 cm. 2016
USD 7000

saatchiart.com/account/profile/325613

The sole intention and purpose of my work is to communicate with the unknown in our subconscious mind. To find the connection with our true selves which I believe is something common we all possess. Another goal is to create artwork that would be some kind of new and if not new then original kind of work.

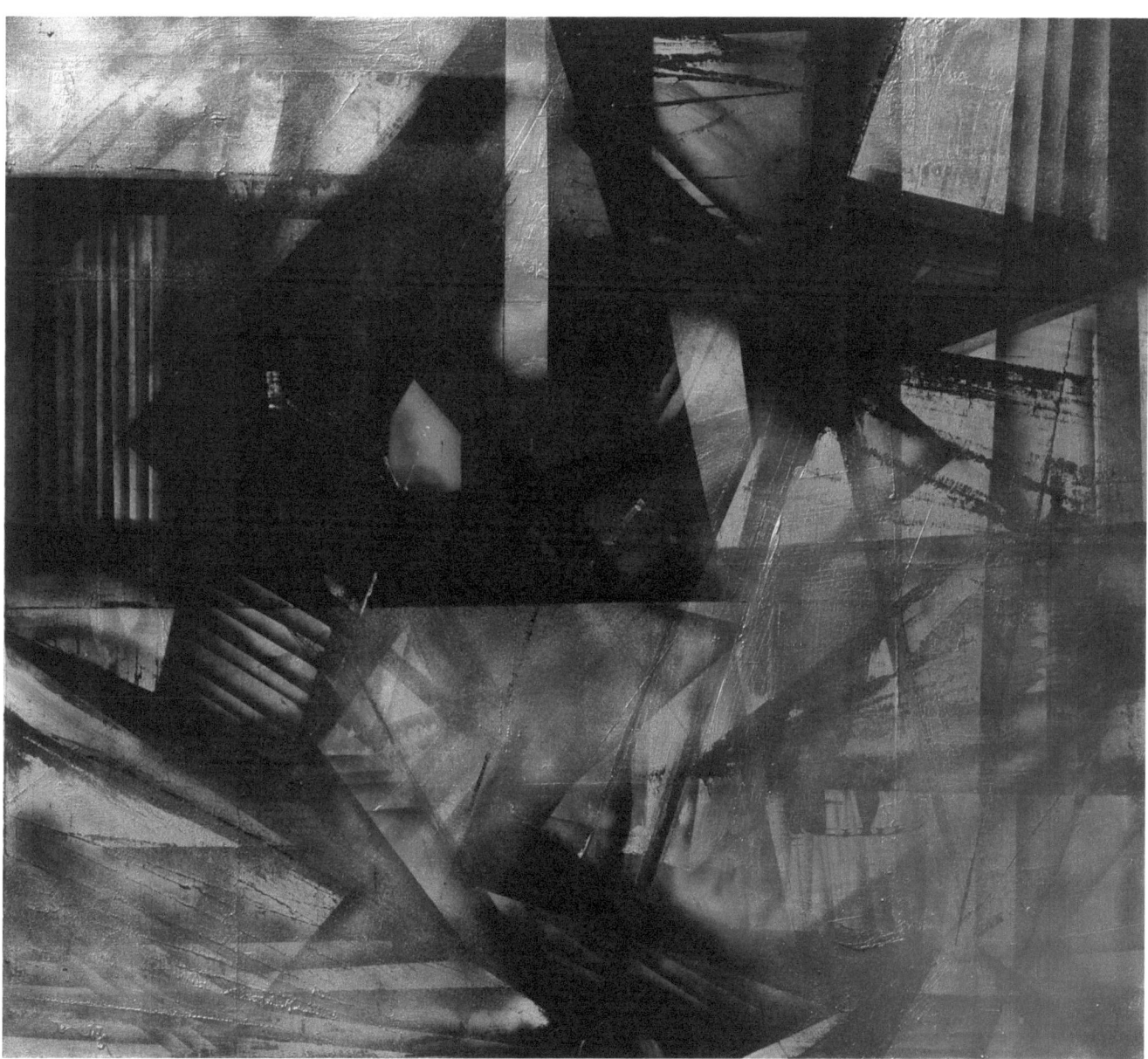

Technique | Painting
Price Range | USD 2500 - USD 8000
Sales Report | USD 4400 (2018) - USD 3000 (2019)
Active Years | 25 years

Skier
Oil, acrylic, spray paint on canvas, 140x160 cm. 2018
USD 5000

Paul Ygartua
カナダ | Canada

イギリス、チェシャー（リバプール）、ベビントン出身でカナダ、フランス、スペイン、イギリスを拠点にしているPaul Ygartua氏は、画家、そして壁画家である。単独で世界最大の壁画や、カナダやアメリカで最大の公共スペース向けの壁画を多く手がける。工業デザイナーであり、金銀細工師の資格も持つ。Liverpool Art College in Industrial DesignとFinal City & Guilds of London Institute in Gold and Silversmithingの学士号を取得。Liverpool School of Artを卒業後すぐに画家になり、そこから絵画は彼の全てとなった。現在美術、写実主義、表現主義、抽象表現主義、抽象概念、超現実主義、超現実抽象主義などいくつものスタイルを合わせ持っている。

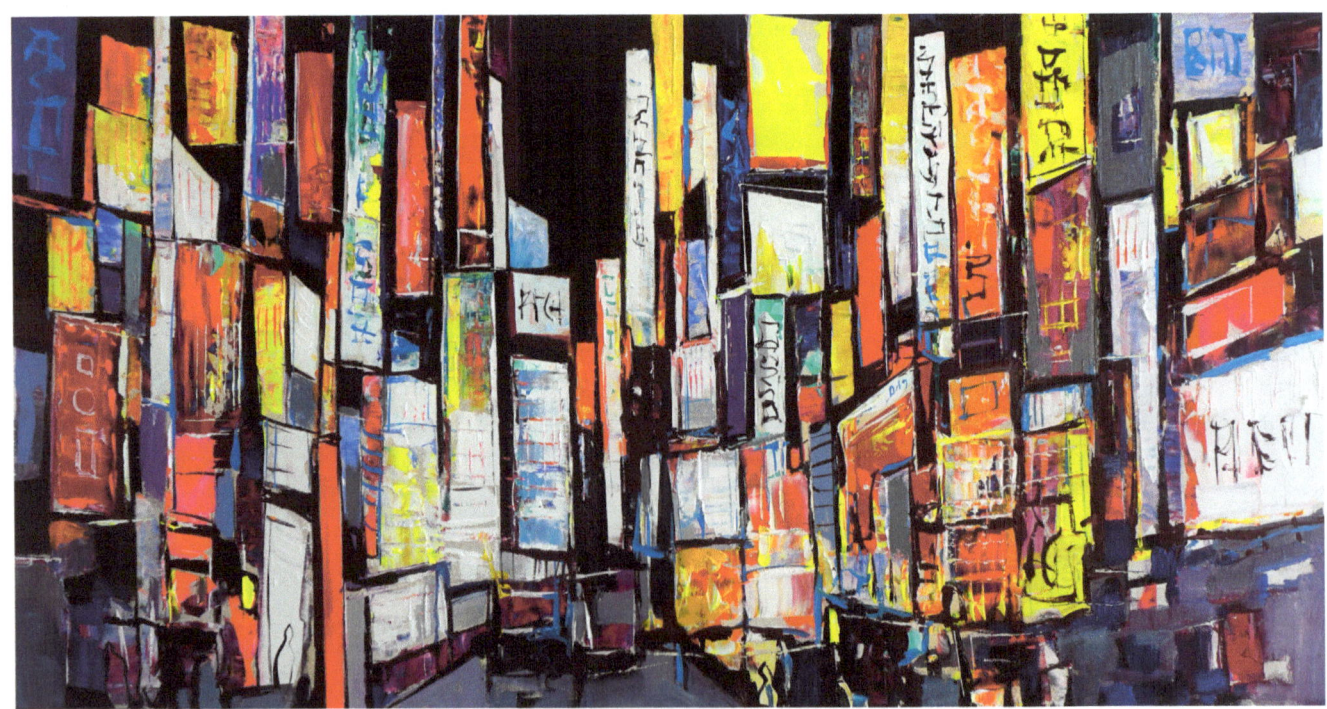

技術 | 絵画
価格帯 | USD 500 - USD 60000
販売レポート | USD 100000 [2018年] - USD 125000 [2019年]
有効な年数 | 50年

Tokyo City of Lights
160 x 780 cm. Acrylic on canvas
USD 5000

thisisarttokyo.com

Paul Ygartua is a painter and muralist with bases in Canada, France, Spain and England. He has single handedly painted the World's largest mural and some of the largest public space murals in Canada and the United States. He was born in 1945 in Bebington, Cheshire (Liverpool) England. He is an Industrial Designer and qualified Gold and Silversmith. He received his degree from the Faculty of Arts, Liverpool Art College in Industrial Design and Final City & Guilds of London Institute in Gold and Silversmithing. Paul turned to painting immediately after graduating from the Liverpool School of Art in Great Britain and from then on painting became his whole existence. His styles include Contemporary, Realism, Expressionism, Abstract Expressionism, Conceptual Abstraction, Surrealism and Abstract Surrealism.

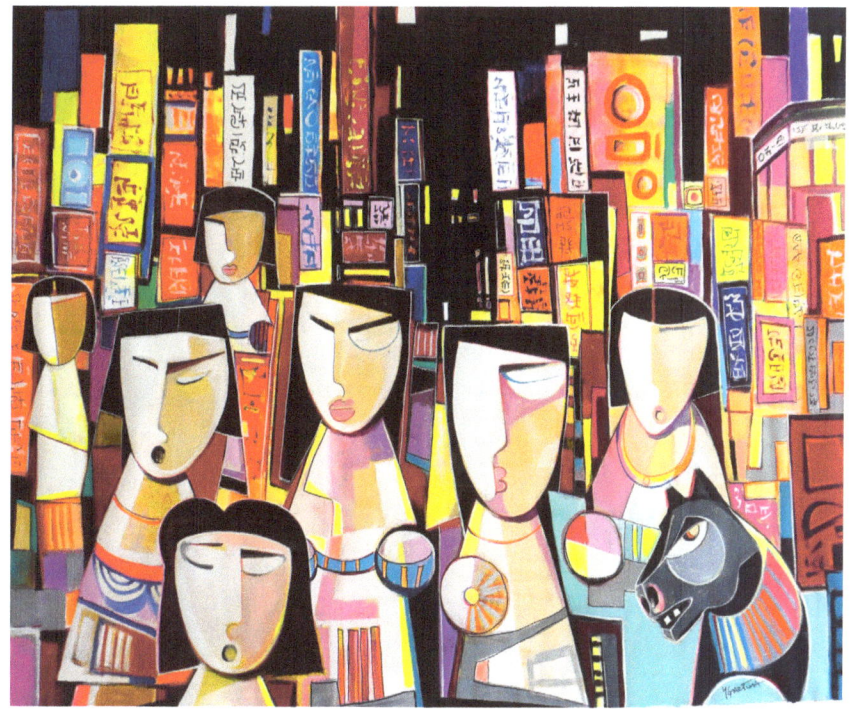

Technique | Painting
Price Range | USD 500 - USD 60000
Sales Report | USD 100000 (2018) - USD 125000 (2019)
Active Years | 50 years

Shibuya Girls
152 x 121 cm. Acrylic on canvas
USD 6000

Pia Kintrup

ドイツ | Germany

Pia　Kintrup氏の公開シリーズ作品のテーマは、パラレルワールドを作るために設計された場所の境界の影響と最終責任についてである。この風景は人工的な設定と構造で、私たちの日常生活に対立を生んでいる。特定の領域については、過剰な演出、真実や自然の構造の模倣であふれている。シリーズ全体は小説のような構造になっており、読者が様々な場所や地球について知らなかったことを学べる。イメージは創造力の隠喩的な場所を作る網の要点になる。重要なのは、写実的なミクストメディアを確立し、支配、演出、監視、価値などの普遍的なテーマに対して新しい視点を持てるようにすることであると考えている。

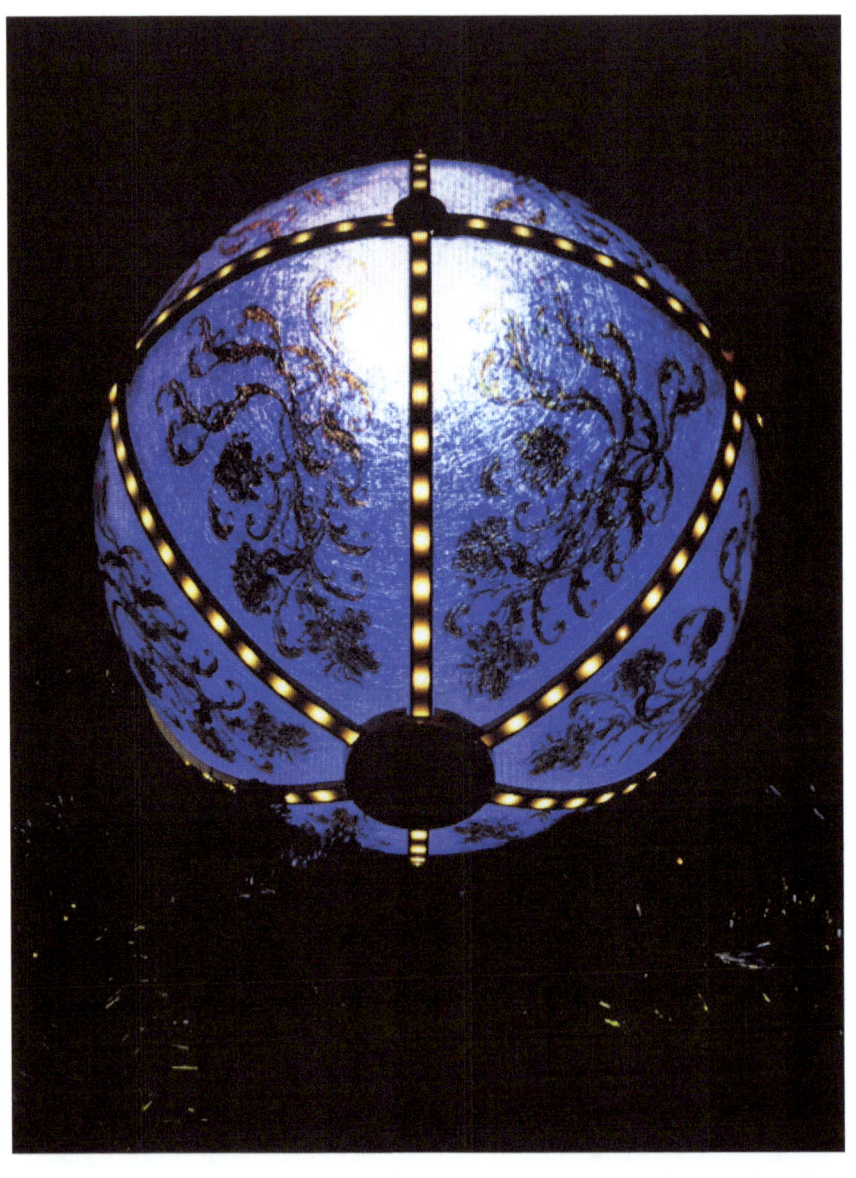

技術 | 混合メディア - 写真

価格帯 | USD 900 - USD 6700

販売レポート | USD 7500 [2018年] - USD 10000 [2019年]

有効な年数 | 2年

the loop, as part of the series: the nonexistent areas are of particular interest,
Print on aluminum lightbox, 60 cm x 45 cm x 15 cm, 2019, Edition 2+1AP

USD 2900

piakintrup.com

The theme of my open series is the impact of borders and ultimate control in places that are designed to create a parallel world. These sceneries are artificial settings and constructions which create conflicts within our everyday life. The particular areas are excesses examples for staging, an imitation of the reality, and natural structures. The whole series is build-up like the story in a novel, where the reader receives more and more information about a place or a planet, the reader didn't know before. The images are points of a net, which create a metaphorical place of imagination. The issue is to create a photographic, mixed media installation that brings a new perspective about universal themes such as control, staging, surveillance, and value.

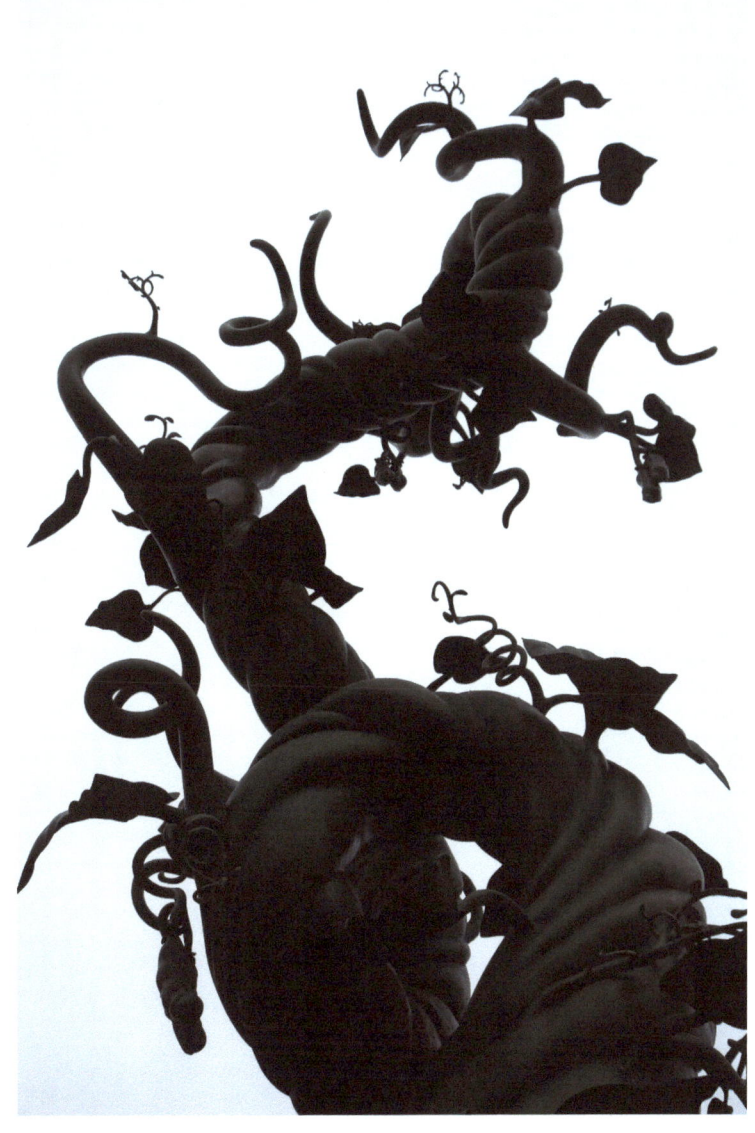

Technique | Mixed Media - Photography
Price Range | USD 900 - USD 6700
Sales Report | USD 7500 (2018) - USD 10000 (2019)
Active Years | 2 years

the spiral, as part of the series: the nonexistent areas are of particular interest, C-Print mounted and framed in a black shadow frame, 100 cm x 66 cm, 2019, Edition 2+1AP

USD 3333

Ursa Schoepper
ドイツ | Germany

Ursa Schoepper氏は教職免許に続き自然科学の国家資格を取得している。また、家族のために家事をおこないながらさらなる高等教育を開始した。Dr. Eckart Pankoke 教授、Dr. Ulrich Krempel 教授さらにはDr. Michael Bockemühl 教授のもとで視覚芸術やニューメディアを学び、文化管理の学士号を取得し、現在は、文化マネージャーとして文化教育システムの分野で様々なプロジェクトの考案と実施を担当している。2001年には、ソーシャルネットワークの考案と実施についての「Museum of Absent Images」でノルトライン・ヴェストファーレン州のメディア賞を受賞。2003年より実験的アート写真分野のアーティストとして活動している。

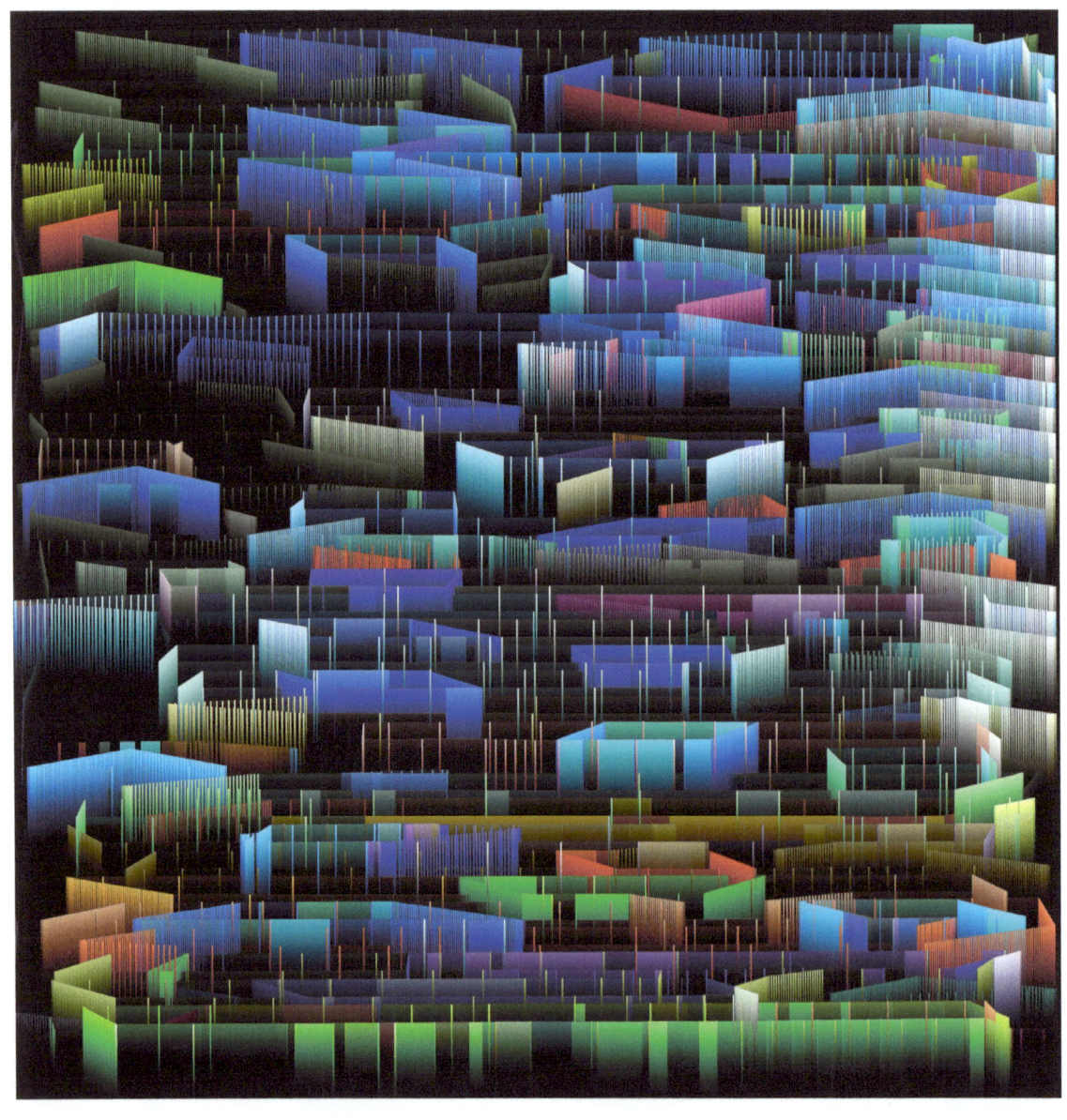

技術 | 写真
価格帯 | USD 1500 - USD 8000
販売レポート | USD n/a [2018年] - USD n/a [2019年]
有効な年数 | 15年

Light Color Room
100 cm x 100 cm
USD 7000

virtuelledenkraeume.de

Ursa Schoepper has a state examination in natural sciences, followed by teaching. In addition to a simultaneous, accompanying family work she was beginning of a new higher education. She has a University degree, studies in cultural management, focused on visual arts, new media, at Prof. Dr. Eckart Pankoke, Prof. Dr. Ulrich Krempel and Prof Dr. Michael Bockemühl. Ursa Schoepper was responsible for the conception and realization of various projects in the field of cultural education systems as a cultural manager. 2001 she received the Media Prize North Rhine-Westphalia for the Museum of Absent Images, a conception and realization as a social network. Since 2003 she is working as an artist in the field of experimental fine art photography.

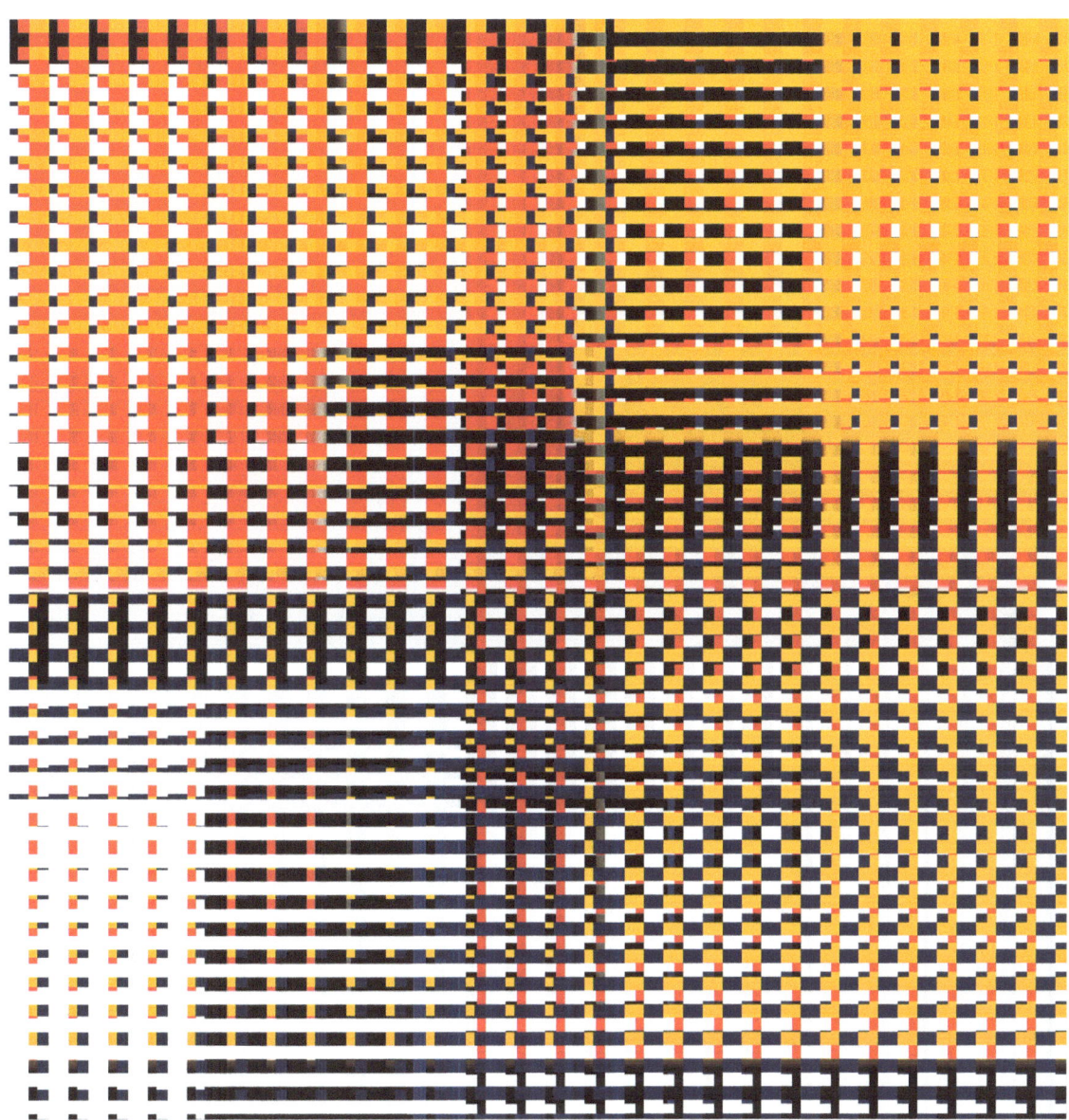

Technique | Photography
Price Range | USD 1500 - USD 8000
Sales Report | USD n/a (2018) - USD n/a (2019)
Active Years | 15 years

Referenz Bauhaus
100 cm x 100 cm
USD 7000

Christo Anto Francis
カナダ | Canada

カナダ出身のイラスト作家Christo Anto Francis氏は、オークビルのSheridan Collegeを卒業後、人々の生活の中の様々なシーンを描写する作品を制作。自身の作品を「コンテンポラリー・リアリズム（現代の写実主義）」と表現し、そこにシンプルさ、優雅さ、奇抜さ、茶目っ気を盛り込んでいる。William Adolphe Bouguereau、John Singer SargentやJon Whitcombなどに影響を受け、様々な場面での人間らしさを描写。それぞれの肖像画はその人物の魅力を余すところなく引き出している。作品は遊び心たっぷりで、生意気で、無邪気な人々の様々な感情を表現している。一貫性のある技法を使用しながらも、伝統的な油絵とデジタルアートをうまく切り替えながら自由にその質感を組み合わせている。

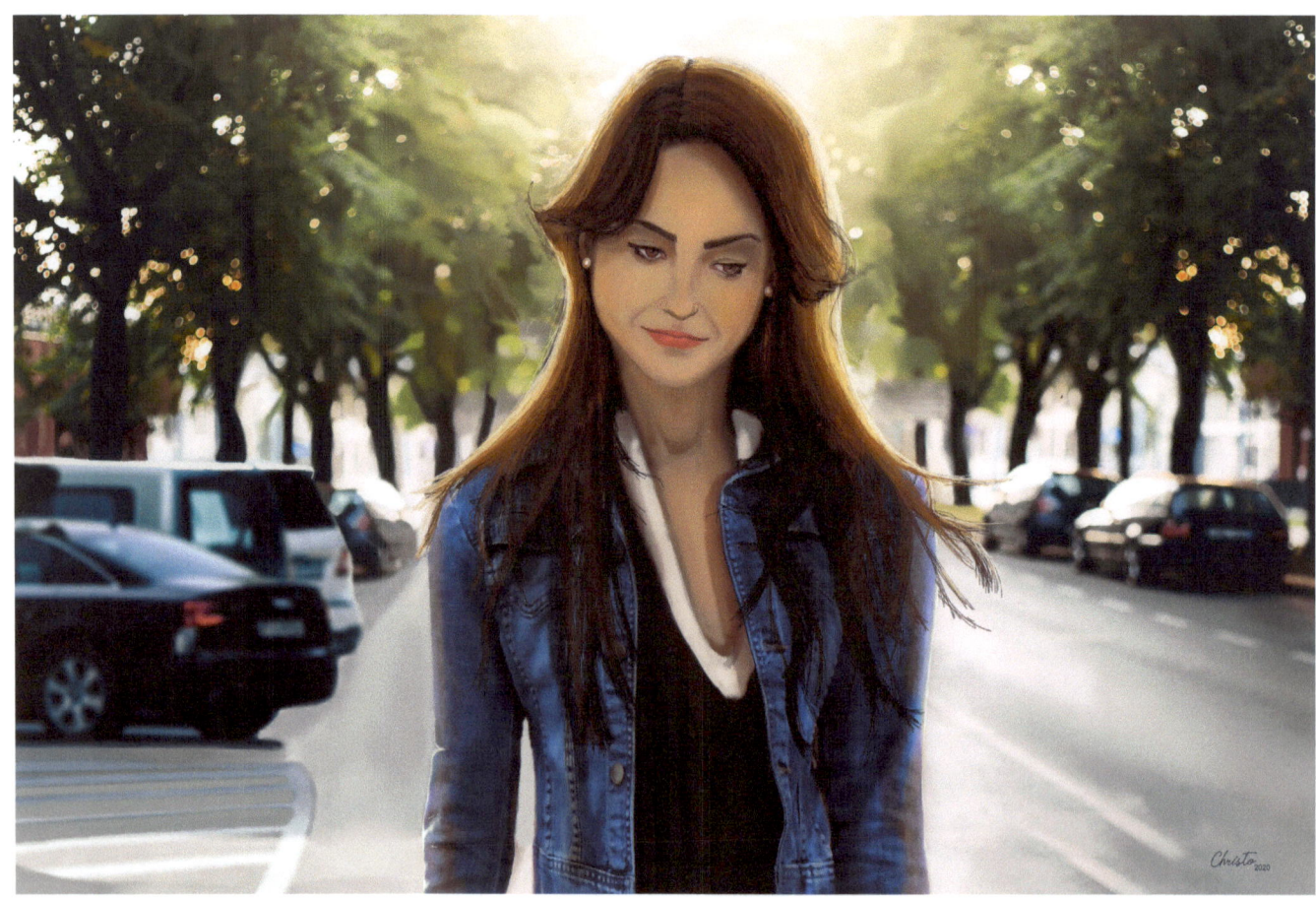

技術	絵画 - 図 - 混合メディア
価格帯	USD 500 - USD 7000
販売レポート	USD 10000 [2018年] - USD 27000 [2019年]
有効な年数	2年

City Life
Digital Painting on metal, 30 x 46 in, 2019
USD 3300

christoantofrancis.com

Educated at Sheridan College in Oakville, Christo Anto Francis, an illustrative painter hailing from Canada captures people at various moments of their lives. Describing his works as 'contemporary realism', he investigates the portraits of showing simplicity, elegance, eccentricity and naughtiness in them. Inspired by the likes of William Adolphe Bouguereau, John Singer Sargent to Jon Whitcomb, he looks at depicting humanity at its various moments. Each portrait draws attention to the person in it and in a direct and up-close way. The portraits are playful, cheeky, innocent and many more; a cornucopia of human emotions which are explored by him. Switching from traditional oil painting to digital and vice versa gives him the freedom to mix and match different textures while keeping the methodology consistent.

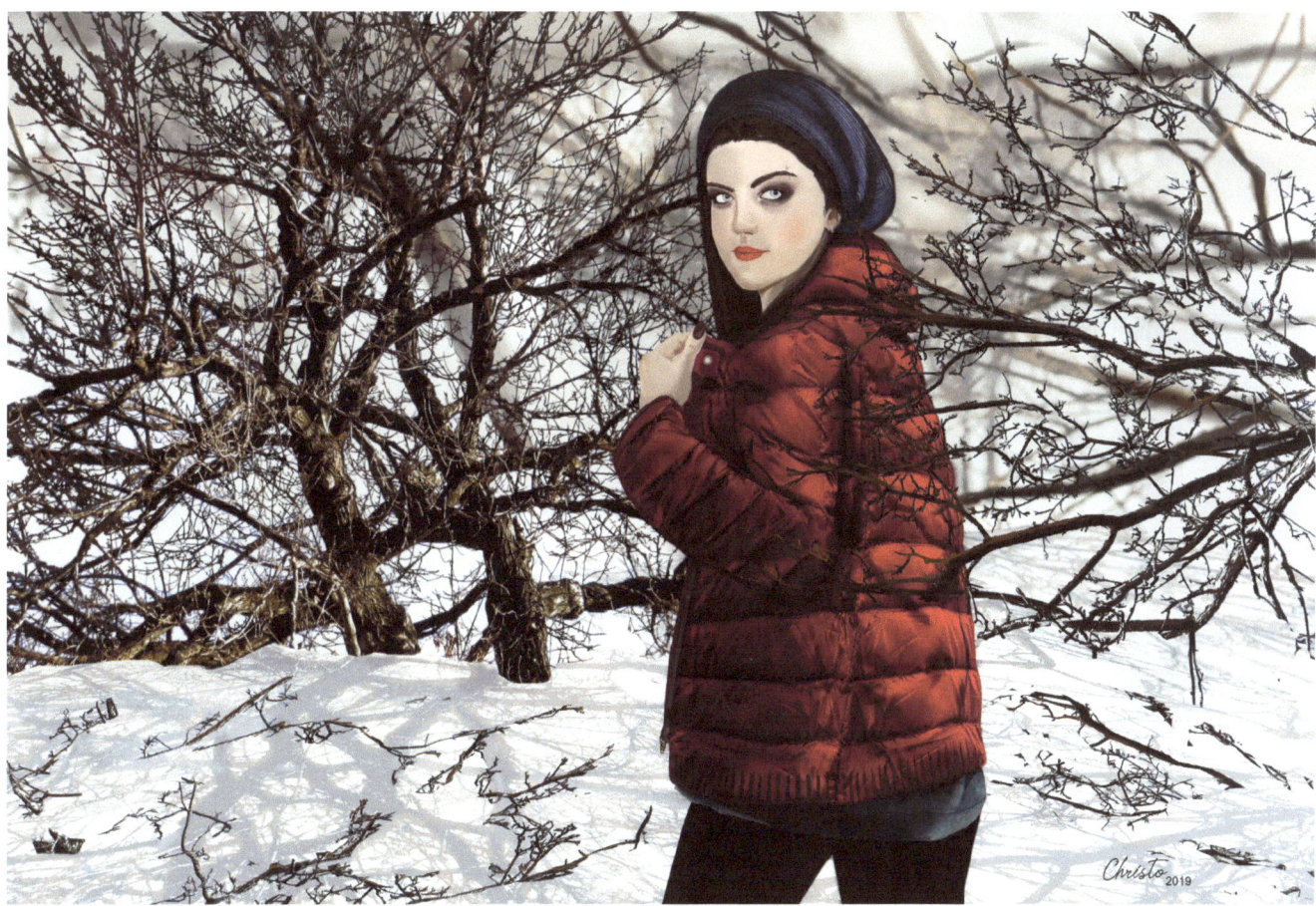

Technique | Painting - Illustration - Mixed Media
Price Range | USD 500 - USD 7000
Sales Report | USD 10000 (2018) - USD 27000 (2019)
Active Years | 2 years

Wandering in Snow
Digital Painting on metal, 30 x 46 in, 2019
USD 3300

Vardan Ghumashyan
アルメニア | Armenia

「人間の最高の幸福とは神が存在することである」神の存在は、人類による最も創作的な活動であり、我々の存在(生命)の基本原理である。幸せな人生を送る誰にとっても時は始まり、また終わる。この圧倒的な美しさが、自然界の神秘の解明につながる。しかし、美しさだけではまだアートとは言えず、人間の存在(生命)は自然との絶対的な調和によってのみ実現するのである。その場合にのみ、自然は神の遺言である愛の中で生まれ変わるという生命の神秘を明かすのである。

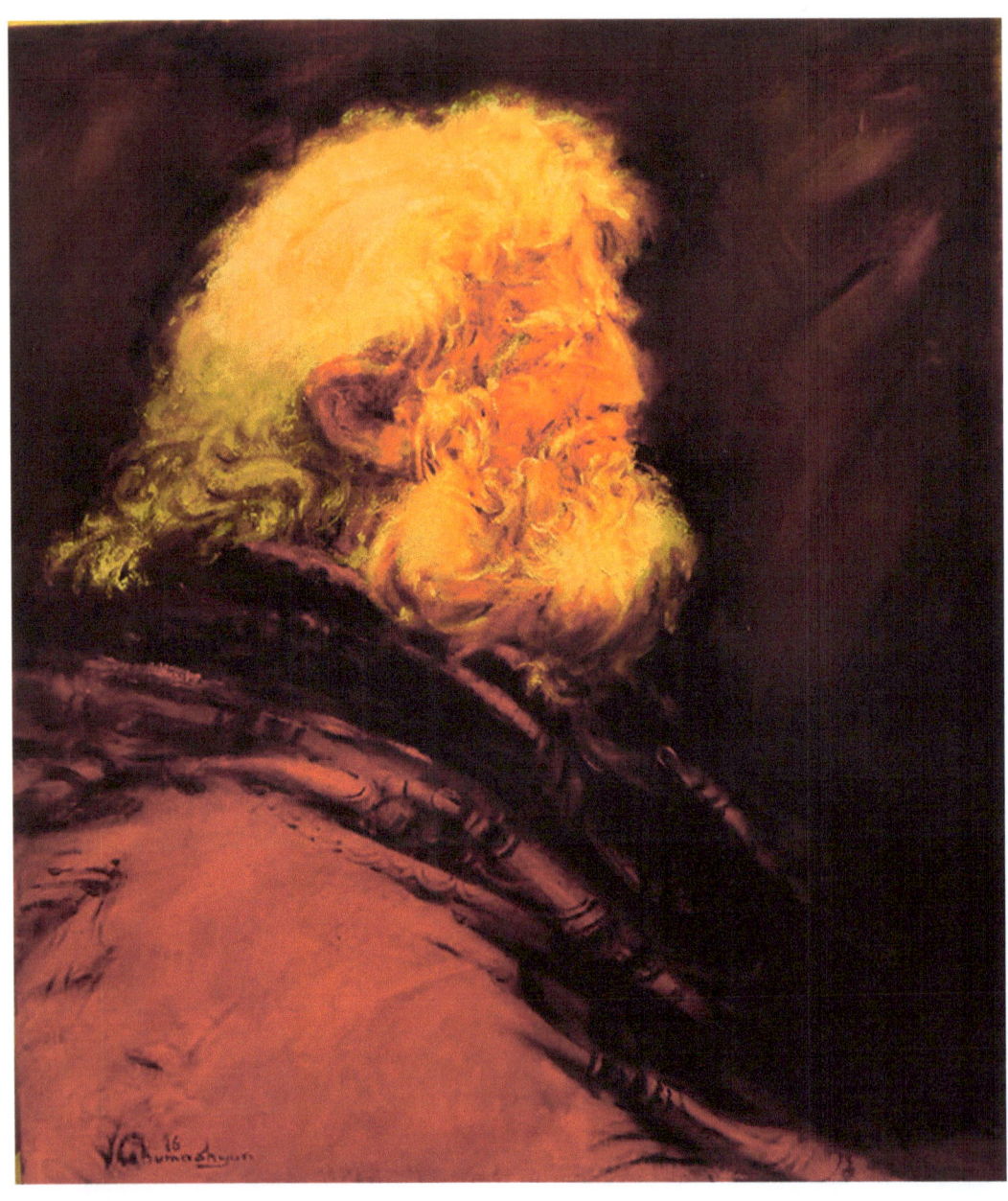

技術 | 絵画
価格帯 | USD 5000 - USD 15000
販売レポート | USD n/a [2018年] - USD n/a [2019年]
有効な年数 | 27年

Red Cardinal the soaring Eagle
2016. Oil canvas. 68 x 61 cm
USD 10000

vardanghumashyanpaintings.com

"THE SUPREME HAPPINESS OF HUMAN - THE PRESENCE OF GOD". The presence of God means the highest creative activity of man, the basic principle of which is Being (Life). This time ends and begins with everybody them who will awarded this bliss-Life. This incredibly beautiful us leads to the disclosure of the secrets of nature. But beauty is not yet the art and creation of man in Being (Life) is realized only in absolute harmony with nature. Only in this case, nature reveals its life secrets of rebirth in Love which is God's testament.

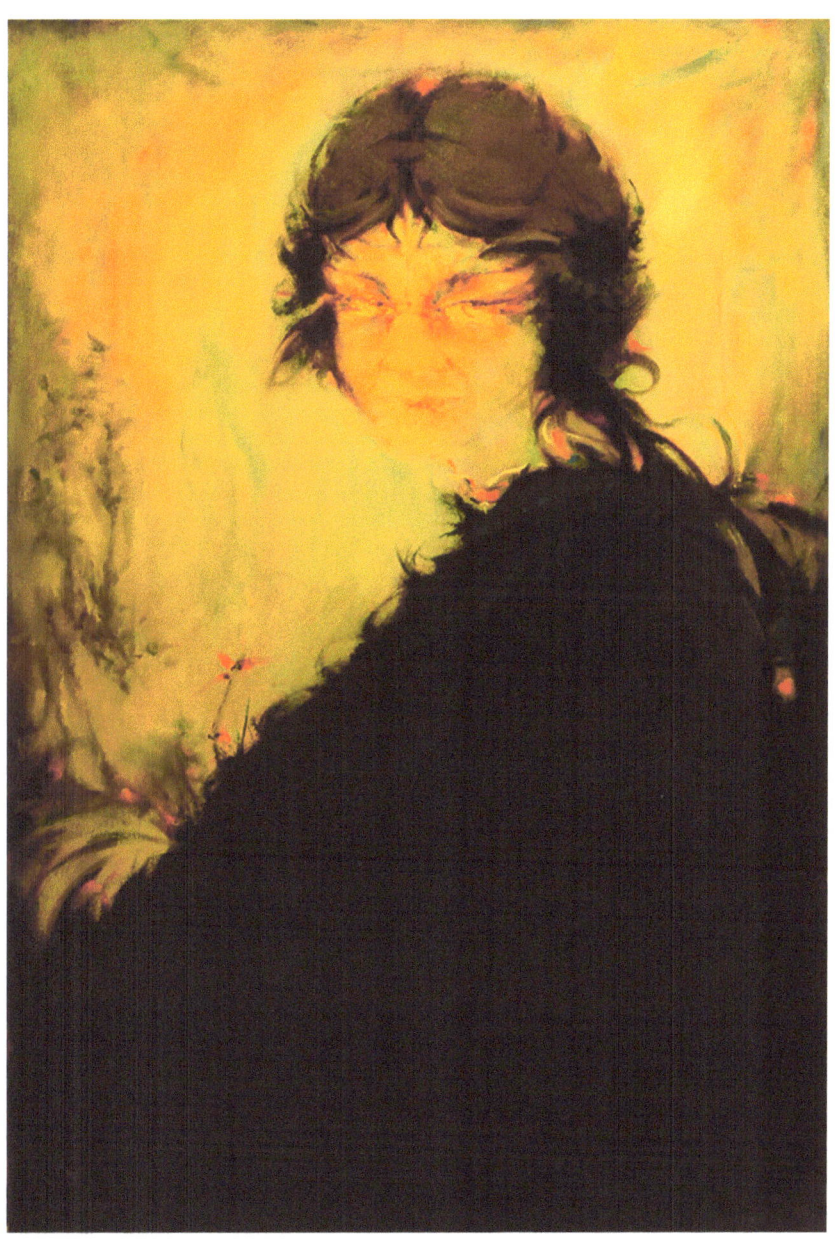

Technique | Painting
Price Range | USD 5000 - USD 15000
Sales Report | USD n/a (2018) - USD n/a (2019)
Active Years | 27 years

Wild Nature
2017. Oil linen. 100 x 70 cm
USD 10000

Belle Roth
アメリカ | United States

Belle Roth氏は、色彩、光、建築的な要素を通して人と人との繋がりを表現している。作品は抽象画で、分解されたフォームをきらめく金色、中間色、鮮やかなアクセントカラーを使った線と形でハイライトしていく。テネシー州メンフィスにある彼女のスタジオでの制作工程や技法は、20世紀の抽象表現主義様式と、ルーツであるフィリピン、旅行、そして多様な文化との交流などからの影響がふんだん取り入れられたものとなっている。貴金属の色である金色の構造を変化させ、黒と対比させる作品は、彼女が経験した階級格差の記憶を象徴している。同時に、彼女の作品は希望に満ちた社会の変容への願いがあふれており、アースカラーを基調としたパレットからは採掘された建築材や家族の団欒を連想させる。

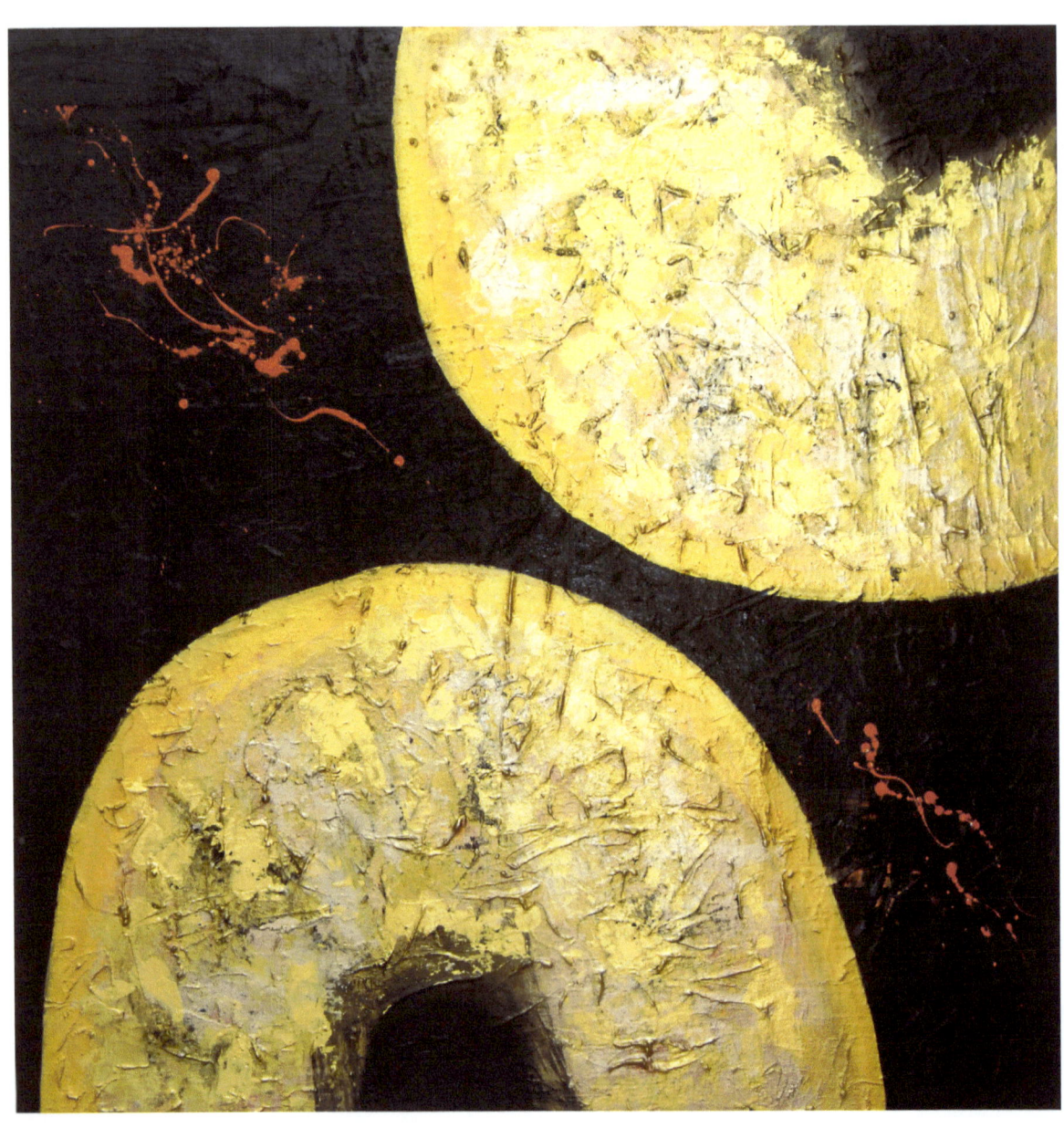

技術 | 絵画
価格帯 | USD 3000 - USD 10000
販売レポート | USD n/a [2018年] - USD 12000 [2019年]
有効な年数 | 1年

Building Paris, Day 1
USD 7000

bellerothstudios.com

Belle Roth explores human interconnection through her use of color, light, and architectural influences. Roth's compositions are rooted in abstraction; deconstructed forms are unearthed and highlighted by both line and shape that coincide with shimmering gold, neutral color fields, and vibrant accent hues. In Roth's Memphis, Tennessee studio, process and media are fortified by 20th-century abstract expressionist vernacular, and impressions from her Philippines upbringing, travels, and interactions with diverse cultures. Roth varies structures of golden noble metals and contrasting black that symbolize memories of the class divide she witnessed. Simultaneously, her work glistens with hopeful societal transformation. Her earth-toned color palette is reminiscent of sources from which building materials are mined and on which home and hearth stand.

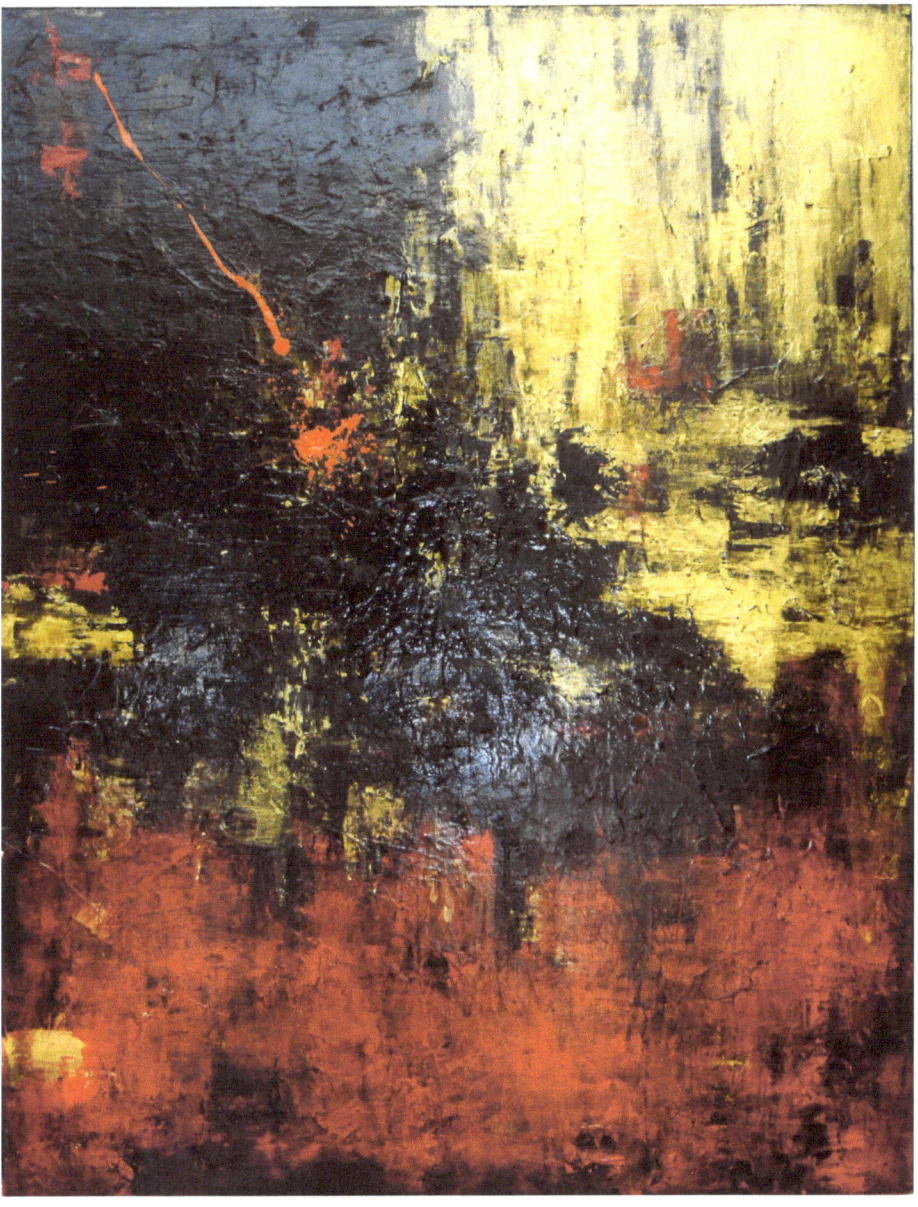

Technique | Painting

Price Range | USD 3000 - USD 10000

Sales Report | USD n/a (2018) - USD 12000 (2019)

Active Years | 1 year

Building Manila, Day 8

USD 7000

Amarnath Viswanath

ドイツ | Germany

絶妙な色の組み合わせによって自然景観への忘れがたい印象を与えることができる才能は画家から鑑賞者への贈りものである。風景はいたるところにあふれているが、絵画は鑑賞者に独自の想像力と見解を与えることができる。自然が見せてくれた忘れられない記憶を再現するために、ほとんどの作品は青を基調に明るい色と組み合わせている。

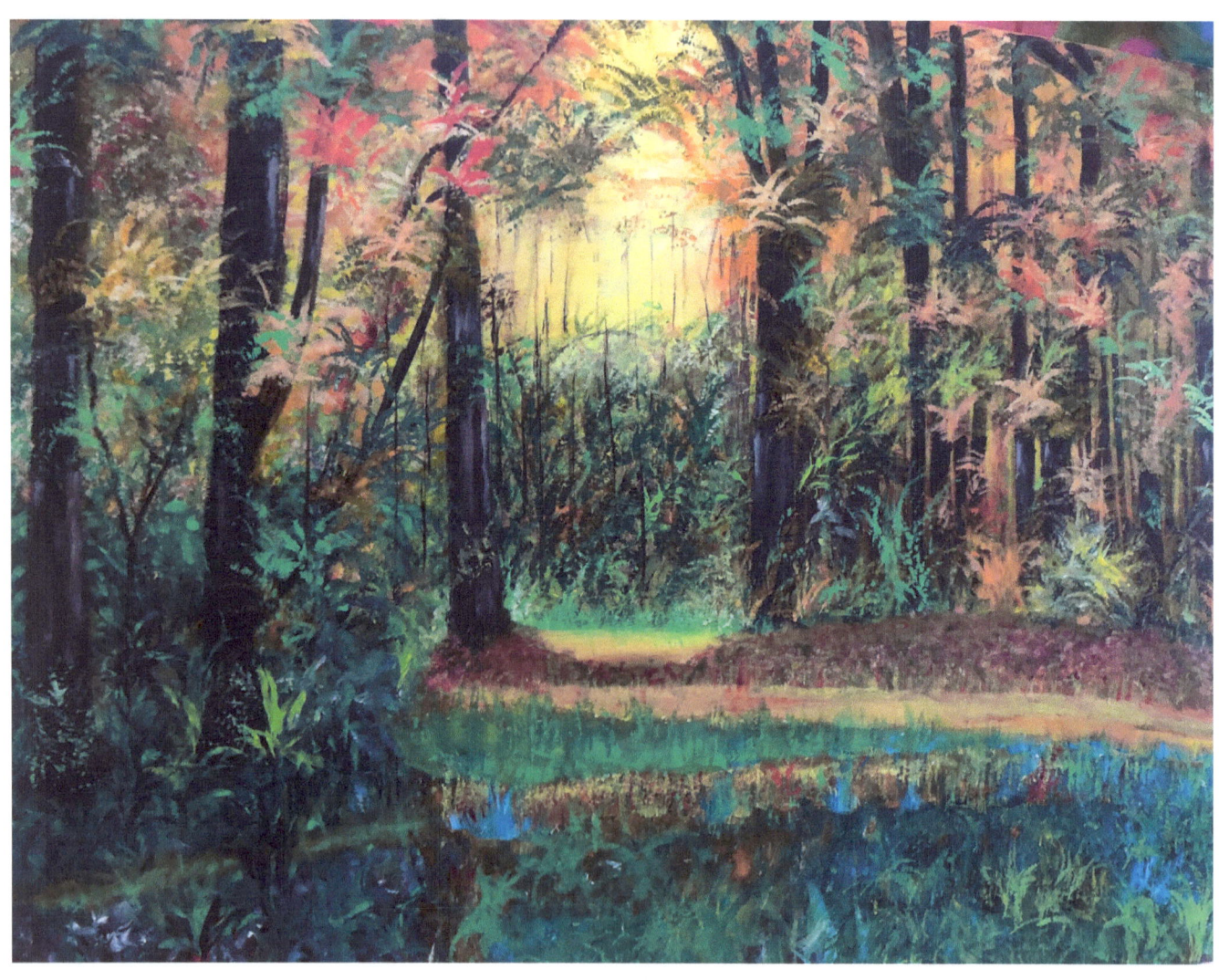

技術 | 絵画
価格帯 | USD n/a - USD n/a
販売レポート | USD n/a [2018年] - USD n/a [2019年]
有効な年数 | - 年

Golden Meadows

Price Upon Request

viswanath.de

The ability to create an unforgettable impression of a natural landscape by experimenting with color mix, is a present a painter can give to the viewers. Although all landscapes are there, the paintings promote viewers to develop their own imagination and thoughts . Most of my paintings are blue colored acrylic which is compensated with bright color mixes and the aim is to bring back some unforgettable memories presented by the nature.

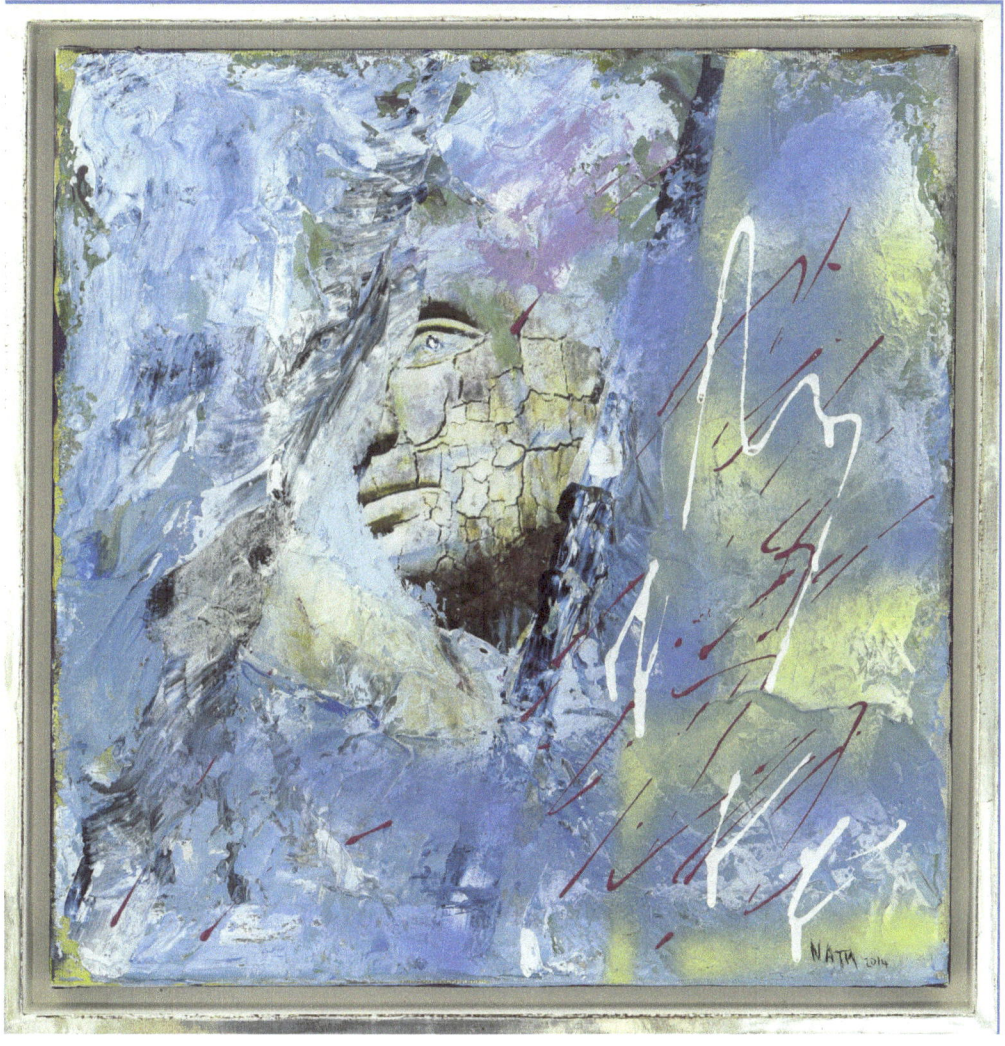

Technique | Painting
Price Range | USD n/a - USD n/a
Sales Report | USD n/a (2018) - USD n/a (2019)
Active Years | - year

Moses
Price Upon Request

Mira Satryan
アメリカ | United States

自身の絵画は感情の周りにある程度ずっと渦巻いているメッセージである。それは魅惑的で、美を感じ取り体験する能力であり、最も親密な経験や感情を合わせたものであり、自然や、他者との相対関係への強い興味などである。作品の中では、日々の生活の中でのつかの間のできごとから生じる懸念とリスクを表現している。絵画は表現や情緒性を伝える領域であり、それは自身の作品の共通のテーマでもある「無常さへの自覚」にも通じる。時にその作品は異なる彩度の色合いの対比した色を強調したドラマチックな形を成している。私たちが存在する仕組みはとてもはかないものであるとしている。

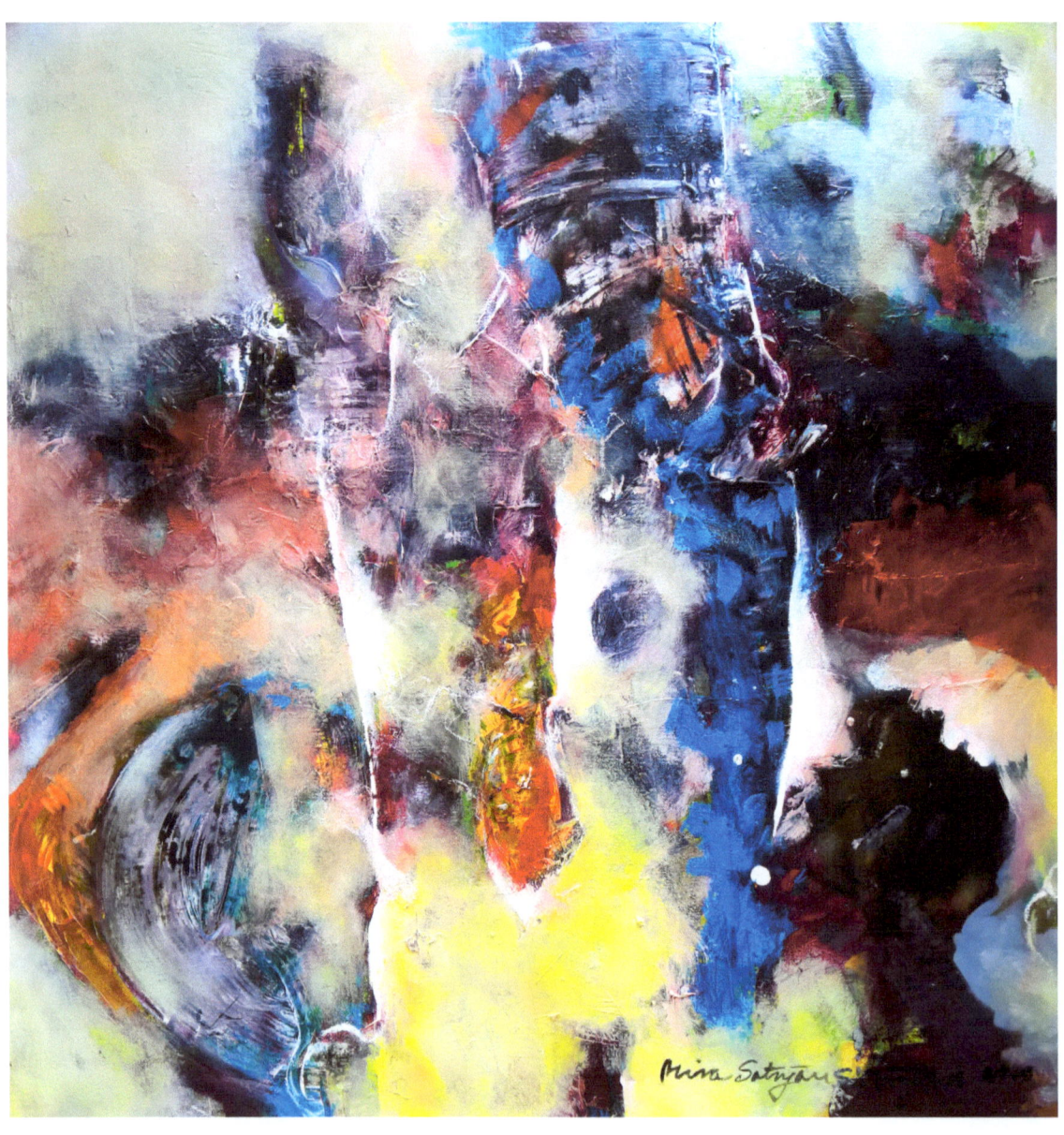

技術 | 絵画
価格帯 | USD 850 - USD 20000
販売レポート | USD 10500 [2018年] - USD 15000 [2019年]
有効な年数 | 25年

Imagining That
USD 3800

facebook.com/Art-Studio2-287702051387315

My painting is a message evolving around emotions, eternal to some degree, primary, one could say... It is the fascination, the ability to perceive and experience beauty, a union of most intimate experiences and emotions, the fascination with nature as well as with a relative relationship with another human being. I express in my painting the concerns and risks that result from a fleeting structure of circumstances defining our everyday lives. Painting is the realm of communicating expression and emotionality that are a common theme of sorts in my paintings - the awareness of impermanence. Sometimes my painting has a dramatic form, emphasized with a contrast color of varying intensity of the hue. The structure of our existence is very fleeting.

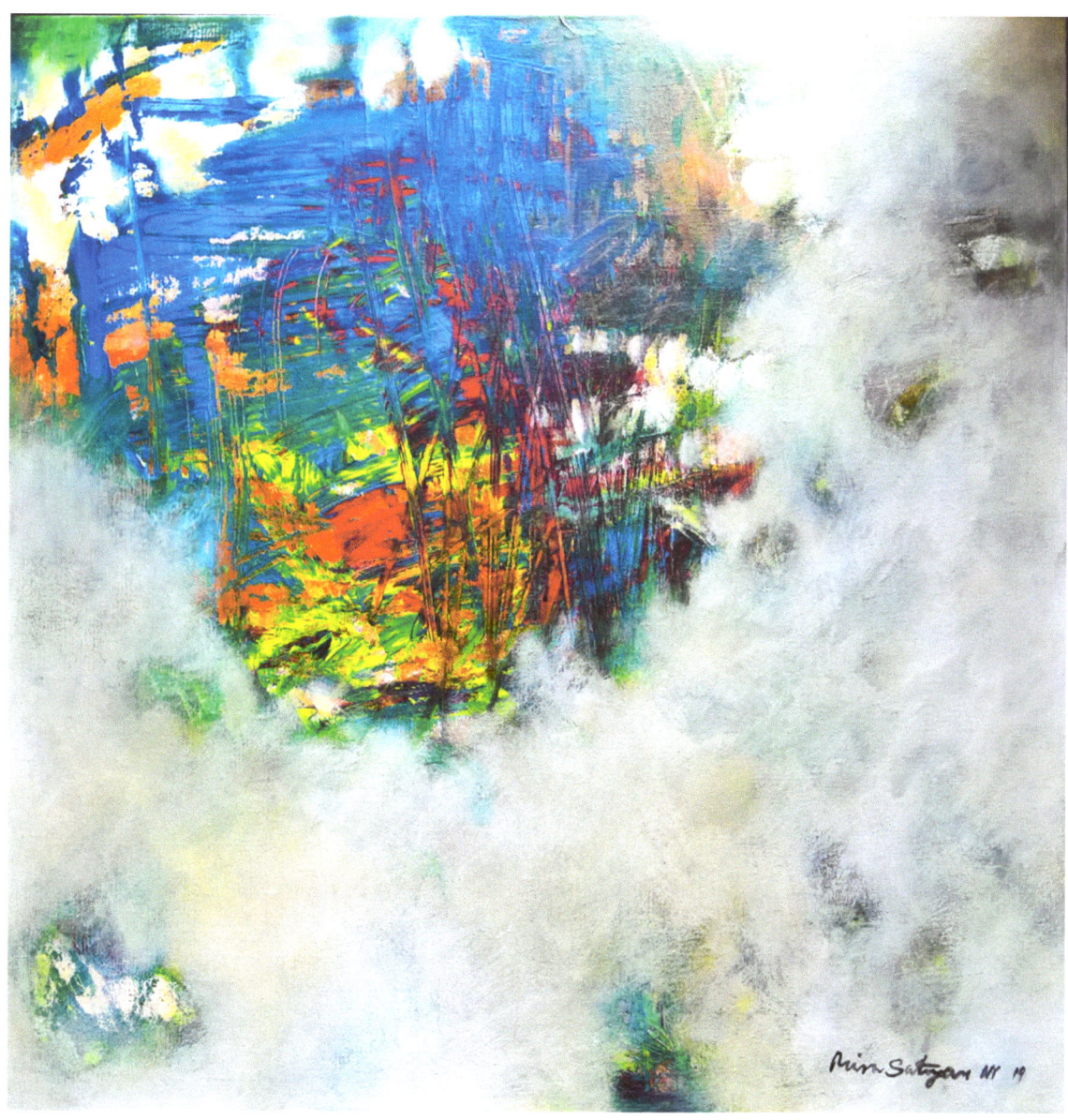

Technique | Painting
Price Range | USD 850 - USD 20000
Sales Report | USD 10500 (2018) - USD 15000 (2019)
Active Years | 25 years

In the Place
USD 3850

Derwin Leiva
アメリカ | United States

ダーウィンはキューバで育ち、音楽は彼の人生の一部でした。たとえほんの一瞬であっても、彼にとって音楽やダンスを聴くことは、日常を忘れられる方法でした。彼の作品はピカソ、ボッチョーニ、ヴィフレド・ラムなどのアーティストの影響を受けていますが、最もキューバ音楽は常に彼の想像力の源となっています。彼の作品はリズムと動きを使用することで、レイバはキューバ音楽を通して自由な体験を反映したいと考えています。レイバの作品は国際的に認められており、最近では「国際カラヴァッジオ賞-芸術の巨匠」、「国際ボッティチェリ賞」、Artexpoニューヨーク「最高新人出展者賞」を受賞しました。彼はマントヴァアートエキスポで「2019年アーティスト・オブ・ザ・イヤー賞」を受賞しました。

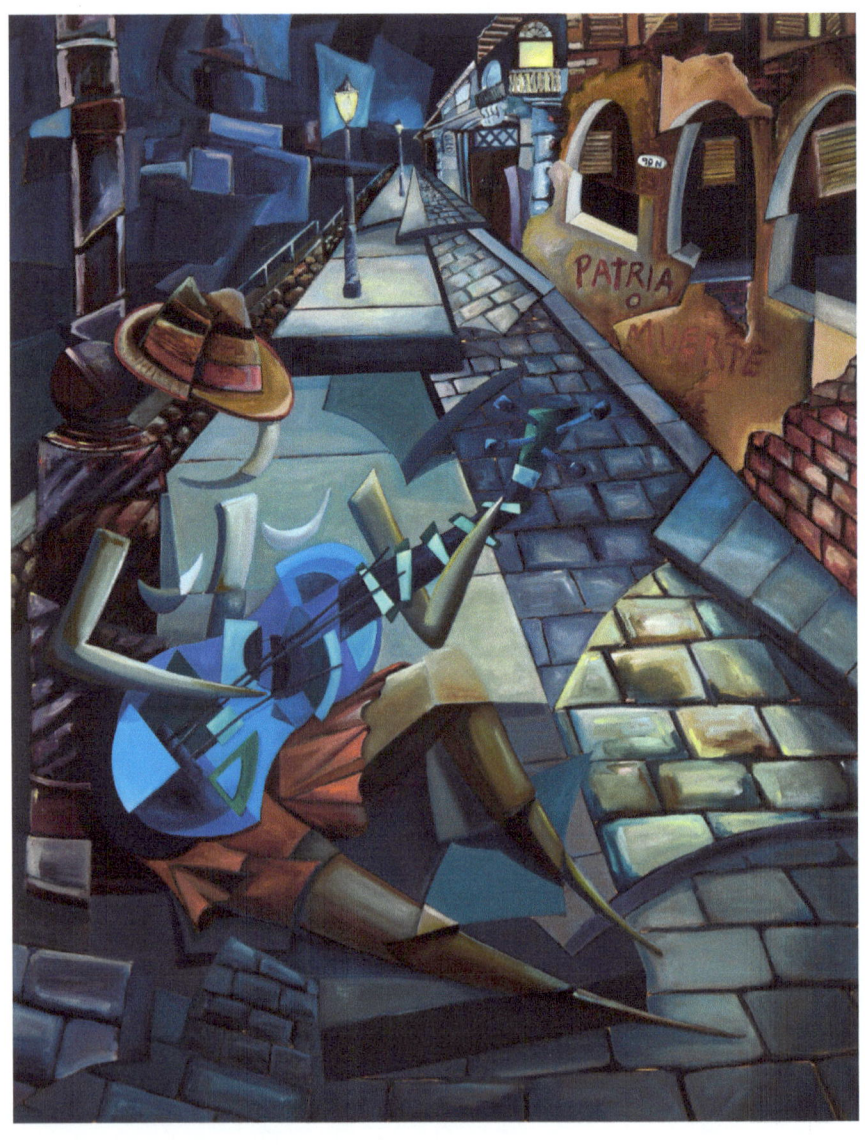

技術 | 絵画
価格帯 | USD 10000 - USD 100000
販売レポート | USD n/a [2018年] - USD n/a [2019年]
有効な年数 | 10年

"The Blue Guitar" 2018
Oil on Canvas, 152 x 122 cm
USD 100000

derwinleiva.com

Derwin grew up in Cuba where music was part of his life. Listening to music and dancing was a way to forget, even if just for a moment, about the necessities of daily life. Although his work has been influenced by artist like Picasso, Boccioni, and Wifredo Lam; Cuban music has always been a constant backdrop to his work. Through the use of rhythm and motion in his work, Leiva wants to mirror the experience of freedom found through Cuban music. Leiva's work has been recognized internationally and recently he received the "International Caravaggio Prize – Great Master of the Art," "The International Botticelli Award," Artexpo New York "Best New Exhibitor," and he was recognized at Mantova Art Expo as "Artist of the Year 2019."

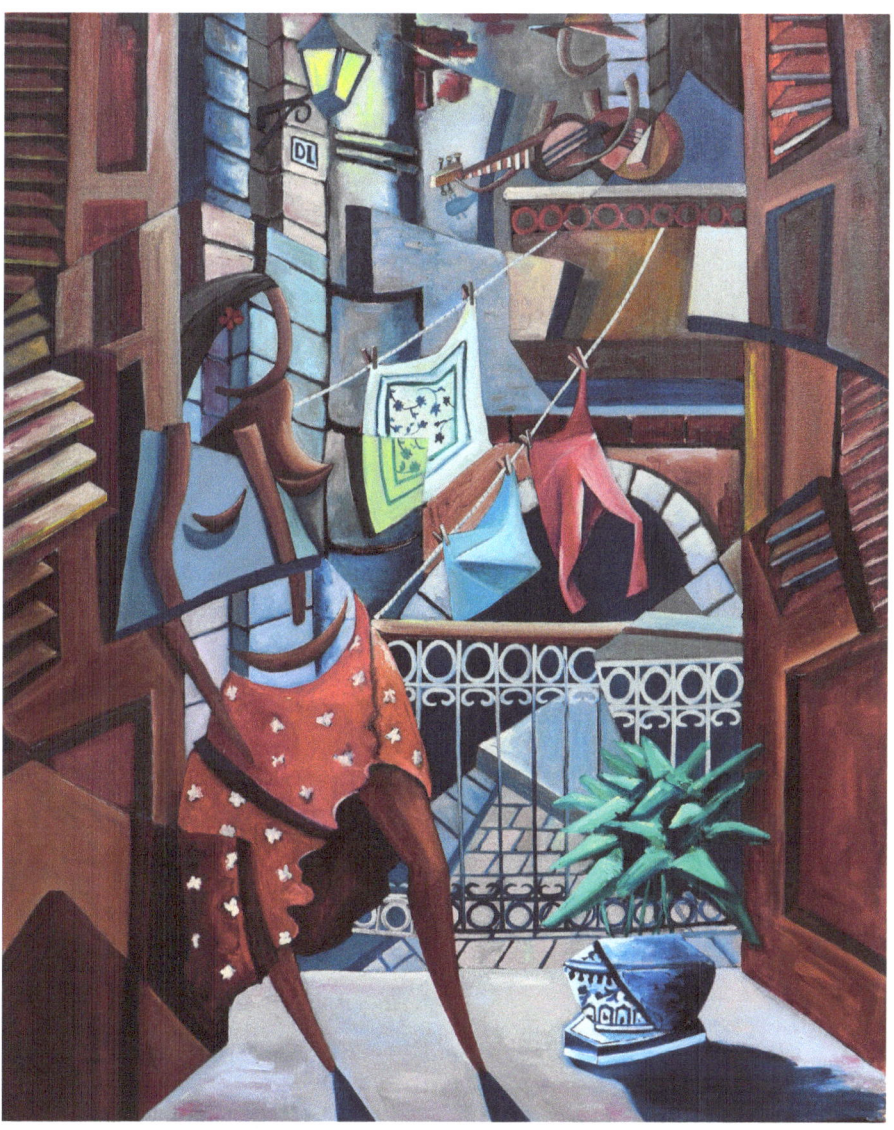

Technique | Painting
Price Range | USD 10000 - USD 100000
Sales Report | USD n/a (2018) - USD n/a (2019)
Active Years | 10 years

"Amor de Balcones" 2019
Oil on Canvas, 91 x 76 cm
USD 38000

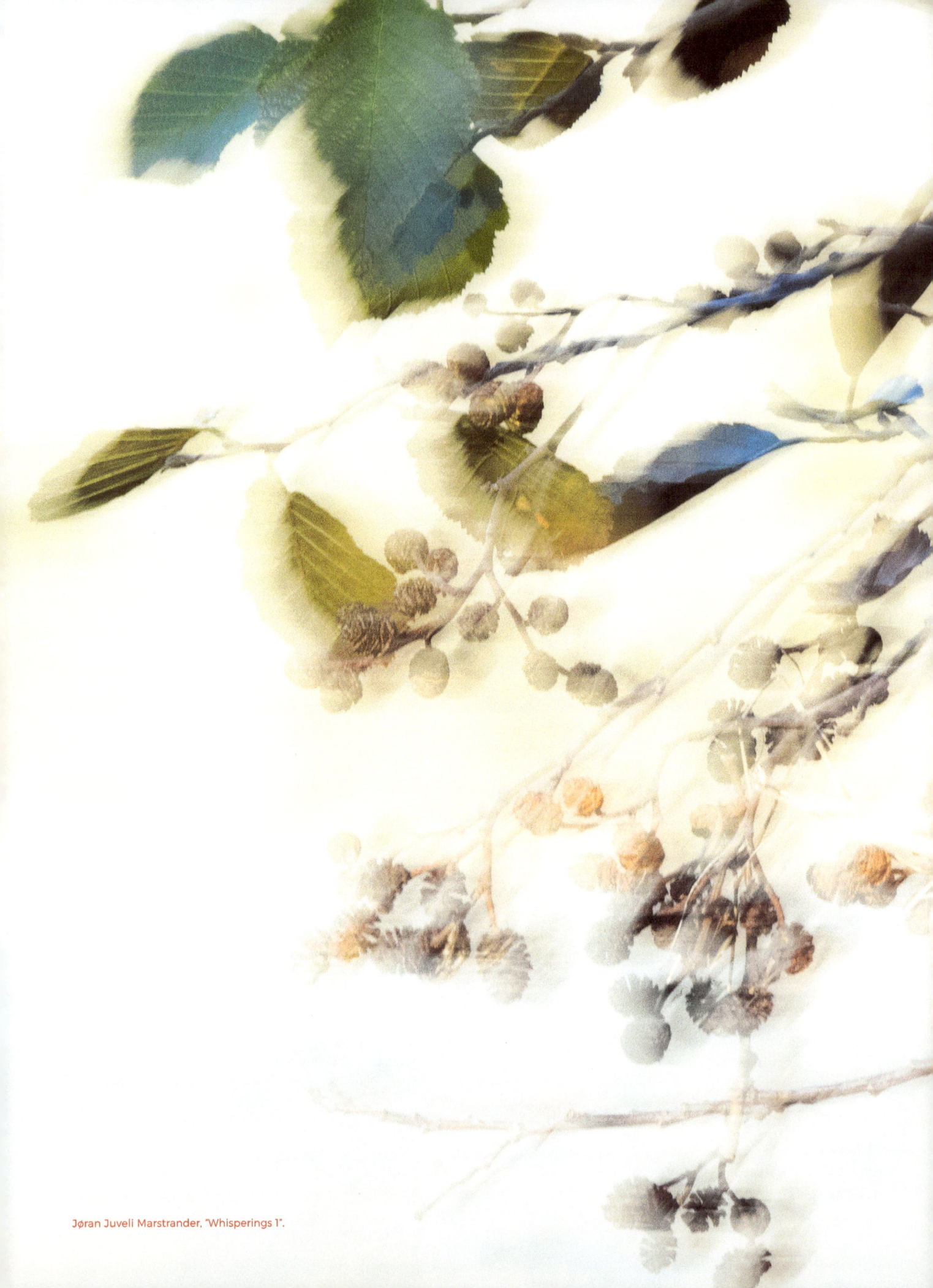

Jøran Juveli Marstrander, "Whisperings 1".

アーティストとのインタビューを読む:
Read the interviews with the artists:
contemporaryartstation.com/acc-japan-book

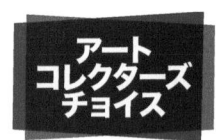

イギリスで印刷
UK Book Publishing発行

Printed in the United Kingdom.
Published by UK Book Publishing

2020 © Contemporary Art Station
ICM Group Ltd. | ICMグループ限定
www.contemporaryartstation.com

www.ingramcontent.com/pod-product-compliance
Lightning Source LLC
Chambersburg PA
CBHW051147220526
45473CB00003B/686